Shaping World History

Kevin Reilly, Series Editor

Shaping World History

Breakthroughs in Ecology, Technology, Science, and Politics

Mary Kilbourne Matossian

M.E. Sharpe
Armonk, New York
London, England

Library of Congress Cataloging-in-Publication Data

Matossian, Mary Allerton Kilbourne.
Shaping world history : breakthroughs in ecology, technology,
science, and politics / Mary Kilbourne Matossian.
p.   cm.—(Sources and studies in world history)
Includes bibliographical references and index.
ISBN 0-7656-0061-7.—ISBN 0-7656-0062-5 (pbk.)
1. Science and civilization. 2. Technology and civilization.
I. Title. II. Series.
CB478.M35   1997
909—dc21   96-29807
CIP

Printed in the United States of America

The paper used in this publication meets the minimum requirements of
American National Standard for Information Sciences—
Permanence of Paper for Printed Library Materials,
ANSI Z 39.48-1984.

BM (c)   10   9   8   7   6   5   4   3   2   1
BM (p)   10   9   8   7   6   5   4   3   2   1

CONTENTS

LIST OF FIGURES AND TABLES

Figures

Tables

FOREWORD

World histories are shaped by the questions their authors ask. The great Toynbee asked how civilizations developed and declined. Anthropologists once led historians to ask how the world's cultures were similar and different. Recently many historians have followed William McNeill in asking how the peoples of the world interacted and became one.

An older tradition, strains of which were called Christian, Whig, positivist, and Marxist, asked how the entire course of world history changed, evolved, or progressed. While sometimes dismissed as naive by cautious twentieth-century specialists, this older tradition continues for a simple reason. It asks the questions most of us want answered. What have been the most important changes in human history? How have these changes come about?

Mary Matossian begins with these questions. But there is nothing old-fashioned about the way in which she answers them. Her tools are among the most contemporary the historian has available. Recent studies of climate, nutrition, disease, and population, Matossian's specialties, can now provide outlines of long-term history and measures of major changes. Matossian is able to argue, for instance, that the development of agriculture, settled life, and cities corresponds to an extended period of warming from the sixth to third millennium B.C.E. She shows how the height of the Roman and Han empires and the twelfth-century flowering of European and Chinese civilizations also occurred in warm, moist periods when crops prospered, populations expanded, and governmental revenues increased.

One cannot read this book and deny the importance of climate on human history. But Matossian's argument is not limited to climate (even in all of its ecological and demographic implications). Rather she argues that three other factors have also been crucial in speeding change. They are the role of political elites, the effect of technologies of communication and transportation, and science.

These choices lead the author to rich veins of narrative and explanation. A few examples suggest her range. An analysis of the role of microtoxins and forests in agriculture explains religious prohibitions against eating pork. A lucid discussion of writing systems leads to the argument that alphabetic systems were related to Phoenician and Greek maritime trade and Homeric poetry. There are incisive interpretations of a wide variety of technological breakthroughs: the domestication of horses and camels, the building of printing presses and full-rigged sailing ships, the discovery of electricity and X rays, to name only a few.

Some histories of change lack proper names, as if individuals play no role in the grand sweep of long-term processes But this is not history without names and human stories. It is a history full of individuals: Gutenberg, Copernicus, Newton, Watt, Darwin, Roentgen, Pasteur, Faraday, Ford, Edison, Wright, Sikorsky, Marconi, and Norbert Wiener, among many.

To ask what changed rather than what happened is to ask for knowledge rather than information. Matossian's history provides such knowledge with compassion and clarity. It is a world history for veteran and novice alike.

Kevin Reilly
Series Editor

PREFACE

Until we ask a question, we cannot find its answer. If the unsolicited answer passes before our eyes, we do not recognize it. So this book is designed to raise questions. It contains suggestions and ideas, but is not a grand synthesis.

Shaping World History

INTRODUCTION

Major Causes of Breakthroughs

This is a book about the most significant innovations in world history. It is not an account of all world history. My concern is primarily positive innovations.

I realize that most innovations have negative consequences for some people. A businessman is not pleased when a competitor adopts a promising new technology. An established professor is not pleased when a junior colleague wins acceptance for a revolutionary idea.

Innovators often are surprised at the unintended negative consequences of their work. There is much irony involved. Yet I think it is possible to distinguish innovations with mainly positive consequences from those with mainly negative consequences.

When one examines all major innovations in world history, one finds that in a given era there was usually one region in which most of the innovations occurred. This center changes sooner or later. In 3000 B.C. the Near East was the center of innovation. It included the lands around the eastern Mediterranean, the Nile Valley, and the Tigris-Euphrates Valleys. It was where the first "civilizations" began.

During most of the period A.D. 500–1500 China was the leading power in Eurasia. The period, long known to European historians as the Medieval Millennium, might be better described as the Chinese Millennium. The Chinese invented many new technologies and systematically co-opted political talent.

During the Chinese Millennium, except for its universities Europe was an undistinguished region. From 1450 (invention of printing with movable type) until 1939 (outbreak of World War II) Europeans enjoyed their days of glory. However, by the end of World War II (1945) the political, economic, and scientific hegemony of the United States was established.

Africans and native Americans did not participate in these advances. There were two important reasons for this. One was geographic isolation. The Sahara Desert and the tropics of Central Africa were strong barriers to the southward movement of more advanced technologies. The Atlantic and Pacific Oceans provided equally daunting barriers to the connection of the Americas with Eurasia.

A second reason for the relatively modest progress made on these isolated continents was that their peoples lacked an efficient writing system. Moreover, they had no widely shared language in which to write. Without such a language and an efficient writing system, human groups have difficulty building cumulative knowledge.

Major Causes of Innovation

Climatic Changes

Prior to about 1750 climatic changes were a major factor in the course of human history, influencing the quantity and quality of food available. As I will show, contaminated food weakened human resistance to many infectious diseases. Epidemics of these diseases were probably the principal constraint on population growth. Meteorologists allocate responsibility for these causative climatic changes between the movements of the sun in relation to earth, on the one hand, and on changing levels of volcanism, on the other. Volcanic eruptions, when sufficiently strong, send dust into the stratosphere, blocking the sun's rays and causing the surface temperature of the earth to decline. During historic times (since 3500 B.C.) there have been forty eruptions with a VEI (Volcanic Eruption Index) score of 5 to 7, which classifies them as "very large." Observers described such events as "cataclysmic," "colossal," "terrific," etc. There have been only two 7-level eruptions: that of Baitushan in east China in A.D. 1050, and that of Tambora in the Lesser Sunda Islands in A.D. 1815. There have been fifteen eruptions at the 6 level, the most famous of which was Santorini (an island in the Aegean Sea) in 1650 B.C.[1] A single severe eruption probably does not influence the course of history, but a sequence of severe eruptions such as that of 1580–1640 was associated with cold, stormy weather and a cessation of population growth or a decline in population in most countries. This was a period of rebellions and warfare across Eurasia.

Communication and Transportation Technologies

After the seventeenth century climatic influences on world history lessened. Improvements in communication and transportation technology had greater effects. As communication technology improved, people could learn faster. Scientists increased the stock of knowledge and developed new scientific disciplines. By extending communication systems political elites could gain greater control over their home territory and distant colonies. At first messages traveled fastest by water. Only in the nineteenth century, with the development of railroads, the telegraph, and marine cables, did communication by land and across oceans significantly improve. With better systems of transport, it became easier for governments to move troops from place to place. Lawmen suppressed highwaymen and pirates. By securing trade routes, government enabled localities to specialize in products that were complementary to each other, and this in turn raised labor productivity.

Political Elites

Political scientists believe that political elites ("dominant minorities") have ruled all civilized societies. But no families were permanent elite members in a given place. Most elite families eventually died out, squandered their wealth, or moved away. Either slowly or quickly, the composition of political elites changed. Most elites were at least to some degree open to new entrants. Competition at the top and for entrance to the top was fierce, and those in power had to meet challenges and keep their edge to stay there.

Scientific Progress

After about 1850, when science married technology, competitors for great power and wealth could not afford to ignore science-based technologies. But they had to pay a price for their acceptance of these new technologies. Unwittingly scientists were undermining the social control systems upon which political elites had relied for almost two thousand years. Specifically, scientific discoveries undermined belief in an anthropomorphic god, in heaven and hell, and in the action of supernatural powers on earth. The concept of divine providence as a factor in history went into abeyance. The notion of an immortal soul became less plausible. In scientific thinking, the soul appeared to be nothing more than the mind; the mind, nothing more than the conscious functioning of the brain; the brain, no more than a part of the body. Darwin's work rendered the anthropomorphic god unnecessary as an explanation of design in nature. If one puts aside this hypothesis, then "God" has no mind or brain with which to design nature.

Let us see how well these four causal factors account for breakthroughs in history.

Summary of Chapters

I begin with the initial situation of human beings (*Homo sapiens sapiens*) on earth. Chapter 1 is concerned with geography and ecology. How did environmental conditions influence human prehistory and history? In particular I discuss the influence of land-water relationships on the fortunes of populations in different regions. I also discuss the association between temperature and moisture variations with the growth and decline of human societies. Chapter 1 also poses these questions: What was the "natural" behavior of hominids and the first human beings? What can we learn by studying other primates? This chapter serves as a point of reference for subsequent changes.

Chapter 2 covers the extraordinary beginning of settled life and the inventions of the first farmers. Global warming, which came about 10,000 years ago in the Near East, probably had an important influence on the Farming Revolution.

In Chapter 3 I discuss the birth of "civilization" in Eurasia. It begins with the appearance of intensified warfare, the creation of city-states, and important technological innovations: the invention of writing and the invention of the wheel. Other innovations appear to have been reactions to climatic deterioration and increased military insecurity.

Chapter 4 takes up the Roman and Chinese elites, who by 200 B.C. had conquered and held large empires with diverse languages and cultures. They wanted to establish uniform rules to facilitate the control of these empires. This is the origin of Roman law, still influential today. Neither Latin in the West nor Greek in the East could prevail throughout the whole empire. The Chinese failed to develop a systematic body of law from which no emperor could exempt himself. Why?

The Roman political elites became more receptive to the moral insights of prophets and philosophers. They finally assimilated the Christian Church and used it as a means of social control. The Chinese elites co-opted the Confucian philosophers to the same end. They were successful in establishing a single written language, mandarin Chinese, throughout their empire. This served to create cohesion within their own ranks, although not among the common people of different regions. Cultural diversity kept the common people in chains.

Chapter 5 delineates why, during the millennium A.D. 500–1500, the Chinese were the most advanced people in the world. They invented rag paper, block printing, the compass, and much else. They developed an examination system to recruit the most able individuals for the civil service.

In Chapter 6 I address the invention of universities and of the printing press. Better transportation systems and urban development also played an important role.

In Chapter 7 I consider the environmental and social origins and the political consequences of the Protestant Reformation. I use continental political culture as a contrasting arrangement.

Chapter 8 covers the scientific revolution of the seventeenth century. With new mathematics, lenses, and physics scientists began to draw a new map of reality.

Chapter 9 covers the steady population growth that began in the first half of the eighteenth century. I suggest that dietary improvements, improving transportation systems, and commercial growth were mainly responsible.

Chapter 10 covers the first Industrial Revolution in Britain (c. 1780–1870). Its most important new technology was steam production from coal burning. This in turn opened hinterlands and overseas continents to commerce and facilitated population growth.

In Chapter 11 I discuss social controls as employed in Europe since 1789. The French revolutionaries, by breaking down regional differences in language, reduced cultural diversity and spread a new kind of political ideology across Europe and eventually to faraway lands. This new political ideology especially inspired single young men in cities. Other new social controls in the nineteenth century were civil service examinations, compulsory elementary education, compulsory military service, democracy, nationalism, and mass entertainment.

Chapter 12 covers the economic and intellectual origins of Darwin's ideas and the religious and political consequences thereof. Darwinism tended to subvert all religious myths serving the purpose of social control.

Chapter 13 deals with the "marriage" of science and technology that began about 1870. As a result there was a revolution in transportation technology. Entrepreneurs produced electrical appliances and businesses ran on electricity.

In Chapter 14 I describe the dazzling array of scientific breakthroughs from the time of James Hutton (fl. 1796) to Robert Wilson and Arno Penzias (fl. 1965). Some changed our image of the cosmos and our understanding of the history of life on earth; others were linked to revolutionary technological implications.

Chapter 15 contains a discussion of the origins of the third communication revolution (1948 to the present), and we are rolling with the consequences.

Note

1. Environmental historians may find that the Smithsonian-sponsored work *Volcanoes of the World* (2d ed.), by Tom Simkin and Lee Siebert, is indispensable. It contains a list of all known volcanic eruptions since 10,000 B.C.

1 FROM HOMINIDS TO HUMAN BEINGS

Biology, Geography, and Climatic Change

Man is an exception, whatever else he is. If it is not true that a divine being fell, then we only say that one of the animals went entirely off its head.

—G.K. Chesterton

Anthropologists have named us *Homo sapiens sapiens,* the clever, clever hominid. Over a century ago certain scientists abandoned the Western creation myth and began to seek human origins in nature among the primates (apes and monkeys). If apes and people had many resemblances, what kind of creatures linked the two species? When and where did this linking happen?

The discoveries of physical anthropologists and geneticists have indeed established that we belong to the primate family. The line of hominids (bipedal apes, apes who walk on two legs) differentiated from that of other apes about five million years ago. We share with chimpanzees and bonabos (pygmy chimpanzees) between 98 percent and 99 percent of our structural genes. Who can watch primates in a zoo without experiencing a shock of recognition?

In December 1992 in Ethiopia, Tim White, an anthropologist from the University of California at Berkeley, and his team discovered the earliest hominid yet known. They announced their discovery in September 1994. Anthropologists believe that the bones discovered are almost 4.5 million years old. These hominids walked upright, were four feet tall, and lived in a woodland setting. Their skull capacity was about one third that of ours.[1] They lived very close to the time of separation between hominids and apes estimated by geneticists—five million years ago.

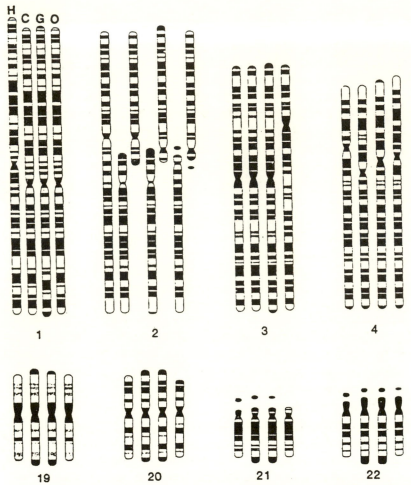

Figure 1. **Schematic representation of late-prophase chromosomes (1000-band stage)** of man, chimpanzee, gorilla, and orangutan, arranged from left to right, samples 1–4 and 19–22, visualizing homology between the chromosomes of the great apes and humans. (Reprinted with permission from J.J. Yunis and O. Prakash, "The Origin of Man: A Chromosomal Pictorial Legacy," *Science* 215 [March 19, 1982], p. 1527. © 1982 by the American Association for the Advancement of Science.

In August 1995 Maeve Leakey and her team discovered in Kenya similar hominids that were 4.1 million years old. These hominids are estimated to have weighed between 101 and 121 pounds.[2] This is the most recent of a long sequence of discoveries. It now seems likely that hominids differentiated from apes in northeast Africa, in or near the

Great Rift Valley of Ethiopia, Kenya, and Tanzania. Hominids had habitually upright posture and walked on two legs. They lived mainly on the ground, not in trees. These attributes appeared long before their brain expanded and they began to make tools.

About fifteen million years ago the environment in East Africa was changing. The earth's crust was splitting apart in places, while highland domes of up to nine thousand feet formed in Ethiopia and Kenya. These domes blocked the west-to-east airflow and threw the land to the east into rain shadow. Lacking moisture, the continuous forests in the east fragmented into patches of forest, woodland and shrubland. About twelve million years ago the Great Rift Valley, running north to south, appeared in East Africa.

This development had two major biological consequences. First, the Great Rift Valley was an east-west barrier to the migration of animal populations. Second, although the apes in the dense jungle on the west side of the valley were already adapted to a humid climate and thus were not forced to adjust to a new environment, in the east a rich mosaic of ecological conditions emerged. Biologists believe that mosaic environments drive evolutionary innovation, since competing successfully in such an environment requires new adaptations. The hominids—bipedal apes—developed in such a place. This is the first example of the influence of climatic change on prehistory.

According to Peter Rodman and Henry McHenry, on the east side of the Great Rift Valley, where woodlands were scattered, a bipedal ape had an advantage. It could move more easily from one grove of food-bearing trees to a more distant grove. An ape who walked habitually on two legs was more energy-efficient than an ape who walked on four. Upright posture was also more efficient for cooling the body in the daytime heat. Other anatomical changes made it easier for hominids to stride and to run. The beginning of brain expansion in hominids began in Africa around 2.5 million years ago with *Homo habilis* and was associated with the appearance of the earliest stone tools. By 1.8 million years ago a more advanced hominid, *Homo erectus,* was making sharp-edged tools. The process involved knocking one rock against another, chipping off a sharp flake from the "core" stone and using the flake as a knife. Hominids could use this knife to cut through the hides of most animals and get to the meat quickly. Evidence shows that with this innovation hominid meat eating soon increased.

There was probably a positive feedback loop between the expansion of the hominid brain and meat eating. The hominid brain is three times as big as that of an ape of similar body size. Meat is an excellent source of protein and, because of its fat content, is high in calories; this helps to support the larger brain. At the same time the growth of the brain in relation to body weight favored the improvement of human hunting skills and higher meat consumption. In hominid females, the pelvic opening widened to compensate for the increased brain size of the hominid infant. However, that was not enough, and any greater widening would reduce bipedal mobility. A solution to the problem of increased hominid brain size was the natural selection of those hominids that produced children born "too early," with brain size only one third that of an adult. These infants are slow to mature and so depend on their parents for a longer period. This extends the time that parents can transmit culture (patterns of behavior) to their offspring. In contrast, baby apes are born with a brain one half the size of that of an adult ape. They mature more quickly than hominids do, but have fewer years of dependency to learn from their parents.

What sort of culture did prehistoric humans transmit? Cultural anthropologists who have studied the way of life of foragers (hunter-gatherers) today say that the usual size of a human band is twenty-five persons, including children and adults. A larger unit, the dialectical tribe, includes about five hundred persons. Foragers use only temporary camps and move about on their range. Since longevity was usually only twenty-five to thirty years, many children were raised by relatives, their parents being dead. The band, not the nuclear family, was the principal social unit.[3] A band acquires food cooperatively, by hunting and gathering, and shares it. Adults teach their children, who are born self-centered, to become sensitive to the needs of others and to share food.

Is such sharing, social behavior unique to humans? Frans de Waal, a researcher at the Yerkes Primate Research Center in Atlanta, Georgia, discovered that chimpanzee groups consist of caring, sharing individuals who form self-policing networks. He believes that the roots of morality may be far older than we are. A chimpanzee seems to realize that social disorder is a threat to its individual well-being. When rivals embrace, signaling an end to their fight, the whole colony may break into loud, joyous celebration.

However, chimpanzees share food and other treasures only when it is to their advantage. They cheat when they can get away with it by hiding a private stock of food. When cheating, they try to deceive other members of the group. Fortunately, they live in groups of less than a hundred, so they can watch each other and identify the cheaters. Older chimpanzees deny food to young cheaters by excluding them from sharing in the next windfall.[4]

It appears that both our moral and immoral tendencies are part of the natural order. Both "good" and "evil" are aspects of our adaptive and competitive strategies. We can imagine that human goodness developed out of the need to adjust to a cooperative group. By belonging to such a group an individual had a major advantage in the struggle to survive and reproduce.

No more can we think of stone-tool making and sharing behavior as unique to our species. Nor are we unique in our capacity for tactical deception and savagery. Rather, we have a place in a natural mammalian continuum.

The only behavior unique to humans appears to be the ability to communicate quickly with a large number of phonemes (discrete sounds). We can make fifty phonemes; apes can make only twelve. Humans can speak more quickly and articulately than any other species. The placement of our vocal organs makes this possible.

When did our ancestors acquire spoken language involving more than twelve phonemes? Some anthropologists think it was as far back as 2.5 million years ago (the time of *Homo habilis*). Most agree that complex spoken language goes back at least thirty-five thousand years to the time of the cave paintings in Europe. They think that language evolved as a means of social interaction, allowing individuals to prevent fights or settle them more easily.[5]

Recent discoveries in the Pavlov Hills of the Czech Republic indicate that ceramics and weaving go back twenty-seven thousand years—to before the beginning of settled life. These skills were probably the innovations of women, because women could make pots and weave while they took care of children.[6]

When did people exactly like us, anatomically speaking, appear? Many anthropologists think that our species *(Homo sapiens sapiens)* differentiated around two hundred thousand years ago in either south or northeast Africa. From northeast Africa people spread across the earth. They went to the Near East, Europe, China, Southeast Asia, Australia, the Pacific Islands, and the Americas.

Lucky humans settled on lands suited to agriculture. Only they could look forward to sustained population growth and civilization. They were especially lucky if the relationship between land and water in their region was favorable for water transportation, as the cost of moving bulk goods by water for a given distance was one eighth to one twentieth that of moving them by land. Waterborne commerce may have been just as fundamental as the development of farming for the birth of civilization.

Geography and Prehistory

Given limited prehistoric shipbuilding skills, the tamer the water the better. Navigable rivers that did not dry up in the summer were important in moving goods from the interior of continents to settlements on the shores of lakes, inland seas, and oceans. Primitive sailors, without navigational instruments, preferred coastlines with well-marked natural features and deep harbors. The Mediterranean Sea, a tideless inland sea with stepping-stone islands, was a magnet. Seas and oceans with predictable winds and currents, such as those of the northern Indian Ocean, were more attractive than rough and capricious waters, such as those of the North Atlantic.

Eurasia had great geographical advantages. It included a variety of environments, animals, and plants. Its long east-west belt of fertile soil and temperate climate made it highly suitable for food production and exchange. Certain parts of Eurasia had particular advantages. The Middle East was centrally located, controlling east-west trade routes. It included territory such as the Suez Isthmus and the easily navigable extensions of the Indian Ocean: the Red Sea, the Gulf of Aqaba, and the Persian Gulf. The alluvial valleys of the Nile, Tigris-Euphrates, and Indus Rivers had rich soil that could support a dense population.

China had two great rivers, the Yellow and the Yangzi, which could be linked by canals. It had great botanical diversity to draw upon for food. But unlike Europe, it did not have an inland sea. Much of the Yellow River was not navigable and frequently flooded. The rocky north and central Chinese coast lacked good harbors. These factors constrained the commercial development of China.

Northern and western Europe were blessed with many navigable rivers linking the interior with the coasts. Water and land interpenetrated: Europe was a peninsula of peninsulas. The North, Baltic, Black, and Mediterranean Seas moderated the climate and served the needs of waterborne commerce. Europe had long coastlines and many harbors. It had 4 kilometers of coast per 1,000 square kilometers of land, while Asia had only 1.7 square kilometers of coast per 1,000 square kilometers of land. This too was an asset for traders.

From a global perspective, most of the water surrounding Europe, even the Mediterranean Sea, was cold. This meant that shipbuilders could use iron nails to fasten together the parts of a ship without fear of early rusting and wood decay. Nailed ships were structurally fit to sail in rough waters. On the other hand, South and East Asia were surrounded by warm water, in which nails quickly rusted and wooden structures accordingly decayed. The boats sailing in these waters were most often held together by fiber ropes—coconut, hemp, etc. Such ships were not sturdy enough to sail in rough waters over long distances.

From a human point of view the Americas, Africa, and Australia were disadvantaged continents. None had an inland sea. All except South America had large interior deserts. Africa and South America contained extensive tropical jungles with soils unsuited for agriculture. They were suited instead to the propagation of voracious disease-bearing insects.

Except for the Niger River there were few navigable rivers in sub-Saharan Africa. Consequently connections between the interior and the coasts were often poor. North America had the great Mississippi River system running north and south, but no water connections from the Great Lakes to the west coast. High north-south mountain ranges (the Sierra Nevada and the Rockies) obstructed east-west land travel.

The Americas lacked native animals suitable for traction. The llama could be used as a pack animal, but there were no camels, horses, or cattle. Consequently the native Americans had no use for wheeled vehicles. Moreover, without traction animals they could not use plows to break the sod on the great plains of North America and southeastern South America.

In 1492 some native American peoples were skilled in gold, silver, and copper metallurgy, but few could produce bronze and none could smelt iron to make tools and weapons. They confronted the Spaniards without daggers or swords, not to mention guns.

It took until the twentieth century for peoples of the Americas, Africa, Australia, and Southeast Asia to enter the main theater of world history. However, during prehistory they independently domesticated staple starch plants: maize and potatoes. Europeans brought these crops back across the Atlantic, and they contributed to the population explosion in Eurasia.

How Climatic Changes Are Reconstructed

In 1714 Daniel Fahrenheit invented the mercury thermometer. During the eighteenth century in various spots in Europe and North America, educated people used thermometers to keep a daily temperature record, usually for only two or three decades. These were direct contemporary measurements of climate, which we now call instrumental records. Beginning in the Medieval Millennium Chinese and European annalists made note of unusual weather, such as severe winters, floods, and droughts. These are called documentary records: they were made at the time of the event, but without instruments, and they tended to omit mention of normal, ordinary weather.

In the twentieth century scientists discovered proxy variables for defining climatic trends. The first was the tree ring; the study of a series of tree rings is called dendrochronology. Tree rings, like other proxy variables, provide continuous information about a climate variable. Unlike annals, they do not omit ordinary years from their time-series data.

The problem with tree rings is that in many latitudes, such as the mid-Atlantic states of North America, they give ambiguous signals. In order to grow, a tree must have both warmth and water. Tree rings, which measure simultaneously the effects of both temperature and moisture, merely show how much the tree grew each year, but not the weather that determined that growth. Trees that reveal past climatic changes are found in either warm, dry areas or cold areas. Those in warm, dry areas, such as the southwestern United States, almost always have enough warmth to grow, but lack sufficient water. Their tree rings are markers of rainfall each year. The best indications of past temperatures in northeast America may be found in trees located in Canada. They almost always have enough moisture to grow, but lack sufficient warmth.

In Europe the rings of ancient trees found in northern Scandinavia and Russia, in the Alps, and in northern Scotland indicate past temperatures. In China the scientific study of ancient trees from Tibet has provided what may be the best indication of temperatures in China since 1500.[7] In the 1970s scientists discovered a new proxy variable representing past temperatures in the Northern Hemisphere. They measured the varying fallout of sulfates in cores of ice cut out of the Greenland ice sheet. Sulfates indicated past volcanic eruptions strong enough to send dust and ash into the stratosphere. Sulfuric acid aerosols from an eruption left a sulfate "signal" in the ice core. Such signals often, although not inevitably, indicate a decline in temperature on the surface of the earth after the eruption. This effect might linger up to two years.

The information in Figures 2 and 3 may be useful to historians in explaining the past. Changes in temperature have coincided with peaks and troughs in population and in political centralization. We can see that the beginning of civilizations in the Nile and Tigris-Euphrates Valleys around 4000 B.C. coincided with a period of warm temperature. We can see that the invasions of the Bronze Age, 2000–1000 B.C., coincided with a trough in temperature. The peak in the power and population of the Roman and Han Empires, 200 B.C. to A.D. 200, coincided with another peak in temperature. The next peak, the "medieval warm," A.D. 1100–1300, coincided with a peak in population growth in Europe and China.[8] These observations suggest that warm weather tends to coincide with population growth and power.

Variation in moisture is more localized, but its effects can be powerful nevertheless. Wet weather encourages plant growth, but it also encourages fungal colonization of plants in the fields and in storage. Microfungi in food may produce poisons that cause infertility and destroy human and animal resistance to infectious diseases. Cold winter weather traumatizes food plants and makes them more vulnerable to fungal colonization during a wet spring. Dry weather, whether in arctic areas such as Scandinavia and northern Russia or in a hot desert area such as North Africa and northwest China, discourages fungal colonization of plants. Unfortunately, it also discourages plant growth. Hot, wet tropical regions, such as Central Africa, are unfavorable for agriculture because harvested food in such regions molds very quickly. It is more practical to grow food on trees (such as bananas) or underground (tubers), and harvest only as much food as one can immediately consume.

The activity of microfungi and the poisons they produced served to link climatic changes to food quantity and quality. Food quantity and quality influenced population size. Population size, in turn, powerfully

18

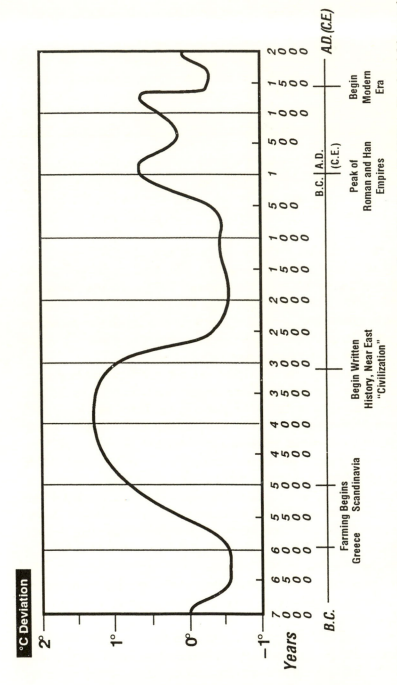

Figure 2. **Volcanism and temperature in the Northern Hemisphere and turning points in world history.** (Reprinted [abstracted/ excerpted] with permission from G.A. Zielinski et al., "Record of Volcanism Since 7000 B.C. from the GISP2 Ice Core and Implications for the Volcano–Climate System," *Science* 264 [1994], p. 948. © 1994 by the American Association for the Advancement of Science.)

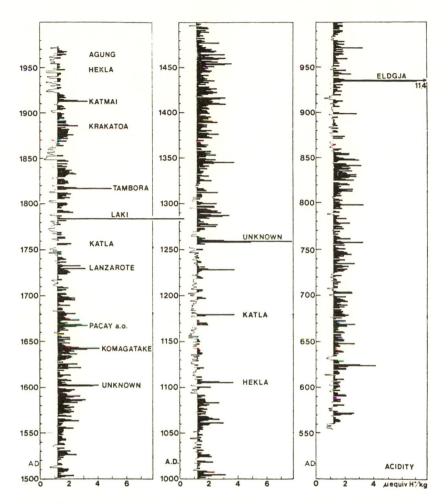

Figure 3. **Record of volcanism, A.D. 553–1972, in ice core from Crete, Central Greenland.** The greater the fallout of sulfuric acid, the greater the volcanic activity, and the cooler the climate. (Reprinted with permission from *Nature* 288 [November 1980], p. 230. C.U. Hammer et al., "Greenland Ice Sheet Evidence of Postglacial Volcanism and Its Climatic Impact." © 1980 by Macmillan Magazines Limited.)

influenced the amount of tax revenues a government could collect. These revenues determined how many bureaucrats and soldiers that government could employ.

Nothing known in nature has just one cause. Of course there were other factors involved every step of the way. However, I think that the

20

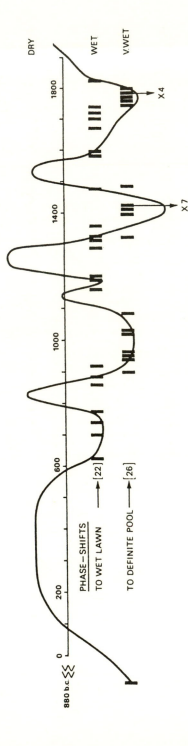

Figure 4. **Wetness, northwest England**, A.D. 1–1900. Note the dry period, 1200–1300, coinciding with the "medieval warm." Population in both Europe and China rose. Note the increase in wetness, 1300–1500. In this period the population of Eurasia declined by about one third. The period 1570–1850 was both wet and cold, yet around 1750 the population explosion began. Some weighty new factors were probably involved in this burst of population growth. (From K. E. Barber, "Peat Stratigraphy and Climatic Change: Some Speculations." In *The Climatic Scene*, ed. M.J. Tooley [London: Allen and Unwin, 1983], pp. 175–185. Reprinted by permission of A. A. Balkemu. Please order from: A. A. Balkemu, Old Post Road, Brookfield, Vermont 05036; telephone [802] 276-3162; telefax [802] 276-3837; email info@ashgate.com.)

influence of climatic changes on human life was very important until the mid-seventeenth century. Climatic changes, it should be remembered, influence human life not so much by causing seasonal discomfort, but through their influence on the foods that human beings need.

Notes

1. Tim D. White et al., "Australopithecus Ramidus: A New Species of Early Hominid from Aramis, Ethiopia."

2. Maeve Leakey et al., "New Four Million Year Hominid Species from Kanapoi and Alia Bay, Kenya."

3. Richard Leakey, *The Origin of Humankind*, pp. 40–58.

4. Frans de Waal, *Good Natured: The Origins of Right and Wrong in Humans and Other Animals.*

5. Leakey, *Origin of Humankind*, pp. 119–38.

6. Elizabeth W. Barber, *Women's Work: The First 20,000 Years;* Brenda Fowler, "Find Suggests that Weaving Preceded Settled Life."

7. X.D. Wu, "Dendroclimatic Studies in China," p. 441.

8. C.U. Hammer et al., "Greenland Ice Sheet Evidence of Post-Glacial Volcanism and Its Climatic Impact"; G.A. Zielinski et al., "Record of Volcanism Since 7000 B.C. from the G1SP2 Greenland Ice Core and Implications for the Volcano-Climate System."

2 THE FIRST FARMERS

*The Lord sent them forth from the Garden of Eden to till the
ground whence he [Adam] was taken.*

—Genesis 4:23

About twelve thousand years ago the glaciers began to retreat. By 8000
B.C. the global climate was warmer; this was the beginning of an
interstadial period that continues even today. A peak of warming occurred between 5500 and 2500 B.C. In those three millennia some
foragers first learned to farm and to domesticate animals rather than
hunt them. But even after they learned how to cultivate, foragers did
not immediately adopt farming as a way of life. They probably chose it
reluctantly, for farming was a more laborious way of getting food than
hunting and gathering.

The label Neolithic, which means "new stone age," is inappropriate
for this period of early farming. It is true that the stone tools farmers
used were superior to those used by the foragers of the preceding
Paleolithic, or "old stone age." The more important change was a
change in lifestyle from foraging (hunting and gathering) to settled
agriculture and animal husbandry.

The Origins of Agriculture

Richard McNeish believes that there were four centers of pristine
(original) agriculture: the Near East, the Andes, Mesoamerica, and the
Far East.[1] There may have been a fifth center in Southeast Asia, but
archaeologists have done relatively little work there. Bruce D. Smith

has made a case for a sixth center in eastern North America.[2]

Archaeologists seem to agree that agriculture began in the Levant (the area that includes present-day Israel, Palestine, Lebanon, and Syria). This was part of the Fertile Crescent, which included Mesopotamia as well. When the climate warmed, the Natufians (inhabitants of the Levant) left their caves and began to live in the open. They collected wild grass seeds (wheat and barley), nuts, peas, and lentils, plants that grew wild on upland sites.

Most seeds and nuts are nontoxic and full of nutrients; they also have a low moisture content and so are less likely than other plant parts to mold in storage.

In particular, the Natufians learned that wheat and barley were very desirable foods. Wheat is rich in iron; it is also high in gluten, which makes it ideal for making leavened bread. Leavening bread is desirable because this tends to neutralize phytates, natural compounds in wheat that prevent people from absorbing iron and zinc.[3] In order to thrive wheat needs rich, nonacid, moisture-retaining (but not soggy) soil. Barley contains less iron and zinc, and lacks gluten, so it cannot be made into leavened bread. However, it is hardier than wheat. It grows in the thin limestone soils of the Levant and Greece. While germinating in the ground it has less need for rain, and it can tolerate wider extremes of temperature. Since it takes a shorter time to mature, barley is less likely to suffer from disease.

Donald Henry thinks that the expansion of the woodlands and cereal grasses to the hills, which occurred as a result of the warming of the climate, was of critical importance because it pulled the Natufians into a more specialized economy. When the wild cereals were ripe in one spot, the Natufian foragers could harvest them in three weeks. Then the band could move to a higher elevation and find more cereals to harvest (the higher the elevation, the later the harvest time). The Natufians could collect so much food in the winter and spring that it would last through the long arid season (May to October). It became profitable for them to build settlements in which they could store the food they had gathered.

Then the climate developed a more marked seasonality. There was a warm, arid season (May to November) in which the Natufians had less success in finding food.[4] This more arid climate was not good for plant growth. The Natufian food supply shrank, and the number of settlements dwindled from twenty-three to five. In a few places, however, there were springs, where the water supply remained reliable. These became centers of settlement. Using hoes, the Natufians prepared the soil on the land around their settlements. Then they planted seeds, watering them with spring water when rainfall was deficient.

In these arid conditions annual plants with large seeds were selected. These plants had short reproductive cycles. They were self-fertilizing, and so their desirable characteristics tended to be stable instead of being lost through cross-fertilization with wild varieties. A disadvantage of plant domestication was that people selected plant specimens that lacked protective devices, both physical (for example, thorns) and chemical (natural poisons). This made plants more vulnerable to animals, insects, and microfungi. Moreover, a large expanse of a single food crop in village fields was more tempting to pests than the same plant dispersed among other plants less attractive to pests.

The Near Eastern farmers added two other important elements to their diet. Recently archaeologists have discovered unmistakable evidence of Neolithic era wine similar to today's retsina wine. The dregs of the wine in great jars have been dated to 5000 B.C.[5] Grapevines have deep roots and can survive a dry summer. Like grapevines, the olive tree has deep roots and so can find water during the summer. Olive oil is now a fundamental ingredient of various Mediterranean cuisines. Unlike animal fats, this oil does not clog arteries, which raises the odds of a heart attack.

Contaminated Food and Mortality

Food storage is relatively easy in arid conditions such as those of the Levant from May to November. Grain stored in a dry place is not likely to germinate, and the lack of moisture also discourages the growth of microorganisms (microfungi, bacteria, and yeasts).

Microfungi (molds) are the greatest threat to plants in the field and in storage. This is because they can grow in foods with only 16 percent moisture content, whereas yeasts and bacteria usually need 30 percent or more.[6] The storage life of grain is determined by its dampest point. Damp pockets in the grain favor microorganism growth, and the longer people store unprotected grain, the moldier it gets.

Moldy grain is not just distasteful; it may be lethal. Many microfungi produce poisons (mycotoxins) that damage the immune system of people and animals. With a damaged immune system it is hard for people and animals to resist the microbes that cause infectious diseases. While it has been commonly believed that infectious disease was the principal cause of death in Western societies prior to the twentieth century, especially for infants and children (and still is in many less developed regions of the world), I suggest that the status of the immune system had a strong influence on mortality rates. The status of the immune system depended in turn on the body's exposure to mycotoxins in food. This observation may help to account for variance in the occurrence of an infectious disease. Why was a given malady common in one year and rare the next? Why was it epidemic in one village and rare in a neighboring village? Why was there an association between high grain prices and high mortality?

In 1698, a famine year, Andrew Fletcher told the Scottish parliament in Edinburgh that "from unwholesome food diseases are multiplied among the poor people."[7] Why? Most people realized that moldy grain was bad for them, but when grain prices were high, the poor were forced to eat moldy grain anyway. They would then be more likely to come down with infectious diseases, and mortality would increase.

Weaned infants and children were the most vulnerable to death from infectious diseases. This may be explained by two circumstances. Weaned infants began to be exposed to cooked grain and other foods that might be moldy. (Since this exposure coincided with the eruption of teeth, English records attributed many deaths of weanlings to "teething.")

Further, infants and small children grow very fast and consume more food per unit of body weight than adults. If that food is poisonous, small children would ingest more poison per unit of body weight than adults. These toxic, immunosuppressant chemicals in spoiled food made children more vulnerable to infection.

Mycotoxins can have an impact on population in another way, too. Not only are many mycotoxins immunosuppressants;[8] some, such as zearalenone and certain ergot alkaloids, are fertility suppressants.[9]

Animal Husbandry

Although cultivation of grain crops can both encourage population growth and, under certain circumstances, increase the vulnerability of a population to infectious diseases, settlement also leads to the development of animal husbandry. About a thousand years after domesticating cereal crops, the Natufians domesticated sheep and goats. Sheep and goats were walking larders that the Natufians could utilize when they needed milk or meat. These animals could survive for long periods in drought-prone areas with little food. Like cattle, they are ruminants, and so they do not have to consume proteins to make proteins. Instead, they can make proteins by breaking down cellulose and combining it with nitrogen.

By domesticating plants and animals, the Natufians domesticated themselves. They had to become people of steady habits: crops could not wait for water, nor animals for feed. At the right moment in the fall crops had to be sowed; when ripe, they needed to be harvested; when harvested, they had to be winnowed and stored. Animals needed to be cared for, driven from pasture to pasture, and given feed when pasture was insufficient. Moreover, they could die of fungal poisoning and as a result their flesh was contaminated.

Agriculture Outside the Near East

Europe

By 6000 B.C. farmers had moved from the Levant by way of Anatolia and Greece into Europe. By 3000 B.C. they reached England and Scandinavia. In Europe there was enough rainfall for dry farming (farming without irrigation).

The European soils that Neolithic farmers preferred were those with high fertility and a light texture that made them easy to work. The best of these soils was loess. When it turned into dust the wind blew it away and redeposited it elsewhere. When enriched by partially decomposed wild grasses, loess turned dark and became the famous "black earth," or chernozem. In arid conditions such as those of northwest China the loess was yellow. Uncultivated loess is often covered with grass, but in early Neolithic central Europe it was covered with dense deciduous forests.

Pigs were the most efficient converters of plant food energy into meat. They could convert 35 percent of this energy, compared with 13 percent for sheep and 6.5 percent for cattle. They could live on mast (acorns, beechnuts that fell to the ground, and chestnuts) in the abundant forests of northern Europe.

This being so, anthropologists have wondered why there was so little pig husbandry in Europe south of the Alps and Pyrenees and in North Africa and the Levant. They have wondered why Moslems and Jews choose not to eat pork. Marvin Harris has argued that caring for pigs is not cost-effective in unforested areas because pigs require more shade and water than sheep and goats.[10] Moreover people cannot shear, ride, or milk these animals. They are unsuited to pulling a plow or wagon.

If they lack something better to eat, pigs will eat human feces. So people consider them "dirty." However, this does not explain why north of the Alps and Pyrenees religious authorities permitted pork consumption while those to the south of these ranges forbade it. Moreover, in ancient and medieval times the forests of the Mediterranean basin were more extensive than they are today and could have provided enough shade and water for pigs.

When forests were scant, farmers might feed spoiled human food to pigs. This spoiled food might be poisonous. Mycotoxins such as ochratoxin-A in pig feed can damage cellular and humoral immune functioning of humans who consume pork. Moreover, J. Fink-Gremmels found that ochratoxin-A in pork sausages could be transmitted from mother to infant by breastfeeding.[11]

In ancient and medieval northern Europe, however, as long as there were abundant forest clearings where pigs could safely graze, pork was less likely to become contaminated. Farmers did not have to keep pigs in pens and feed them spoiled human food. The same was true of British North America before deforestation, where forests were abundant and accessible pork was relatively safe to eat.

Wild oats and rye spread to Europe as weeds. They could be grown in the sour soils of the cold higher altitudes and latitudes of Europe and northern Russia. Around 1000 B.C. oats and rye became important as field crops.

Nile and Tigris-Euphrates Valleys

Meanwhile, between 6,000 and 5,070 years ago, when the weather became more arid and cold on the desert margin of the Nile Valley, grazing animals did not thrive as before. So hunters were more attracted to the uncultivated land in the valley. This rich soil had accumulated during the preceding warm and wet period, when rivers such as the Nile often overran their banks, depositing silt on land instead of carrying it to the sea. Here again we see the influence of climatic change on prehistory.

People soon discovered that the soil of the Nile Valley was easy to work and fertile. Here and in the valley of the Tigris-Euphrates there was not enough rain for dry farming, and agriculture depended on irrigation with river water. Note that farmers were well established in the Levant, Anatolia, and Europe before they began to farm in the river flood plains of Egypt and Mesopotamia.

Africa

In Africa wheat and barley could be cultivated only in cool, dry highlands. They could not withstand the molds and other microbes that flourished in conditions of high temperature and humidity, as in tropical Africa. Sometime between 4,000 and 2,000 years ago Africans probably domesticated millet and sorghum on the grasslands north of the tropical rain forest. Before the first millennium A.D. there was no settled farming in the tropics. One reason may have been that a metal cutting tool is necessary to clear scrub, bush, and woodlands. When iron smelting technology reached southern Africa, farming began.[12]

Indus Valley

Between 2500 and 1700 B.C. conditions in the Indus Valley of India were quite wet. Here the people of Harappa and Mohenjo-daro cultivated an area greater than that of the Nile and Tigris-Euphrates Valleys combined. Their houses had running water. They sowed the same staple crops as those in the Near East.

The Americas

Some scientists think that in the Americas at the end of the Pleistocene Era (the glacial era) there was a reduction in grasslands. Around 11,000 years ago three fourths of the big game (megafauna) went completely extinct. This forced native Americans to seek other food sources.

The domestication of the precursor of maize (teosinte?) occurred in southern Mexico about 8,000 years ago. In the next millennium on the coast of northern Peru farmers cultivated squash, beans, chili, and cotton. By 3000 B.C. in southern Mexico farmers cultivated all these crops, together with avocados, gourds, and pumpkins. Between A.D. 800 and 1100 there was a rapid shift to maize cultivation in eastern North America.

Between 8000 and 7000 B.C. in the Andes native Americans domesticated potatoes. By 4000 B.C. they added corn to their diet. In the varied microenvironments of the Andes farmers discovered many other attractive food plants that they could domesticate.

East Asia

Around 6500 B.C. in north China farmers began cultivating the yellow loess soils of the Yellow River basin. They domesticated millet, soybeans, peaches, pigs, and chickens. The summers were wet from monsoon rainfall and the winters were dry, just the opposite of Mediterranean conditions. Northern China was drier than southern China, and consequently food could be preserved more easily. This may serve to explain why agriculture began in the north of China.

By 5000 B.C. the Chinese had become the earliest known cultivators of hemp (*cannabis sativa,* marijuana) and were aware of its psychoactive characteristics. In Chekiang they began cultivating rice; this is the first evidence of rice domestication in China. Around 3000 B.C. they borrowed wheat, richer than millet in energy and minerals, from the Near East.

Around 1000 B.C. the Chinese domesticated soybeans, which produce more usable protein per acre than any other legume or cereal. Soybeans are a source of calcium, phosphorus, and iron and improve the soil by fixing nitrogen. As the Chinese population grew, the supply of pastureland became more and more limited. Therefore soybeans became increasingly important as a source of protein.[13]

South and Southeast Asia

In eastern India, Burma, and Thailand monsoon rains were predictable. About 5,500 years ago farmers engaged in dry rice cultivation. By 2500 B.C. they were practicing wet rice cultivation in the river valleys of Southeast Asia, especially the valleys of the Chao Phraya, Mekong, and Red Rivers. In the first millennium B.C. this practice expanded to south China and north India, supporting the development of dense populations. By planting rice, farmers could obtain more calories per hectare of land than they could with any other crop. But wet rice cultivation is limited to level ground where an adequate supply of water is available, most often from monsoon rains. [14]

Pre-Writing, Trade, and Metallurgy

Even before people invented writing, farming societies developed devices for predicting natural events. The first calculating devices may have been megalithic monuments. In maritime Western Europe we find stone circles that may have been celestial observatories; Hawkins, for example, suggests that Stonehenge was used to determine solstices and predict eclipses.[15]

According to Denise Schmandt-Besserat, in Neolithic Syria farmers took basic steps forward in information storage and transmission.[16] Some made ceramic tokens in geometric shapes: cones, spheres, discs, cylinders, rectangles, triangles, etc. People apparently used them for keeping account of food and animals to be stored or traded. They put some tokens inside clay envelopes, which they labeled when wet with impressions of the tokens themselves. This may have been the beginning of an efficient writing system.

The counting system was primitive. There were no tokens representing numerals. For example, to indicate three similar items, three tokens were used; each token was related to an object on a one-to-one basis, and they could be counted to obtain totals.

The tokens may have been helpful to traders. Early farming communities engaged in commerce. The four most important goods traded were flint, obsidian, copper, and salt. In Europe flint was an important article of trade, and to find flint mines Neolithic people, using antler picks, dug thirty to sixty feet through chalk. Obsidian, or volcanic glass, was also significant, as it could be given an edge sharper than a surgical scalpel.

Another important item traded was salt.[17] Salt is plentiful on or near the surface of the earth but is not evenly distributed. As long as people hunted and ate meat regularly, they did not need salt, but once settled farming began, many needed to trade in order to obtain salt. Domesticated animals were too valuable to slaughter, so people took from them wool, eggs, milk, and energy for traction.

Compared with foragers, the early farmers were probably involuntary vegetarians. In order to maintain hydrostatic balance they needed to ingest salt. In dry, hot areas where fresh animal and plant foods were unobtainable salt was very important. Europeans used it in the making of butter and cheese and for preserving meat and fish.

Prior to 5000 B.C. the only metals used were gold, copper, and silver, which were commonly found in their elemental form. (In places where elemental copper was found there would often also be brightly colored minerals such as malachite, turquoise, and lapis lazuli, which are copper compounds.) Between 5000 and 4000 B.C., Egyptians mined and smelted copper, the first metal to be widely used and traded. By 4300 B.C. Europeans independently invented the art of copper smelting. Copper ore is oxidized copper. To release elementary copper it is necessary to reduce the ore, creating an atmosphere poor in oxygen and rich in carbon with a temperature of at least 1,084 degrees Celsius. Ceramic makers probably helped to develop copper smelting. When fired at only 450 degrees Celsius clay can be hardened. However, a charcoal fire cannot exceed 700 degrees Celsius. To produce more rigid pottery it is necessary to heat it for hours in a kiln above 1,400 degrees Celsius. This temperature would have been more than enough to smelt (reduce) copper.[18] Once smelted, copper was used for all sorts of tools.

The first known copper smelting furnace was found in the Sinai and has been dated to 3800 B.C. The discovery in the Tyrol in 1991 of the nearly intact frozen body of a man who lived around 3300 B.C. and was carrying a copper ax provides us with the earliest known example of such a tool.

Transportation Technology and Trade

Once people settled in a village on a river, lake, or seashore they built more boats so that they could trade with their neighbors. The earliest trading expeditions were probably waterborne. People built dugouts and log rafts first, and the first means of propulsion were probably poles, paddles, and oars. Plank-built wooden boats required the use of metal tools in their construction and did not appear before the fourth millennium B.C.

Thor Heyerdahl made a career out of demonstrating that rafts of balsa logs and boat-shaped reed rafts could cross oceans. Both were available in pre-Columbian America; boat-shaped reed rafts, made of reed bundles lashed together with a continuous spiral cord, were found in ancient Egypt and are made in contemporary East Africa as well.

The reed raft is surprisingly safe because it is self-buoyant—water washes through it. Some reeds even get stronger during prolonged submergence in ocean water. On the open ocean a reed raft moves over and between swells with ease. Likewise, balsa logs, if cut green and full of sap, are water-resistant. Rafts of these logs can be maneuvered by centerboards.[19]

Skin boats (such as kayaks) made on frames of willow or other pliant wood were dominant north of latitude 45 or 50 degrees. They kept their occupants relatively dry (wash-through rafts are not practical in cold regions) and were light enough for easy portage.

Trade tended to support the development of market towns located on trade routes. It probably brought market towns an unperceived benefit, for settlements that traded in food had more diversified food resources available to them and were no longer dependent on locally grown food. Imported food might be less contaminated at point of origin than local food—clearly a benefit. Food could not be imported over long distances without spoiling. It was mostly carried in coastal trade. But if contaminated with mycotoxins it was harmful on short voyages. In addition, even if all food from diverse sources was contaminated at point of origin, it would be likely to contain small amounts of various fungal poisons, which is probably less dangerous than a large amount of one locally grown poison.

It follows that the development of cargo-carrying coastal sailing ships was also an advance. The greater the volume of trade, the greater the diversification of food sources, and the lower the mortality.

Toward the Birth of Civilization: A Shift to Violence

Marija Gimbutas, a great European archaeologist, has argued that the mother-goddess-worshiping farming communities of the Neolithic Balkans and Anatolia were more civilized than the states of Egypt and Mesopotamia that succeeded them.[20] Before the late fifth millennium B.C. archaeologists found no weapons for killing people among the artifacts of these matristic societies. It is not clear just why violence began and why it intensified in the ensuing millennia. What we do know is that violence and the birth of "civilization" went together. To be "civilized" in the historical sense, it was not, as many think, necessary to be peaceful, much less to have good manners.

Notes

1. Richard S. McNeish, *Origins of Agriculture and Settled Life.*
2. Bruce D. Smith, *Rivers of Change; Essay on Early Agriculture in Eastern North America.*
3. Mark N. Cohen, *Health and the Rise of Civilization,* pp. 59–61.
4. Donald O. Henry, *From Foraging to Agriculture: The Levant at the End of the Ice Age,* pp. 12–13.
5. John N. Wilford, "In the Annals of Winemaking, 5000 B.C. Was Quite a Year."
6. Clyde M. Christensen and Richard A. Meronuck, *Quality Maintenance in Stored Grains and Cereals,* p. 41.
7. Hubert H. Lamb, *Climate, History and the Modern World,* p. 212.
8. James J. Pestka and Genevieve S. Bond, "Alteration of Immune Function Following Dietary Mycotoxin Exposure"; Pestka and Bond, "Immunotoxic Effects of Mycotoxins"; A.C. Pier and M.E. McLoughlin, "Mycotoxic Suppression of Immunity"; J.M. Beardall and J.D. Miller, "Diseases in Humans with Mycotoxins as Possible Cause."
9. Mary Matossian, *Poisons of the Past,* pp. 59–69; "Climate, Crops and Natural increase in Rural Russia, 1861–1913"; "Effects of Natural Fungal Toxins on Fertility and Mortality in Connecticut, 1660–1900."
10. Marvin Harris, *Good to Eat: Riddles of Food and Culture,* p. 67.
11. T. Kuiper-Goodman, "Risk Assessment to Humans of Mycotoxins in Animal-derived Products"; Pestka and Bond, "Alteration of Immune Function"; J. Fink-Gremmels, "Mycotoxins: The Situation in Europe with Special Emphasis on West Germany."
12. G. Mokhtar, ed., *General History of Africa,* vol. 2, pp. 300, 326, 385.
13. E.N. Anderson, *The Food of China;* Frederick J. Simmons, *Food in China: A Cultural and Historical Inquiry.*
14. Charles Hingham, ed., *The Archaeology of Mainland Southeast Asia,* pp. 6, 30; D.R. Sar Desai, *Southeast Asia, Past and Present,* 2d ed., p. 7.
15. G.S. Hawkins, *Stonehenge Decoded.*
16. Denise Schmandt-Besserat, *Before Writing: From Counting to Cuneiform,* vol. 1.
17. S.A.M. Adshead, *Salt and Civilization;* Robert P. Multhauf, *Neptune's Gift: A History of Common Salt.*
18. Robert Raymond, *Out of the Fiery Furnace: The Impact of Metals on the History of Mankind.*
19. Thor Heyerdahl, *Early Man and the Ocean, passim.*
20. Marija Gimbutas, *The Civilization of the Goddess,* p. viii.

3 THE BIRTH OF "CIVILIZATION"

4000 to 500 B.C.

Pride goeth before destruction and a haughty spirit before a fall.

—Proverbs 16:18

At the beginning of civilization two new technologies started a cascade of other innovations. The invention of writing set off the first communication revolution. The invention of the wheel and the wagon set off the first revolution in land travel. With these in place, we begin to have evidence of various political elites controlling a city-state. These early states consisted of a town and its food-producing hinterland. The city-states were not "democratic," nor did their rulers respect the rights of individuals. The ruler and his men did not build judicial establishments; rather, the law represented the will of the strongest. The ruler was primarily a war leader.

A city needed a strong tax base to survive, so the larger the population the better. Just before the birth of civilization the climate in Mesopotamia turned warm and wet, favoring good harvests. As the food supply increased, so did the population. As the population increased, so did tax revenues. As tax revenues increased, the larger and more powerful a government could be.

Plowing and Irrigation

An optimum climate in the Near East occurred around 3000 B.C. It coincided with intensification of agricultural production in the valleys of the Nile and Tigris-Euphrates. The farmers in these valleys improved on their good luck by inventing new technologies, including the plow and elaborate irrigation systems, and by so doing so made possible intensified agriculture. Plowing allowed plants to use more of the soil's nutrients. It served to loosen the surface of the soil, pulverizing it and clearing it of weeds. But there were drawbacks to plowing. It required traction animals, which farmers had to feed all year round. Plowing also exposed topsoil to wind and water erosion. Referring to soil damage, Daniel Hillel said that in the history of civilization, "the plowshare was far more destructive than the sword."[1]

Farmers probably practiced small-scale irrigation in the Nile Valley, the Tigris-Euphrates Valley, and the Indus River Valley. By the third millennium B.C. the inhabitants of all these valleys had built large-scale irrigation systems. Unfortunately, among the byproducts of irrigation were silt and salt. Silt deposits on river bottoms raised the level of their beds, causing flooding, and clogged irrigation canals. All water used in irrigation contained dissolved salts, which tended to accumulate in the soil, and in arid regions natural rainfall was insufficient to leach them out and keep root zones from being poisoned. In Mesopotamia in spring, when the snows melted in the Anatolian highlands, the rivers flooded. Water evaporating during the summer left salt deposits.

In Egypt, on the other hand, the Nile, fed by the monsoon rains that had fallen in East Africa, began to rise in mid-August and peaked in early October. By this time the summer heat had killed weeds and aerated the soil. The bed of the Nile was deeper than that of the Tigris and Euphrates Rivers, its flood plain was narrower, and its irrigation canals were shorter. Farmers trapped the Nile flood waters in basins surrounded by banks. Before they sowed their crops they allowed the water to soak into the soil. Then they drained off excess water. In this way the salts remained dissolved and were flushed away.[2]

The Chinese also used irrigation to feed their growing population. The Yellow River carried loess silt from the dry northwest to the Yellow Sea. This river was notorious for flooding and changing its course, destroying crops, animals, and human life. People began irrigating here by 2200 B.C., but these projects did not become important until 800 B.C.

The Invention of Writing in Eurasia

The needs of political elites and traders prompted the invention of writing in the Near East around 3500 B.C. As they built their city-states, the Sumerians unwittingly began a revolution in communication. In the city of Uruk in 3730 B.C. they progressed from the use of simple tokens representing commodities to tokens representing manufactured products. These products included bread, oil, beer, perfume, and metal goods. Complex tokens had linear and punched marks on them. Scribes represented such marks by using the sharp end of a stylus, a wedge-shaped tool, to make impressions on a wet clay tablet. The earliest pictographs reproduced the shapes of tokens and contained lists of goods. This happened at about the same time that Sumerian officials were creating monumental architecture, establishing standard weights and measures and archives, and, to support all this, developing systematic taxation. Temple priests kept inventories of the taxes in kind that they received from the people.

Clay tablets were an improvement over tokens because a tablet held information permanently, whereas tokens could be separated from each other. Tablets could also provide more information because they assigned parts of the field to recording particular data.

In the archaic system of listing commodities and goods there was a one-to-one correspondence between symbols and what they represented. For example, three sheep's-head tokens represented three sheep. In the new writing system, numerals, such as 3, were abstract concepts. They could represent three of anything. They were more efficient for counting than three sheep's-head tokens and the like.

Once the Sumerians created abstract numerals, by the same process they created other symbols, both abstract ones such as squares, circles, and triangles, and iconic ones such as eyes. Then they phoneticized these symbols. To use an English-language example, an eye icon could represent not just an eye but also the word *I* or any other syllable or word with the same sound.[3] This was important because many words cannot be represented by drawing an object. They can, however, be represented by drawing an object whose name has a different meaning but the same sound. To take some other English-language examples, the word *cannot* can be represented by images of a tin can and a knot. The idea of a clause can be represented by an image of "claws." It is easy to represent a bear, hard to represent *bare*. So the scribe could use a bear to represent the sound of the word, no matter what its meaning; the reader would have to infer the meaning from context.

The process of phoneticization, so necessary to a successful writing system, required that the graphic sign of an object be linked with a linguistic sign (a spoken word). Two changes had to occur for this to happen. The first change was the simplification, or abstraction, of the visual sign. This reduced the strength of its connection with a visible object. It also reduced the time needed to write it. The second change was a tightening of the connection between the visual sign and the linguistic sign (spoken word). In time the visual sign became readable; meanwhile, the linguistic sign (a sound) became writable.

The Akkadian people in northern Mesopotamia spoke a Semitic tongue quite different from Sumerian. They wished to write their own language in the Sumerian script (cuneiform). Scribes, in their efforts to use this Sumerian script for Akkadian and other languages, developed their writing into a universally useful tool. By 2500 B.C. they were able to write anything, not just lists.[4]

In the third millennium B.C. the Egyptians developed a writing system, hieroglyphics, based on the same principles. Between 2500 and 2000 B.C. they began to write on papyrus, a paper made from a tall sedge native to the Nile Valley. Since papyrus was brittle, it could not be folded and had to be rolled up into scrolls. It was easier to store papyrus scrolls than sun-baked clay tablets. How could a bureaucrat function without such an inexpensive, easily stored, and quickly retrievable writing material? It seems likely that just as bureaucrats multiplied documents, papyrus multiplied bureaucrats.

Priests probably invented the first Near Eastern writing systems, cuneiform and hieroglyphics. It took a priestly scribe many years to master these systems. Many people who kept written records needed a simplified, more user-friendly writing system. Phoenician merchants, those who "went down to the sea in ships, and did business in great waters" (Psalm 107:23), deserve the credit for the invention of the alphabet. In the eighteenth century B.C. their alphabet consisted of twenty-seven or twenty-eight signs; by the mid-seventeenth century B.C. the Phoenicians had reduced it to twenty-two signs, each a consonantal phoneme. There was no need for vowel signs because in the Western Semitic language family, to which the Phoenician language belonged, all syllables began with a consonant. They used the principle of acrophony, which means they represented a sound by a picture of an object whose name began with that sound. Merchants using only twenty-two signs could represent all the language's syllables.

For example, in the Phoenician alphabet, *aleph,* meaning an ox head, stood for *a* (a consonant in Semitic). All syllables that began with that sound were represented by the same figure (the letter A, an upside-down oxhead). Scribes used *beta,* meaning "house," for all syllables starting with *b.* They used *dalet,* meaning "door," for all syllables beginning with *d.* The equivalent Greek letter, *delta,* is an equilateral triangle. The Greeks, however, did not start all their syllables with a consonant, and so needed to add vowels to the Phoenician alphabet.

According to Barry Powell, the Greek alphabet was invented on Euboea between 800 and 750 B.C. The motivation of its inventors, he thinks, was neither political nor commercial. Rather, they wanted to make a written record of the epic poetry of Homer.[5] Many Greeks were traders, however, and probably picked up the idea of writing quickly because they found it useful.

The priestly class in Egypt and Mesopotamia did little to simplify their complex writing systems, probably because they wanted to maintain their valuable cultural monopoly. The Phoenician and Greek traders did not have to contend (for a time) with a powerful land-based centralized government. Therefore they had the motivation and the means to make their writing system more user-friendly.

By the time of the Shang Dynasty (1500–1451 B.C.), the Chinese had invented their own system of writing. In the future archaeologists may find evidence of an earlier origin for writing in China, because we know that by the Shang period the writing system was already well developed.

The use of the alphabet, although it spread from Phoenicia to India, stopped at the western frontiers of China. The Chinese writing system, as reformed in 221 B.C., is much the same today as it was then. There are thousands of Chinese characters, one for every word. Instead of reducing the number of characters to be memorized, the Chinese increased them.

The consequences of this were serious. Because Chinese writing took a long time to learn, only an elite could use it. The literate Chinese mandarins, or gentry scholar-bureaucrats, dominated Chinese society. Like the Mesopotamian and Egyptian priests, they had no motive to develop a user-friendly writing system.

Why didn't the merchants of China create a more user-friendly writing system, as did the Phoenicians? I do not know, but I have a suggestion. China had no inland sea like the Mediterranean, where a merchant-dominated society could build a seaborne empire. China's merchants could not easily escape the surveillance of its land-based government and create a more user-friendly writing system.

When the climate turned cold and arid, the Chinese government usually faced increased pressure from the nomads to the north or east.[6] The resistance effort absorbed a great proportion of the government's resources. With population declining and profits down, this would be the time for Chinese merchants to seek a cost-cutting innovation, as did the Phoenicians. But at this time the mandarins were apparently not disposed to accept a simplification of their complex writing system. That might threaten their monopoly on power. Chinese merchants, having neither a maritime state nor a nation of their own, had only two realistic options: to adapt to the imperial system, or to emigrate.

Social Control

How did rulers in the ancient Near East and China attain and maintain their power? Apart from using coercive forces to suppress revolts, what did they do to keep order? I suggest a study of the political implications of ancient religions.

In the past there were two functions for religion. The first was to influence the beliefs and moral values of individuals. Religion in that function might help individuals under stress and give them the power of self-correction when they went wrong.

Many religions also have political functions. Political elites have used religion to motivate people for secular ends. For example, during World War II, Stalin and company used the Russian Orthodox Church to keep up the fighting spirit of the people, though it was riddled with Soviet police informers.

During the beginnings of civilization in Mesopotamia, the people apparently came to see the universe as governed by an assembly of gods, not one god. The people of each city served their local god. The highest servant of a local god was the secular ruler of the city. People regarded him as a vessel of divine power. He was also responsible for keeping law and order and was the military commander during foreign wars.

The temple of the god, "managed" by the king, was the greatest landowner of the state. Most people were sharecroppers, servants of the king and nobles, or servants of the god. Their destiny was to take care of the god's material needs. For them the good life was an obedient life.

The Mesopotamian priests said that the god lived in the temple, inside a statue made of precious wood and overlaid with gold. A varied staff served the god: cooks, bakers, musicians, scribes, priests, and caretakers. The temple kitchen staff prepared daily meals for the deity. They clothed the statue with costly garments, bathed it, and escorted it to bed in the divine bedchamber. Some royal princesses "married" the god and lived in the temple as nuns.

In ancient Egypt the religion was much the same. Each town had a cult of the local god, who lived in a temple. The servants of the god fed and dressed it. Priests managed large tracts of land with workshops that supported the temple.

The king (pharaoh) of Egypt was portrayed as a god. He was the sole priest for all the local gods of Egypt; the other priests acted for him. The rulers of Egypt spent great amounts of money for their tombs. The thousands of workers who built them were servants of the god-king and were considered to be engaged in an act of piety.[7]

By identifying themselves with gods, the kings of the ancient Near East gained a number of advantages:

- They appeared more authoritative, the source of their power being divine.
- If things went well, the authority of the king was enhanced.
- If things went badly, the king could blame the god.
- If the people believed they were serving a god, they were less likely to resent the king's demands upon them.
- Above all, Near Eastern gods were powerful. The ruler encouraged people to believe in the power of the god and turn to it for favors and protection. People were told they had to obey the god and its servant, the king. If they disobeyed, they would be punished.

Climatic Change for the Worse

The timing of the appearance of city-states was probably not random. During the period between 5500 and 3000 B.C. in Mesopotamia, warm, wet conditions prevailed. The mean temperature was two to three degrees Celsius higher than it is today. It is reasonable to suppose that this was a good time for food plant growth and that the population grew. In the period between 2500 and 500 B.C., however, conditions in Mesopotamia became cooler and drier.[8] Consequently people tended to settle around larger watercourses. While the number of settlements declined, the average size of settlements increased.[9]

Sometime between 2334 and 2279 B.C. Sargon of Akkad united the city-states of Sumer and Akkad into a territorial state (empire). He probably had a standing army. For the first time he established direct links between his capital and other towns in Mesopotamia. But around 2200 B.C., during a severe drought, the Akkadian state collapsed.[10]

Speaking more generally of the Northern Hemisphere's climate, as indicated by bristlecone pine rings in California, Thomas Crowley called the period from 2500 to 500 B.C. the "Iron Age cold phase." I call it the Bronze and Iron Age cold phase. In central Europe this change reached a climax in the period between 1400 and 1230 B.C. It was extremely cold (the coldest period in the last eight thousand years).[11]

The cold, dry trend in the climate suggests that population growth was reversed, especially in the second and first millennia B.C. Archaeologists have found that from the late sixteenth to the early twelfth centuries B.C. the population of Palestine was declining. Between 1200 and 825 B.C. they found evidence of decline in the populations of Greece and Mesopotamia as well.[12]

Political Decentralization and Colonization

One consequence of the colder, drier climatic trend that began around 2500 B.C. was a more unfavorable balance between population and resources. In the eighteenth century B.C., perhaps because the population had declined significantly, the Babylonian Empire disintegrated. A powerful government needs a dense population to support it.

The severely cold, wet Lobben Phase in European climate (1400–1230 B.C.) coincided with hard times. The "Sea Peoples" (Philistines, Europeans?) invaded Crete, Palestine, and Egypt. It seems likely that the immigrants were of European origin. They destroyed the royal palace at Knossos, Crete, in 1400 B.C. After this, the Minoan civilization did not recover.

Between 1300 and 1100 B.C. the small states of Mycenaean Greece fought and destroyed each other. In the twelfth century B.C. the centralized Egyptian state was declining.

In northern China during the period from 721 to 481 B.C. there were 170 warring states. The period from 402 to 221 B.C. was another period of warring states that ended with integration into one empire.[13]

From the tenth to the seventh centuries B.C. the Phoenicians and Greeks were colonizing the shores of the Mediterranean Sea. At first glance this is surprising, for today we associate emigration with overpopulation in the home territory of the emigrants. In the past this was not necessarily so. Expansion might imply change in the mother country, change in the colonized country, or both. The region that was colonized might be lacking inhabitants with sufficient ability to resist.

As for the emigrants, all societies before the mid-nineteenth century normally tended to be top-heavy. This meant that more affluent and high-ranking men and women were more successful in producing and rearing children than poor and low-ranking couples. This variance in reproductive success was in accord with Darwin's theory of natural selection, but in such societies there was a chronic shortage of high-prestige niches (social positions) for the children of affluent families. As the author of Ecclesiastes 5:11 said, "Where there are great riches, there are also many to devour them." David Herlihy found support for this concept by analyzing the statistics from late medieval Italy.

Even in normal times, downward mobility was the dominant trend among elites, and many members of the next generation had to be enterprising in order to continue living in the style to which they were accustomed. *Moreover, in times of general population decline the children of the elite were worse off, since there were fewer poor people to support them in privileged positions.* Thus when labor was expensive, the younger sons of the elite were more likely than commoners to emigrate and become colonists of ill-defended foreign lands.[14] Today tens of thousands of Americans are descended from younger sons of the English gentry who emigrated to America in the early and middle seventeenth century. That period was one of cold weather and high grain prices. This theory may also explain Greek and Phoenician colonization of the Mediterranean in the tenth to seventh centuries B.C. Under the threat of downward social mobility, the younger sons of the elite hoped to find new places in which they could thrive.

Water Transportation

Periodically boats were needed to transport migrants during times of high emigration. Long-distance merchants needed boats on a regular basis. But prior to the nineteenth century, progress in boat and ship-building was slow. Wind, which was free, was the principal means of propulsion. But sailors could not control the winds: they could only try to predict them. They did not even have the compass to tell them their direction of movement.

By 5000 B.C. there were seagoing craft in the eastern Mediterranean. In the fourth millennium B.C. the Egyptians were sailing not only down but also up the Nile. The summer winds over the Mediterranean usually blew from northeast to southwest. In summer it was easy to move upstream with wind from behind.

At first the Egyptians used boats made of reed bundles, but later they imported wood from Lebanon and, using metal tools, built boats from wooden planks. In the second millennium B.C. they dug a canal from the Nile delta to the Gulf of Suez. This connected the Mediterranean with the mouth of the Tigris and Euphrates Rivers and with Iran. The canal joined two active markets, one in the Mediterranean and the other in the northern Indian Ocean.

Domestication of the Horse

The domestication of the horse occurred on the Eurasian steppe, where horses were abundant. The zoologist Juliet Clutton-Brock believes that a prehistoric dun-colored striped horse species found in what is now the Ukraine was the ancestor of all other horse species. The timing of the domestication of the horse probably coincided with the shift to a cold, arid climate during the Piora Oscillation, 4200–3800 B.C. When the climate on the steppe got cold and arid, the horse, since it was so adept at foraging with snow on the ground, tended to replace cattle and sheep. Cheek pieces from a bridle that were found in the Ukraine and which have been dated to around 4000 B.C. provide evidence of the domestication of the horse, as wild horses do not wear bridles or cheek pieces. Fossilized remains from the Ukraine also show signs of wearing on horse premolars, where a bit might have been placed.[15]

Horses are fast and strong compared with other quadrupeds. While a human being walks at 3 mph, a horse walks at 4 mph, trots at 9 mph, and canters at 12 mph.

Invention of the Wheel: Revolution in Land Transport

By the fourth millennium B.C. the Sumerians had invented the wheel, and wheels soon appeared from the Rhine to the Tigris. In the third millennium B.C. the wheel reached India, and in the second millennium it came to Egypt and China. The first wheels were of solid wood, but sawyers did not cut tree trunks transversely, like salami. Such a slice would be vulnerable to radial fracture. Instead, carpenters and wheelwrights made wheels from thick planks taken from a hardwood tree trunk, often oak.

Once there were wheels it was possible to build a wagon. This invention caused a revolution in land transport. Before, it was easy to sail a boat down the Tigris-Euphrates River to the Persian Gulf, but it was hard to transport goods upstream. There was no reliable wind to do the job (as in the case of the Nile River). Now a horse and cart moving upstream could carry a load equal to that of twelve pack horses.[16] A horse can pull a cart twice as fast as an ox.

Wagons were extremely valuable in the conduct of commerce between Mesopotamia and its trading partners. Once goods reached the Persian Gulf, merchants could carry them by sea to Egypt, East Africa, and India. Now the return trip to Mesopotamia was profitable.

The spoked wheels used in chariots were much lighter. The outer rim, or felloe, was made of wood bent by heat. The nave of the wheel rotated freely on the axle, secured by a linchpin. Such wheels were first made in Europe around 2500 B.C. and were being used on chariots in Syria by 2300 B.C. Archaeologists have found spoked wheels dating from 2000 B.C. on the steppes of Russia. Wheelwrights could make wheels only near forests. Before roads were built people had to use them on open plains.[17]

Bronze Metallurgy

In almost all lands around the eastern Mediterranean the first responsibility of rulers was to defend their territories. Mesopotamia in particular, having no natural defenses, was vulnerable. Its armies had to rely on offensive strength, and so they needed adequate weapons.

Pure copper is too soft to make axes and swords and must be hardened by combining it with some other metal. The favored one was tin. In its presence the temperature needed to melt copper is only 950 degrees Celsius instead of 1,054 degrees Celsius. The resulting metal is bronze. Bronze is harder than copper even before hammering, and it is easy to cast.

The problem is that tin is rarer than copper. In the Middle East it was found in the Zagros Mountains of Iran and in the mountains of Anatolia.[18] Later, when long-distance trade was developed, traders obtained tin from Cornwall in Britain, Spain, and Bohemia, and from Malaya, Indonesia, Thailand, and China.

The secret of making bronze was known in the Near East by 3000 B.C. It may have come from Thailand or Vietnam, where bronze was made before that time. At first people there used bronze only for decorative objects, not tools and weapons.

The Chinese made sophisticated bronze decorative objects beginning in 1400 B.C. by hammering (forging) or casting in molds. They also used bronze to make battle axes, shields, helmets, armor, axles, and other parts of wheeled vehicles.

Iron Metallurgy

As populations grew, victory in warfare depended on the arming of more and more men. Since tin was relatively rare, bronze tools and weapons were expensive. Iron ore, on the other hand, was common, and the blacksmith did not need to alloy it with another metal to harden it. The problem was that natural iron ore could not be smelted below a temperature of 1,537 degrees Celsius. Even with bellows this was impossible to achieve in west Eurasian Bronze Age kilns.

Sometime between 1400 and 1200 B.C. on the southern Black Sea coast within the Hittite kingdom was a subject tribe of skilled metalworkers called Chalybes. They discovered the secret of making iron harder than hammered bronze. Using local iron ore, they produced "bloom iron" (slag) at 900 degrees Celsius. Then they hammered it until it became wrought iron. By heating, hammering, and quenching the hot iron in water the Chalybes were able to produce steeled iron stronger than cold-worked bronze. After the downfall of the Hittites in 1200 B.C. the Chalybes dispersed in the Near East and Europe, taking their knowledge with them.

Since wrought iron products were cheaper than bronze, more men could afford to obtain arms. Men fought wars on a larger scale. Around 875 B.C. cavalry displaced chariots, and by 500 B.C. massed infantrymen learned how to withstand cavalry attacks. Horses, quite sensibly, were afraid to charge into the massed heads of spears.

The Chinese advanced in iron metallurgy more quickly than the peoples of the western end of Eurasia. By the fourth century B.C. they were able to cast iron in molds. They could build furnaces that raised the inner temperature to 1,537 degrees Celsius, making iron molten. Then they filled their molds with molten iron. Europeans lacked such furnaces and could not cast iron until the fifteenth century A.D.[19]

Conclusion

The evidence we have of the birth of civilization tends to support the following hypothesis: In the temperate zone, the warmer the climate, the better the harvest, the lower the mortality, the larger the population, the greater the urbanization, the more powerful the government. Its reverse is also true: the colder the climate, the worse the harvest, the higher the mortality, the smaller the population, the less the urbanization, and the less powerful the central government. Political disintegration and colonization by elites are to be expected. These relations did not apply in tropical and arctic zones.

In early civilizations, as now, people invented new technologies to deal with new problems. The most important was the invention of writing. This invention survived the death of the people who created it. It brought the first great communication revolution. The wheel, which revolutionized land travel, survived the death of Sumerian civilization.

Before the twentieth century political elites used religion as their main means of social control. From the birth of civilization to the twentieth century they used priests to manipulate the beliefs and feelings of the common people.

During the period of climatic cooling and population decline, traders and raiders in Eurasia broke up the order of civilized life. Originating to the north and east, bands of armed men moved around the eastern Mediterranean in search of loot and slaves. Civilized peoples responded by developing new military technologies: the horse and chariot, bronze and iron weapons.

Notes

1. Daniel J. Hillel, *Out of the Earth: Civilization and the Life of the Soil,* p. 75.
2. Ibid., pp. 82–91.

3. Schmandt-Besserat, *Before Writing,* vol. 1, pp. 165–79.

4. Hans J. Nissen, *The Early History of the Ancient Near East, 9000–2000 B.C.,* pp. 138–39.

5. Barry B. Powell, *Homer and the Origin of the Greek Alphabet,* p. 181.

6. Jin-Qi Fang and Guo Liu, "Relationship Between Climatic Change and the Nomadic Southward Migrations in Eastern Asia During Historical Times."

7. H. Frankfort and H.A. Frankfort, *The Intellectual Adventure of Ancient Man,* pp. 64–65, 90, 185–88, 200–5, 228–30, 506.

8. Werner Nutzel, "The Climatic Changes of Mesopotamia and Bordering Areas, 14,000 to 2000 B.C."

9. Nissen, *Early History,* pp. 137–38.

10. Boyce Rensberger, "Severe Drought Doomed Earliest Empire."

11. Thomas Crowley, *Paleoclimatology,* p. 94.

12. J. Neumann, "Climatic Changes in Europe and the Near East in the Second Millennium B.C."; Robert B. Coote, *Early Israel,* p. 90; Barry Weiss, "The Decline of Late Bronze Age Civilization as a Possible Response to Climatic Change."

13. Pao-Kuan Wang, "On the Relationship Between Winter Thunder and Climatic Change in China in the Past 2200 Years."

14. David Herlihy, "Three Patterns of Social Mobility in Medieval History"; Jacques Heers, *Family Clans in the Middle Ages,* p. 62; Harry Miskimin, *The Economy of Late Renaissance Europe, 1460–1600,* p. 21; James L. Boone, "Parental Investment, Social Subordination, and Population Processes Among the Fifteenth and Sixteenth Century Portuguese Nobility"; Boone, "Noble Family Structure and Expansionist Warfare in the Late Middle Ages"; George Duby, *The Chivalrous Society,* pp. 74, 115–17; Edward Moise, "Downward Social Mobility in Pre-revolutionary China"; Conrad Totman, *Early Modern Japan,* pp. 255–59.

15. Juliet Clutton-Brock, *Horse Power: A History of the Horse and Donkey in Human Societies,* pp. 59–62, 97.

16. Maxwell G. Lay, *Ways of the World: A History of the World's Roads,* pp. 25, 43, 92.

17. Stuart Piggott, *The Earliest Wheeled Transport,* pp. 14–27; Piggott, *Wagon, Chariot, and Carriage;* John N. Wilford, "Remaking the Wheel: Evolution of the Chariot."

18. John N. Wilford, "Enduring Mystery Solved as Tin Is Found in Turkey."

19. Robert Raymond, *Out of the Fiery Furnace,* pp. 21–45, 61–62.

4 THE ROMAN EMPIRE AND THE HAN EMPIRE

200 B.C. to A.D. 200

> *Where there is neither Greek nor Jew, circumcised nor uncircumcised, barbarian, Scythian, bond nor free: but Christ is all and in all.*
>
> —Colossians 3:11

In Eurasia two large empires, one in western Eurasia and the other in China, reached a peak in population (about 50 million each) at approximately the same time. Was this a coincidence?

Since both Roman and Han rulers took censuses of population, we have some indications of their population size. According to the estimate of McEvedy and Jones, the population of Italy in Roman times increased from five million in 200 B.C. to seven million between A.D. 1 and 200. Then it declined from seven million to five million in A.D. 400. The Roman Empire at its height (c. A.D. 1–200) encompassed some fifty million people, heavily concentrated in the Greek-speaking eastern provinces.

China's population rose from forty-two million in 200 B.C. to sixty million in A.D. 200. By A.D. 400 it had declined to fifty-three million. In this period the Han Dynasty ruled almost all of present-day China.[1] Clearly both regions had enough people to support a large imperial government.

Political Organization

The basic unit of government throughout the ancient Mediterranean world was the city-state, usually with a population of five thousand to

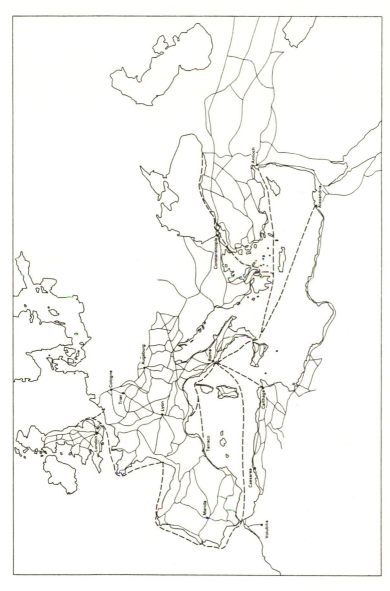

Figure 5. **The principal land and sea routes of the Roman Empire.** The most traveled sea routes were along the northern coasts, while the southern coast (of North Africa), was avoided. (Reproduced with permission from John Wacher, ed., *The Roman World* [London: Routledge and Kegan Paul, 1987], vol. 2, p. 659.)

ten thousand. Athens may have reached a hundred thousand, and the city of Rome may have reached one million. The Greek word for a self-governing town or city, including its satellite villages, was *polis,* hence our word *political.* The Latin word for this was *civis,* hence our words *civic, civil,* and *civilized.*

The government of a city-state may have been originally an exclusive all-male association. Participation in government was limited to those with the right to bear arms. The right to bear arms was the mark of a freeman, a full citizen. The origin of citizen voting probably was the customary right of free warriors to approve or reject the decisions of their leaders.[2] This idea persisted in Europe: After 1150, except for ministeriales (German administrators of humble, even servile origin), unfree persons were not permitted to own weapons.[3]

Italy was centrally located on the Mediterranean Sea, a center of commercial activity. When Romans controlled the whole sea they called it *Mare Nostrum,* "our sea." Protected by the Roman army, Mediterranean merchants prospered.

Roman imperial government had limited functions. The Romans sought to protect their borders and to maintain law and order. In cities the work of maintaining order involved providing bread for the urban poor and entertaining them with spectacles, often violent. We still use the phrase "bread and circuses" to refer to any palliative offered to offset discontent.

The Romans ruled peoples with diverse cultures. Latin was the common language in the western part of the empire, and Greek was used in the eastern part. Given the diversity of the ethnic groups they ruled, the Romans delegated authority to local elites familiar with their own customary law. But when individuals from different ethnic groups with different sets of customary laws had dealings with each other, this did not work. The Roman elite came to believe there should be a body of general law applicable to all ethnic groups throughout the empire. Theoretically no one, not even the emperor, was above the law.

Roman law, conceived in a framework of universal principles of justice, was a major cultural innovation. Preserved by the Christian Church, it became strongly established in twelfth- and thirteenth-century Europe. It has had a great influence on modern European law codes.

The Han rulers united all the Chinese and a few marginal non-Chinese groups. Their empire was relatively homogeneous. The government had many functions. This helps to explain why Chinese government was more centralized and bureaucratic than that of the Romans.

The Chinese did not develop a body of rational, universal law. Individuals and groups had no rights; people were equal only in their duty to obey the emperor, whose will was law. He claimed to be the benevolent father of all the people.

China had no inland sea. Merchants could not create a seaborne empire. As noted in Chapter 3, Chinese merchants were subservient to bureaucrats (mandarins). The mandarins regulated commerce and took a cut of the profits.

Political Thinking

Most ancient political philosophy consisted of exhortations to political elites to be gentlemen (China) or virtuous (Rome) (*vir* is the Latin for "man," and so *virtuous* means "manly"). The philosophers and sages promised that good men would prevail in the end. But ancient history often proved them wrong.

Sometimes ancient literature carried more realistic messages. In the fourth century B.C. in China, Sun Tzu, a general, wrote *The Art of War,* a military (and political) essay intended for political elites.[4] The following passages present some techniques for fighting rivals and enemies.

> All warfare is based on deception. (p. 66)

> Know the enemy and know yourself, your victory will never be endangered. (p. 129)

> Now the reason the enlightened prince and wise general conquer the enemy . . . is foreknowledge. (p. 144)

Climatic Changes

Why did the Roman and Han Empires rise and fall at about the same time? Let us consider climatic changes in Eurasia.

After 500 B.C. climatic conditions improved, growing warm and wet. This was favorable for the growth of food plants. The peak of warmth came between 200 B.C. and A.D. 200, at the same time as the peak in population. (Crowley classified a longer period—500 B.C. to A.D. 500—as warm.) Regional climates differed. In Mesopotamia it was humid; in the Netherlands from 200 B.C. to A.D. 250 it was dry; in north China it was cooler than it had been in the Shang period. In all cases climatic conditions were fair to favorable for the growth of plants and human populations.[5]

Crumley believes that in Europe from 300 B.C. to A.D. 300 a Mediterranean-type climate extended to latitude 48 degrees north, reaching Burgundy and the lower Danube basin. This was in contrast to the preceding cold period (1200–500 B.C.) and the unstable period following (A.D. 500–900). She believes that the warmer climate enabled the Romans to extend the Mediterranean agricultural economy northward.[6]

Industrial Technology

In the Mediterranean world the Roman era was not a time of major technological innovation. The Mediterranean peoples used crops and methods that had proven successful in certain areas and extended them to others.

Did productivity increase? Probably. The principle of specialization with complementarity was at work. Good natural transport conditions on the Mediterranean Sea, together with the peace enforced by Roman armies and navy, made it possible to trade in wine, oil, grain, and manufactures such as cloth, ceramics, and glass.

Since the Chinese lacked an inland sea, they met the increasing food demands of their population by improving their methods of cultivation. In the sixth century B.C. they began to plant their crops in rows and to hoe intensively between rows, a practice not employed in the West until the eighteenth century. Hoeing conserved soil moisture and destroyed weeds.

In the second century B.C. the Chinese invented a rotary winnowing fan operated with a crank. They used it to remove the husks and stalks of rice after threshing. Europeans did not make use of such a device until the eighteenth century A.D.

In the first millennium B.C. the Chinese learned how to smelt iron and cast it to make hoes, plowshares, and cooking pots. Production reached a peak during the Han Dynasty. Plowing with an iron plowshare instead of a wooden scratch plow increased the depth and ease of plowing, releasing more nutrients for food plants. Europeans could not cast iron and mass-produce iron objects until the fifteenth century; they had to make wrought iron by laborious hammering. According to Robert Temple, cast iron, which contains up to 4.5 percent carbon, is stronger than wrought iron and almost as good as steel.[7]

In the late fourth century B.C. (a troubled period before the Han Dynasty) the Chinese began to use heat-resistant clay for the construction of the walls of their blast furnaces. By adding iron phosphate to the furnace they reduced the melting point of iron to 950 degrees Celsius. To raise the temperature of the furnace they invented the double-acting piston bellows, which ejected air on both outstroke and instroke. This device reached Europe only in the sixteenth century.

During the Han Dynasty, in A.D. 31, Tu Shih harnessed water power to work the piston bellows. In the same century others learned to make steel by melting carbon-rich cast iron in a large crucible. The oxygen in the air drew off carbon in the iron until it was less than 1 percent. This was the same process that Henry Cort discovered in 1784.

In the troubled period after the end of the Han Dynasty the Chinese made further improvements in their metallurgy. At the beginning of the fourth century A.D. they began to use coal instead of wood as fuel in making cast iron. Europeans did not do this until the early eighteenth century. In the fifth century A.D. the Chinese melted cast iron and wrought iron together to make steel. This was the process that Siemens and Martin invented in 1863.[8]

I do not want to exaggerate the modernity of the Han economy overall. The Chinese elite mass-produced only salt and iron for sale to the masses. For themselves, the elite commissioned artisans to make by hand silk fabric, porcelain, lacquerware, and other fine products.

Historians have made many attempts to explain the technological backwardness of the Greeks and Romans compared to the creativity of the Chinese. They have tried to explain this backwardness by citing geographic factors. They say there was a deficiency of minerals along the shores of the Mediterranean. They complain of the lack of navigable rivers to link interior lands with those shores. However, the Chinese were no better favored by geography than the Romans. They had no inland sea. The Yellow River was not navigable. They had only the lower Yangzi River basin for commercial transportation.

Other historians say the Roman elite did not appreciate the manual labor of artisans and engineers (who were often slaves or freedmen).

Instead they spent large amounts of wealth for military campaigns and luxurious living.

However, there is no reason to believe that the Han ruling class was any less snobbish than the Greek or Roman ruling class with regard to manual labor. They were no less fond of luxury, nor less generous in equipping their armed forces.

Perhaps Chinese inventiveness was a matter of necessity. Having no inland sea, they had fewer opportunities for economic specialization and complementarity. Their best hope for increasing the productivity of their farmers was to improve agricultural technology. Given their greater vulnerability to invasion from the steppes, Chinese had a compelling military reason for improving their iron metallurgy.

Communication Technology

In the West the invention of the alphabet made literacy a possibility for all. Unfortunately, only Greek and Roman elite males, about 5 percent of the population, had access to schools.[9] The mere existence of an alphabet did not guarantee the spread of literacy.

The Han Chinese did no better. Literacy was a mark of elite status; a little knowledge in the hands of the common people might be a dangerous thing. The Chinese writing system did not become user-friendly.

In the West scribes and clerks used papyrus for routine writing and rolled it into scrolls. They used parchment for sacred writings and laws. To make parchment, workers stretched, scraped, and cleaned hides. One could write on both sides of a sheet. When bound, parchment would not weaken, and it would last almost forever. However, parchment was more expensive than papyrus.[10]

The Chinese first wrote on clavicle bones and wood. In the seventh century B.C. they wrote on silk. In the second century B.C. they invented rag paper, which they initially used as toilet paper and to make clothing. Their first use of paper for writing was in A.D. 110.

In China the disadvantage of the complex writing system was balanced by the advantage of its universality. Chinese elites in different regions, speaking different dialects, could all understand the written language. This served to bind them into a single, widely distributed ruling-class community, familiar with a common literature.

Transportation Technology

In the Roman and Han Empires there were no important innovations in transport vehicles, but the rulers did construct large-scale land transportation systems. They built great networks of roads, tunnels, bridges, and canals over which official couriers passed (see Fig. 6).

The basic roadmaking problem was that natural material soft enough to be formed into a smooth surface was rarely strong enough to bear a loaded cart, especially if the road was wet. Carts required wide, smooth roads.

In 2000 B.C. the Minoans built on Crete the oldest extant stone road. The Romans made little improvement in its design.[11] Richard Gabriel said that in all the Romans built fifty thousand miles of paved permanent roads, designed not so much for commerce as for troop movement. A legion could travel eight miles a day on a dry unpaved road, but thirty miles a day in any weather on a paved road.[12]

Soldiers constructed most Roman roads, as well as bridges, forts, and camps. Roman engineers chose to build roads on well-drained soil and on the sunny side of mountains, so that they would thaw and dry quickly.

In the first century B.C. the Romans discovered possolana, volcanic ash from Puteoli, near Naples. When mixed with lime, sand, and water, possolana made a concrete that would set and keep firm even under fresh and salt water. They used this in the construction of both roads and bridges.

The Romans had good roads, but relatively poor vehicles and equipment for their horses. Their barbarian enemies in Europe had poor roads but better vehicles and horse equipment. This was a problem for the Romans. Once the barbarians pierced Roman defenses, they could use their superior vehicles on superior Roman roads. But if the Romans invaded barbarian territory, they had to use inferior vehicles on inferior roads.

The Chinese government already had a well-organized road system in the first millennium B.C. They had couriers and post houses offering food and lodging. In the third century B.C. they built canals and irrigated extensively. In the first century A.D. they built suspension bridges over gorges using hemp rope and a crossbow to shoot the cable over the river.[13] The Han emperors expanded their territory south and westward, building new roads and linking natural waterways with canals. One canal, from the Yangzi River to Canton, was 1,200 miles long.

Without explosives, how did the Greeks and Romans build tunnels? They did it the "easy" way, by cutting through solid rock. They broke rock by first heating it with fire, then dousing it with cold water. In this way, in the sixth century B.C. the Greeks built a 3,400-foot tunnel on the island of Samos. In 36 B.C. the Romans built a 4,800-foot tunnel on the road between Naples and Puteoli.

In the Mediterranean Sea the trunk routes for ships ran along the north coast. The prevailing summer winds blowing from northeast to southwest made the south coast of the sea a dangerous lee shore. The north side of the sea had many deep harbors; the south shore did not. In the medieval period this was to be an advantage of Christians, who held the north shore most of the time, over Moslems, who held the south shore.

Sailors needed oars to get out of the Mediterranean. In the Strait of Gibraltar there was an adverse current flowing from west to east. At the Straits (common short name for the Bosphorus and Dardanelles) there was an adverse current flowing from east to west.[14] This tended to make the Mediterranean basin a world unto itself (see Fig. 6).

In Egypt the Greek ruler Ptolemy I (third century B.C.) and the Roman emperor Trajan (ruled A.D. 98–117) repaired and rebuilt the Nile–Red Sea Canal. This permitted transit by water between the Mediterranean Sea and the Indian Ocean. Merchants transported grain, wine, and textiles on this canal. In the first century B.C. Greek merchants made regular trips, using the monsoon winds, to the Malabar coast of India and along the east coast of Africa. In A.D. 166 they reached a port in Vietnam, probably Hanoi. They traded only in luxury goods, exchanging glass, gold, and silver for spices.

Roman ships were carvel-built: Workmen fitted the boards of the hull end to end. This minimized water resistance. They were up to 180 feet long and could carry a cargo of over a thousand tons.[15]

Chinese ships were just as good or better. By the second century A.D. they had watertight compartments in their holds, a feature not found in European ships until the eighteenth century.[16]

Long-distance east-west travel across Eurasia could only be accomplished by land, as there were no east-west rivers.

The Silk Road, passing through Central Asia and connecting China with the Near East and Rome, was operational at the beginning of the

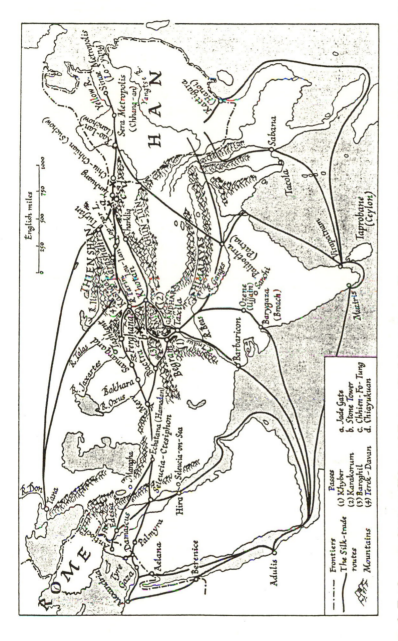

Figure 6. **Trade routes between China and Europe.** On these routes merchants conveyed many luxury goods and ideas. Food and other mass consumption goods went short distances by sea or canal. (Reproduced by permission from Joseph Needham, *Science and Civilization in China* [Cambridge: Cambridge University Press, 1954], vol. 1, p. 171.)

first century B.C. It stayed open until the third century A.D., when fighting disrupted travel. Only pack animals could use the rough Silk Road (few wagons made it), so the cost of transport was high. Generally traders exchanged only luxury goods: silk, jewels, jade, gold, and spices.

Han officials had to build and maintain canals and hydraulic works. They sent out regional inspectors to check on the activities of local officials. They maintained monopolies on salt and mass-produced cast-iron tools and weapons. No wonder, as Peter Garnsey estimates, the Han Empire employed about twenty times the number of officials as did the Roman Empire.[17]

The Struggle for Character

From the beginning of written records we find ideas of right and wrong. We also find condemnations of people who broke the rules of behavior accepted in their society. Most people regarded morality as conformity to social standards. Only when we find individuals who on moral grounds stand in opposition to their society can we talk about the struggle to develop a character. The lives of four men who fit this criterion fell between 600 B.C. and A.D. 100.

The earliest was Siddhartha Gautama (Buddha), c. 563 to 483 B.C., the son of a minor ruler in India. He adhered to universal moral norms (norms that could apply, in theory, to anyone), not those of caste, and welcomed followers regardless of social origin and gender. In a time when much of religion was ritualistic and mechanical, he insisted that ethical conduct was the foundation of spiritual development. Loving-kindness and compassion characterized an ideal Buddhist.

Confucius was a man of humble origins who lived from 551 to 479 B.C. in China. This was a period of anarchy and injustice at the end of the Zhou Dynasty. Confucius believed that heaven had given him a mission to become a perfect gentleman, free of pettiness, greed, and violence. The role of gentlemen was to govern. By setting an example Confucius hoped to create better gentlemen, better rulers.

Socrates of Athens, Greece, who lived from 470 to 399 B.C., the son of a sculptor and a midwife, was also concerned mainly with ethics. He believed that if people reflected persistently about good behavior and a good life, they would tend to lead good lives. If people thought about politics—good government—in time government would improve.

More than any other among the four men considered here, Socrates stressed the power of reason. He saw himself as a "midwife" for clear ideas in other people. He called himself a "philosopher," a lover of wisdom, and there were others like him in the Greek world. Politicians saw the social function of philosophers as teachers of rhetoric—the art of persuading audiences in public gatherings. They paid them to teach the art to their sons. But Socrates believed that the business of the philosopher was to teach goodness and truth, not to make a case for a position that was wrong or untrue.

How did philosophy develop in the Greek world in the fifth century B.C.?

I have a few suggestions.

• The Greeks were polytheists, that is, they believed in many gods, most of whom were thought to be unconcerned about ethical and intellectual issues. Philosophers tried to eliminate the gods and supernatural events from philosophical discussions. They believed in an orderly cosmos, operated by rational law *(logos)* similar to the laws of the Greek city-state *(nomos)*. This later became a fundamental assumptions of natural scientists. The Greeks (and others) experienced orderly government before they could imagine an orderly cosmos.

• The population of the Greek city-states was small. The urban political elites did not encourage an organized Hellenic priesthood to exercise social control.

All these were social control devices. Some philosophers challenged them.

When Socrates was seventy years old he goaded his "stupid" fellow citizens beyond endurance. A majority of these fellows ordered him to commit suicide by drinking poisonous hemlock. They argued that he had a subversive influence on the youth of the city. Although he could have escaped, Socrates did drink the hemlock, serenely.

Jesus (his Hebrew name was Joshua), who lived from about 4 B.C. to A.D. 30, was a carpenter well educated in Hebrew traditions. He lived at the height of the Roman Empire but in a province that was hostile to the Roman government. The upper class of this province was Greek by culture. Upwardly mobile Jews sought to become Hellenized.

Jesus wore unconventional dress. He went about the countryside with his followers, performing acts of healing and holding love feasts with people of all walks of life. He encouraged people to get into direct personal contact with God and each other.[18] Like Siddhartha Gautama he welcomed followers regardless of their social origin or gender.[19]

What Siddhartha Gautama, Confucius, Socrates, and Jesus had in common was commitment to universal moral principles and spiritual brotherhood. Each was successful in defining his own principles and living by them. All lived in Eurasia.

It is likely that all four men were familiar with different ethnic groups and moral standards. This would make it difficult to be strictly ethnocentric. Such exposure is a favorable circumstance for thinking in universal moral terms.

Socrates, Confucius, and Jesus were of humble birth. Buddha was born privileged but not powerful. All rejected the idea that personal merit could be inherited; rather, the individual had to develop it by his own efforts. Jesus said that such development was far more difficult for the rich than for the poor.

Apart from their philosophy, the political elites of a Greek city-state exercised social control by a variety of means. They held public debates, which any citizen could attend. In this way objections to a policy could be examined critically by interaction between speakers and audience, and the policy could be modified. The government gained legitimacy by allowing wide participation.

Some rich citizens built open-air theaters and staged distracting performances for the public. Others sponsored athletic competitions ("games"). Each city had a cult of its patron deity, whose principal function was to protect the city.

Imperial Decline

After A.D. 250 the climate began to deteriorate at the eastern and western ends of Eurasia. It was wet in the Low Countries (which would encourage mold growth in cereals) and cold in China. Climatic deterioration was associated with indications of population decline and political disintegration at the two ends of Eurasia.

However, in inner Asia (the arid zone of nomadism) conditions changed from dry in the third and fourth centuries A.D. to moist in the fifth century.[20] Moist conditions enabled the nomads and their herds to increase. This situation predicted nomad expansion at the expense of neighboring populations.

In the fifth century in some parts of the Roman West the decline was probably much more severe than in others. In a study of agricultural production in the third to fifth centuries A.D., Tamara Lewit surveyed both the relevant documentary sources and rural archaeological sites. She found no evidence of destruction or abandoned land in the third and fourth centuries. During A.D. 200 and 400 the effects of the invasions, she concluded, were localized. They did not generally reduce or impoverish farming in the western Roman Empire.

In the early fifth century, however, she found a widespread and sudden drop in occupation of about 50 percent in most rural sites. In northern France and Belgium the drop in occupation was between 9 and 19 percent of normal, a reduction in population of between 81 percent and 91 percent—more than the toll from the plague (around 33 percent). Lewit thought that epidemic disease, not invasion, caused this depopulation.[21] Ramsay MacMullen also found no population decline until the early fifth century in much of the western empire (ruled from Rome), North Africa, or the eastern empire (ruled from Constantinople).[22]

What caused the sudden population decline in the early fifth century? Did climatic or dietary change cause it? My guess is that lethal epidemics were responsible. Be that as it may, once severe depopulation occurred in a region of the Roman Empire, it became impossible to defend, for defending troops had to live off the land, and dead people produced no food.

The barbarians from eastern Europe and the Russian steppes were pastoralists whose dietary staples were milk, cheese, and meat. They preserved their surplus meat by smoking and drying it. On campaign they foraged, and when local food supplies were exhausted they could drink mare's milk and blood drawn from a vein in the horse's neck. They could also slaughter the animals (horses, cattle, sheep) that accompanied them. As a result they were not likely to suffer from either hunger or iron deficiency.

Moreover, as consumers of animal foods pastoralists would not run the risk of ingesting contaminated plant food. When invading a depopulated territory they would not be very likely to eat grain, since little existed, but would have to live off the food they brought with them. Therefore, if they depended on animal foods they would protect their immune systems and resist infections prevalent in that territory.

This may help to explain why the invaders did not settle down immediately in territory just inside the frontier, but went on to further conquests. If the territory near the frontier was depopulated, there was little to loot and few food producers to feed conquerors. So the invaders kept riding forward on the well-built Roman roads, roads that betrayed the purpose of their builders and served the invaders. As long as they had enough food, the invaders could choose the most vulnerable and attractive targets: weakly defended towns, villas, and monasteries. In this way they spread chaos west and south.

The mechanisms that had served to expand empires now went into reverse. Barbarian incursions disrupted trade and caused the loss to the imperial power of distant markets and taxpaying territories. As the imperial income diminished, the army and transportation systems deteriorated. The diet of the cities became more localized and perhaps more poisonous, and the mortality rate increased. Population declined, and the state disintegrated.

Conclusion

The period from 200 B.C. to A.D. 200 is notable in that favorable climate and population growth made possible two empires of about fifty million people each. These were the largest integrated political units ever seen on earth until that time.

In the period A.D. 250–500 cold weather and population decline contributed to political disintegration. In the fifth century A.D. nomad steppe barbarians consumed the remains of the Roman and Han Empires. Then for five centuries population failed to grow, and power remained fragmented.

Notes

1. Colin McEvedy and Richard Jones, *Atlas of World Population History*, pp. 107, 171. The estimate of the Roman population at its peak is from C. Warren Hollister, *Roots of the Western Tradition; A Short History of the Ancient World*, 5th ed., p. 186.

2. John Boardman et al., eds., *The Oxford History of the Classical World*, p. 207.

3. David Nicholas, *The Evolution of the Medieval World: Society, Government and Thought in Europe, 312–1500*, p. 251.

4. Sun Tzu, *The Art of War*.

5. Thomas J. Crowley, *Paleoclimatology,* p. 94; W. Nutzel, "The Climatic Changes of Mesopotamia and Bordering Areas, 14,000 to 2,000 B.C."; William H. Te Brake, *Medieval Frontier: Culture and Ecology in Rijnland,* p. 173; Jin-Qi Fang and Pao-kuan Wang, "On the Relationship Between Winter Thunder and the Climatic Change in China in the Past 2200 Years"; Jin-Qi Fang and Guo Liu, "Relationship Between Climatic Change and the Nomadic Southward Migration in Eastern Asia During Historical Times"; Emmanuel Le Roy Ladurie, *Time of Feast, Time of Famine: A History of Climate Since the Year 100.*

6. Carole L. Crumley, "The Ecology of Conquest, Contrasting Agropastoral and Agricultural Societies' Adaptation to Climatic Change."

7. Robert K.G. Temple, *The Genius of China,* pp. 42–49.

8. Ibid., pp. 15–20; Robert Raymond, *Out of the Fiery Furnace,* pp. 67–77.

9. William V. Harris, *Ancient Literacy,* p. 325.

10. Leila Avrin, *Scribes, Script and Books,* pp. 174–75.

11. Maxwell G. Lay, *Ways of the World: A History of the World's Roads,* pp. 25, 43, 92.

12. Richard A. Gabriel, *The Culture of War: Invention and Early Development,* p. 105.

13. Temple, *Genius of China,* pp. 58–60.

14. John H. Pryor, *Geography, Technology and War: Studies in the Maritime History of the Mediterranean, 649–1571,* pp. 1–21.

15. Vimala Begley and Richard D. De Puma, eds., *Rome and India: The Ancient Sea Trade,* Introduction, p. 9.

16. Lionel Casson, *Ancient Trade and Society,* p. 269.

17. Peter Garnsey and Richard Salter, *The Roman Empire: Economy, Society, and Culture,* p. 20.

18. John D. Crossan, *The Historical Jesus: The Life of a Mediterranean Jewish Peasant,* pp. 421–22.

19. Orlando Patterson, *Freedom in the Making of Western Culture,* pp. 207, 235, 296–303.

20. L. N. Gumilev, "Heterochronism in the Moisture Supply of Eurasia in the Middle Ages," p. 26. This is based on study of mud deposits in the Caspian Sea basin and other evidence.

21. Tamara Lewit, *Agricultural Production in the Roman Economy,* A.D. 200–400.

22. Ramsay MacMullen, *Corruption and the Decline of Rome.*

5 THE CHINESE MILLENNIUM

A.D. *500 to 1500*

*The dominant direction of social mobility in medieval society had
to be downward. The more rapid expansion of the higher social
strata tended to create a top-heavy social pyramid.*
— David Herlihy

For the last two hundred years European historians have considered the
period A.D. 500–1500 as the Medieval Millennium. From the perspective of world history a better name for it might be the Chinese Millennium.

In A.D. 500 China had a population of about fifty million people. By
1500 this number had doubled, and the Chinese had become the largest
population in the world united under one government. They had a
common market, written language, and political culture.

The Chinese government was the strongest in the world. The rulers
used civil service exams to recruit the best talent they could find as
officials. These officials were able to break the power of successive
warrior aristocrats who threatened the unity of the empire.

The Chinese produced important innovations in technology. Until
the fifteenth century they were responsible for most of the technological advances of worldwide significance. These breakthroughs made
modern history possible.

Climatic Change and Population History

The Chinese Millennium is a good period for studying the impact of
climate on history. At this time overall technological development was

insufficient to offset the damage caused by droughts, floods, and severe frosts. Even minor climatic changes had more influence on population trends than they do today. Moreover, we now have considerable quantitative information about climatic changes and population trends in China and Europe during this time.

The Chinese millennium may be divided into three periods: A.D. 500–1000, 1000–1300, and 1300–1500.

500–1000

During 500–1000, historians agree, Europe had a smaller and less prosperous population than it had in the time of the Roman Empire. Was this because of climatic adversity?

Monastic annals from this period are very poor sources of information about climate. Many years were not covered at all, and some reports were inaccurate. So we move outward in the causal network in search of proxies for factors that influenced climate.

Let us consider the relationship between volcanic activity and climatic trends. Today nonscientists are likely to think that volcanic eruptions have only local, short-term effects. Starting with the work of H.H. Lamb in 1970, geologists and meteorologists have compiled lists of eruptions since ancient times. Their work is part of an effort to reconstruct global climatic history. Their goal was to make better predictions of future climatic changes. The breakthrough discoveries came in the 1980s, when various scientific teams began to study sulfuric acid deposits as traces of volcanism in Greenland ice cores. An ice core is the frozen content of a cylinder sunk deeply into the ice. The ice at the bottom of the core reflects atmospheric quality at the time the snow originally fell. Ice that contains sulfuric acid deposits is the proxy record of earliest volcanic activity; the layer at the top of an ice core represents the most recent activity.

Volcanic eruptions, if sufficiently strong, usually reduce air temperatures on the surface of the earth. Eruptions strong enough to send sulfuric acid clouds into the stratosphere also spew out enough dust and ash to substantially block the rays of the sun for months and even years.

Some investigators suspect that by causing killing frosts in the grain crops in the fields in summer and early fall, volcanic activity increases fungal colonization of crops and the production of mycotoxins. On the

Table 1. **Volcanism and English Grain Prices, 1208–1325**

Peak in volcanism	Location	English grain price peak
1226	Eldeyjar, Iceland	1227
1257–58	unknown volcano, v.e.i. 9	1258
1270	Vesuvius	1271–1275
1287 ?	Sete Ciudad, Azores Crete Index 1287, 340 1290, 284 1291, 252 1292, 261	1291–1295
1311	Katla, Iceland 1312, 262	1315–1318

Sources: Henry Phelps Brown and Sheila V. Hopkins, *A Perspective on Wages and Prices* (London, 1981), pp. 44–45; D.L. Farmer, "Some Grain Price Movements in Thriteenth Century England," *Economic History Review* 10 (1957–58), p. 214; Simkin and Siebert 1994; Hammer et al. 1980.

other hand, a humid atmosphere in spring and fall favors the production of mycotoxins in grain in storage. These may have been important constraints on European population growth.

Recently Eugene Smalley, an American agronomist, observed that the eruption of Mt. Pinatubo (in the Philippines), caused killing frosts in Wisconsin in late summer and early fall and therefore increased fungal colonization of crops and production of mold poisons, or mycotoxins. We may suspect that volcanic activity in the past, by causing cold spells, increased the production of mycotoxins.[1]

The evidence of Greenland ice cores shows that during the period 500–1000 volcanic activity was above average and that the climate was cooler than average but not severely cold. In middle European latitudes (south of Scandinavia but north of the Mediterranean) this implied a wetter climate as well. The so-called Dark Ages may actually have been the Wet Ages (see Figure 4).[2]

In contrast, during the period 650–960 China enjoyed warm weather. The population may have doubled in that time. This larger population supported another integrated empire, that of the Tang Dynasty (618–907), which in its time surpassed all other contemporary states in the world. Originating in northern China, it took possession of the great agricultural resources of southern China.

Meanwhile, the Arabs became major actors in world history. Between 622 and 661 early Arab converts to Islam conquered Arabia, the Levant, Egypt, Iraq, and Iran. The Levant and Egypt had large Christian populations.

The causes of Moslem success in the seventh century are unclear. Our knowledge of changing climatic conditions in the Near East is meager. Between 590 and 647 it was very dry. In Byzantium (the Christianized eastern Roman Empire) there was drought in 591, 593–594, 598, and 605–606.[3] There was drought in Arabia in 630 and in 640, the latter called the "Year of Destruction."[4] Archaeological evidence for this time supports a hypothesis of population decline in settled areas.[5] Drought may have served to reduce the population and tax revenues of settled governments, weakening their defenses against Moslem attack.

It appears that the principal purpose of the early expansion of the Islamic community was not evangelism. The Moslems made little effort to convert their subject peoples. Instead, they made it politically and economically advantageous to be a Moslem. A majority of the conquered population espoused Islam, and many learned Arabic.

By sanctioning polygyny, the Islamic faith served to promote conquest in another way. No Moslem female of childbearing age had to be celibate for lack of a husband. It was the political elite of Islamic society who had the most wives. Given polygyny, which benefits only the more fortunate and usually older males, at any one time there would also be a large supply of young men without wives. *A normally top-heavy society would be even more top-heavy.* In the hope of acquiring female slaves many young men would be motivated to join military expeditions.

After the initial Moslem conquests, from 650 to 770, Nile flood levels indicate that the Mediterranean climate was moist. From 770 to 940 it was intermittently moist. That would explain why intensive agriculture involving irrigation could be practiced in the seventh to ninth centuries in the Near East and the Mediterranean basin. In the tenth century the climate grew more arid. It may not be coincidental that in the early tenth century the breakdown of the caliphate (centralized Moslem authority in Baghdad) was complete.[6]

After their initial conquest the Moslems spread the cultivation of sugar cane (which probably originated in India) in the Levant, Egypt, North Africa, and Spain. Christians later took it to the Atlantic islands (Canaries, Madeiras) and the Caribbean.

Another plant that Moslems disseminated was cotton. Various kinds of cotton were native to India, central Asia, and what is now Peru and Arizona. The Moslems took the annual cotton plants of central Asia, which were suited for planting in arid regions, and spread their cultivation in the Levant, Africa, and Spain.

Citrus fruits probably originated in Assam and north Burma. Moslems introduced the sour orange, lemon, and lime around the Mediterranean. These trees did well in the tropical and subtropical regions of the New World.[7]

Moslems disrupted the infrastructure of Christendom. The Romans had relied mainly on their control of Mediterranean sea routes to hold their empire together. Roman roads had never extended east of the Rhine or north of the Danube, and after the fourth century these roads deteriorated. When the Christians lost control of the eastern Mediterranean to the Moslems, there remained no transportation system to support European political integration. Christendom was divided as well as diminished, and diminished because it was divided. For five centuries the Christians were on the defensive against Islam.

One reason for this was demographic. After the fall of the Roman Empire the European population did not enjoy sustained growth until the eleventh century. Why? Certain possibilities can be ruled out. European peasants had the technology they needed to produce a good supply of food, To this was added the moldboard plow, which made it possible to cultivate not only loess but also wet soils. There was enough good land available to feed a much larger population. Invasions and political disorders were not of such a scale and frequency that they could have disrupted agriculture. They involved small numbers of fighting men. Te Brake thinks that during the ninth century Viking raids did not cause serious depopulation in the western Netherlands.[8]

So what does that leave us? Disease remains the principal suspect for depressing European population growth. But what kind of disease? The population was thinly dispersed, especially north of the Alps and Pyrenees, a condition that did not favor the spread of infectious disease. The spread of the culprit disease or diseases was probably not density-dependent.

Let us examine the possible implications of the wet climate in Europe during the "Wet Ages."[9] I suggest that north of the Alps and Pyrenees cold, wet weather resulted in the appearance of moldy food and musty air in wooden dwellings. Moldy food and musty indoor air are likely to contain certain microfungi that render people vulnerable to all kinds of infections.

The musty air in dwellings was partly the result of a reversion in the fourth and fifth centuries from Roman stone and brick construction to Celtic wooden buildings. Such buildings tended to have damp interiors.[10] Musty air contains spores of microfungi, some of them dangerous. It has been found that those who habitually breathe musty air are more vulnerable to deadly respiratory diseases. In Montreal investigators found that in "sick" buildings intoxication by inhalation was forty times more severe than by oral exposure.[11] In late 1992 and 1993 the residents of some new, poorly constructed condos in Virginia discovered that due to water leaks, their homes had been colonized by the mold *Stachybotrys atra,* which produces dangerous toxins. The residents of these homes suffered from nausea, numbness, loss of memory, vision problems, difficulty breathing, and constant infections.[12]

Moreover, grain grown in wet soils with the help of a moldboard plow has a higher moisture content at the time of harvest than grain grown on loess; this would increase the probability of successful fungal colonization of the grain. Increased cultivation of wet soils would increase the chances that the people would ingest mycotoxins in food. As long as the weather was cool and wet, use of the moldboard plow may have had more negative than positive results.

1000–1300

In southern China the weather was favorable during the period 1000–1300. During the Sung Dynasty, 960–1279, the Chinese developed agriculture nearly to its limits. They extended wet-field rice cultivation and built dams, sluice gates, norias for lifting water, and treadle water pumps. In 1012, on the initiative of the government, Chinese farmers began to extend the planting of Vietnamese Champa rice, which took 60 to 120 days to mature. This allowed double annual cropping of rice, or of summer rice with winter wheat. The standard of good food in south China became polished white rice and fish.[13] At the same time the Chinese developed specialty crops: cotton, sugar, tea, and oranges. These became important items of trade. On the demographic side, from 1000 to 1200 in China the population grew from 60 to 115 million, probably the most rapid growth in Eurasia.

During the Sung Dynasty reformers brought the civil service examination system to a still higher level. The government built schools throughout China so that all talented youths, even those of humble origins, had a chance to compete to become officials.

In northern China and the steppes around 1200 the weather turned cold and dry.[14] The Chinese population, after reaching a high of 115 million in 1200, dropped to 86 million in 1300. Meanwhile warm, wet conditions in Central Asia enabled the Mongols and their herds to multiply and overrun China. This was the first time nomads had been able to do so. But Mongol rule in China, the period of the Yuan Dynasty, lasted only from 1279 to 1368.

Western Europe enjoyed warm weather from 1000 to 1300. Figure 3 shows a peak in warmth at this time equal to that of the Roman period. The European population increased from 36 to 79 million. The dry summers were favorable for cereal maturation, harvesting, and safe storage. The wealth of Europe increased, and there was enough surplus to build cathedrals and universities.

Nile River levels suggest that this was a dry period in Islamic North Africa and the Near East. Demographers guess that the population of these areas remained about the same.

Islamic civilization linked Christendom, Africa, the steppes, Indic civilization, and China. It had a strong infrastructure for its time. With the spread of the faith, Arabic became a lingua franca from Tangier to Jakarta. Moslems moved efficiently by sea and by land. They sailed the Mediterranean, the Red Sea, the Persian Gulf, and the Indian Ocean, conducting commerce in bulky goods. They led camel caravans across the Sahara to black Africa to trade in salt, gold, and slaves, and across Central Asia to China to trade in porcelain, silk, and precious metals.

Moslems were transmitters of other good things to Europe as well, preserving parts of Greco-Roman literature that were unknown in Europe. By land and sea they also transmitted important Chinese technologies. But unlike the Chinese, Moslems did not build enduring governments or introduce technological innovations of world significance. Neither did they systematically recruit bureaucrats; recruitment in Islamic governments (as in most societies) was by patronage, not by civil service examinations.

1300–1500

In the mid-fourteenth century a terrible epidemic of plague, "the Black Death," assaulted Europe, the Near East, India, and China.[15] This epi-

Table 2. **Winter Mildness/Severity Index (Europe near 50° N)**

Country	Period Mean (degrees Celsius) 1311–1479	Series Mean (degrees Celsius) 1100–1969
England	−1.5	−0.9
Germany	−2.2	−0.8
Russia	−6.9	−3.1

Source: Hubert H. Lamb, *Climate, Present, Past, and Future,* vol. 2 (London: Methuen, 1977), pp. 564, 613–14.

Note: Figures represent the number of unmistakably mild months (December, January, February) during 1311–1479 minus the number of unmistakably severe months in the same period.

demic was associated with wet weather. High mortality in China occurred during the period 1331–1354; in Europe and the Near East, during the period 1348–1350. After the Black Death the climate of China became cool and dry. The population grew from 75 million in 1400 to 100 million in 1500.

Europe's climate between 1350 and 1480 was cold and wet. In a study of documentary sources Lamb rated winter severity as shown in Table 2.

The wetness of this period was also notable. In Ireland the rings of trees preserved in peat bogs, as well as written sources, show a pattern of unusual wetness. From 1314 to 1316 there was a great famine in western Europe associated with severe cold and wetness. In 1339 rain and cold destroyed much European grain; the yield (estimated from prices) was below normal. The years of the Black Death, 1348–1349, were unusually wet, and in 1349 the yield was much below normal. It was very wet and cold also in 1434 and 1435, a time of famine.[16]

Pastoralists profited from the moisture. In the region of Lake Saki in the Crimea, water levels suggest that the weather of the fourteenth century was wet. This may have favored the growth of pasturage and herds. So did the mild winters in Anatolia that began in the mid-thirteenth century.[17] It was at this time that the Ottoman Turks made major gains at the expense of Christians in western Anatolia and the southeastern Balkans.

In the fifteenth century, when European population was still low, the Ottomans continued to expand from Anatolia into southeast Europe. They made their last major acquisitions of European territory during the reign of Suleiman the Magnificent (1520–1566). In 1550 the Ottoman Empire had a population of about 28 million, while its European opponents (Austria, the Holy Roman Empire, and Poland) controlled about 33.5 million people. Except in Podolia, the Christians now held their ground.

In the second half of the fifteenth century the population of Europe began growing and reached its preplague level (81 million) by 1500. This was about four fifths the population of China. Such a population, if united, probably could have supported a centralized secular bureaucracy like that of China. But the various countries did not unify. No secular ruler had the wealth and manpower needed to conquer and unify the whole territory.

The wealthy Roman Church had a centralized bureaucratic government, international in scope, with a language of its own (Latin). No feudal monarchy was in a position to make war on the Church. Consequently the resources of Europe were divided not only among kingdoms but also among two kinds of elites, secular and ecclesiastical. The secular elites had little unity, and great families contending for power kept power decentralized. Christendom was united in name only.

Nile flood levels indicate that the climate of Egypt was especially dry from 1315 to 1380 and from 1400 to 1450. Such weather was bad for population growth, agriculture, and trade. In the early fifteenth century industrial production in the Near East was near collapse as a result of a rise in the cost of labor.

However, in the fourteenth and fifteenth centuries Moslems moved into subtropical and tropical regions: India, Indonesia, and sub-Saharan Africa. I suggest that even if the total population of Islam was not growing, the Islamic elite, practicing polygyny, continued to produce surplus offspring. This contributed to political instability and emigration to peripheral areas.

After 1450, when European population was increasing, the Moslem population in the Near East declined. Agricultural production was inadequate, so many in Cairo had to shift from eating white bread made from wheat to millet and dhura bread. By this time European economic superiority was established. Europeans sent Moslems industrial goods in exchange for spices; Moslems could no longer compete in cloth, paper, or sugar production.[18]

Evidence of a Top-Heavy Society

Statistics show that in late medieval Tuscany the reproduction success rate of the rich was higher than that of commoners. Herlihy found that in Florence in 1427 the correlation between family size and wealth was .87 (three quarters of the variance accounted for). The richer the family, the greater the number of children who were born and survived childhood. Commoners did well if they just replaced themselves, with two children who reached adulthood.

This well-documented society was top-heavy with the offspring of the more fortunate families. Downward social mobility for many young members of the elite was to be expected. Lacking enough money to support a family, many younger sons were unable to marry at all.

As noted before, downward social mobility for many sons of the elite was a mechanism of natural selection. Younger sons experienced competitive pressure in order to marry. It forced those who remained in the elite to keep their competitive edge. The overproduction of elite offspring thus served to maintain elite quality. (See Figs. 7 and 8.)

The younger offspring of the elite might find an outlet in colonization. The late medieval period was a time not only of mass migrations of settled peoples but also of small-scale exploration and settlement of islands on the western periphery of Europe. The probing of frontiers is characteristic of even sparse populations.

In some places the overproduction of elite offspring probably contributed to political instability. England and France fought the Hundred Years' War (1338–1453). Then the English nobles fought each other in the Wars of the Roses (1455–1485), while "free lances," or mercenaries, in late medieval France challenged the authority of rulers. It seems reasonable to suppose that knights, coming from privileged families, were not in short supply. (See David Herlihy and Christiane Klapisch-Zuber, *Tuscans and Their Families*, p. 286; David Herlihy, "Three Patterns of Social Mobility in Medieval History.")

Improvements in Communication and Transportation Technology, 500–1000

The Chinese Millennium, as I call it, was a time when Chinese artisans and other manual workers, many of whom remain anonymous, made major contributions to world technology.

Communication

The Buddhists in China were the first to mass-produce their messages. In order to relieve suffering, they wanted to reach as many people as

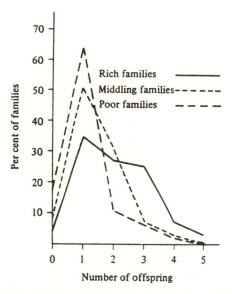

Figure 7. **Wealth and children in a top-heavy society: a parish in medieval England, 1350–1400.** Rich couples could hope for three children who survived long enough to reproduce, while poor and middle-income families typically produced only one such child. (Reprinted with permission from Zvi Razi, *Life, Marriage, and Death in a Medieval Parish* [Cambridge: Cambridge University Press, 1980], p. 143.)

possible. In A.D. 764 they block-printed a million copies of a scroll containing a charm. In 868 they published the Diamond Sutra, the earliest complete printed book extant. It took the form of a scroll.

The Chinese Buddhists carved a whole page of text on a reusable wood block. Since every word in Chinese had a different character, and there were about forty thousand characters (five thousand in frequent use), it seemed efficient to mass-produce a text by the page instead of by the character. Although artisans devised a number of systems to print Chinese with movable type (ceramic, wood, tin), none was ever widely adopted. Anyone who wanted to set the Chinese language that way would have had to jettison the entire Chinese writing system.[19]

In time the demand for copies of the Confucian classics increased to the point that printers found it profitable to mass-produce them. This was especially the case after 977, when the Sung government established schools in the provinces to train candidates for the civil ser-

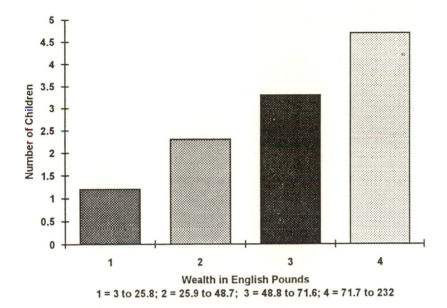

Figure 8. **Wealth and children in a top-heavy society: New Haven, Connecticut, a colonial American town, 1702.** Conditions in colonial America were better than in medieval England. Here rich couples (category four) could hope for four children who survived long enough to reproduce, while other families (categories one to three), on the average, could expect to produce two such offspring. (Data from C.J. Hoadley, ed., *Records of the Colony and Population of New Haven,* vol. 3 [New Haven: Case Tiffany, 1857], pp. 209–24.)

vice.[20] Most of the brightest boys in all China aspired to work for the emperor, as this was the surest way of acquiring wealth, power, and prestige for themselves and their families, and they found that studying the Confucian classics was the best first step to take. In the tenth and eleventh centuries printers using 11,846 wood blocks published 130 volumes of the Confucian classics.

Block printing in China was probably a precursor of printing with movable type in western Europe. The Chinese demonstrated that the mass production of written texts was possible.

Meanwhile, Chinese technology spread. The Arabs were the first to learn the secret of making rag paper. In 751 they captured some Chinese paper makers at Samarkand in Central Asia and learned the art. In 793 they set up a paper mill in Baghdad, and one in the tenth century in Spain. In the rest of Europe, where there were few government officials and little commerce, there was little demand for paper at this time. However, during the tenth century, in Cordoba, Spain, Sicily, and northern Italy, Christian scholars from many lands gathered to translate "lost" Greek classics from Arabic into Latin, and original Arabic works into Latin. They carried these manuscript scrolls back to Christendom.

Transportation

Between 500 and 1500 the Chinese made the greatest improvements in infrastructure in Eurasia. Their bargemen engaged in large-scale river haulage. To be sure, there were rapids and floods, but engineers could solve some of these problems by building canals to divert traffic from the rough places.

Ever since ancient times Chinese governments had built canals for irrigation. The more the Chinese moved into south China, the more canals they built. By the early seventh century China had an integrated canal system. The network of canals created for irrigation also provided a cheap means of transportation.

The improvement of canals to enable vessels to navigate gradients began in China in 984, when Ch'iao Wei-Yo invented the pound lock. To create a pound lock, he arranged gates so close together that they could admit only one or two canal barges. Then it was easy to raise and lower barges by changing the water level.

The Grand Canal, connecting the Yangzi at Hangchow with Beijing on the Yellow River, was the principal commercial artery of China. The Chinese began its construction in 70 A.D. and completed it in 1327. They used it for carrying rice and other food from south China to north China, ensuring China's territorial integration. The canal system enabled particular regions of China to specialize in complementary products, thus increasing the productivity of labor.

The greatest innovation in land transport in North Africa and the Middle East was the camel caravan.[21] The camel driver and rider were the real conquerors of the desert. They stitched together the more populous nodes of the Islamic world.

Camels had a history. Around 2000 B.C., in a period of cold, arid climate, the Arabs and Aramaeans began the domestication of the camel, and by the first millennium B.C. merchants of Arabia were using camel caravans. In the first century A.D. regular camel caravans crossed North Africa.

With the invention of the north Arabian saddle between 500 B.C. and A.D. 200 the camel could carry between three hundred and five hundred pounds. Its arched back enabled it to carry more per unit of body weight than horses could. Also, a single man could manage six camels, compared to only two horses or oxen. Without strain camels could cover twenty miles in six hours and endure four to fifteen days without water. In winter they needed no watering, for they could get enough water from the plants they ate. If there was no pasturage for them, they could draw upon fat stored in their humps. Consequently in the desert camels enjoyed physiological superiority over all other pack animals. They did not need roads. They were less likely than a wagon to break down, and they required little human labor in their management.[22]

Between the seventh and eleventh centuries A.D. Mediterranean shipbuilders shifted from building the shell of a ship first to building its skeleton first. Since less woodworking skill was required, this made possible the construction of larger vessels more cheaply. Lateen (triangular) sails tended to supplement square sails; the Portuguese put them on two or three masts. Thus they could maneuver the ship more easily and use a beam wind (wind blowing crosswise to the direction of the ship).[23]

Technological Improvements, 1000–1300

Communication

Before 1270 European scribes used parchment for official and religious purposes. They wrote other messages on brittle papyrus. Since official documents had a small market, parchment and papyrus sufficed. Few aristocrats had a library or study. Most communication was oral.

The parchment then in use in Europe was an expensive writing material. The production of one Bible required 300 sheepskins or 170 calfskins.[24] This was tolerable in an oral culture, in which the priest placed a large Bible on a lectern and read it aloud to a congregation. However, the use of parchment for Bibles precluded widespread individual reading.

Even before Gutenberg, written communication improved because rag paper became available in European markets. Entrepreneurs began to make rag paper in Italy in the 1270s and Germany in the 1320s. By the end of the fourteenth century the price of paper was one eighth that of parchment; by 1450 it was one sixteenth; by 1500, one thirty-second.[25] There were no printed books just yet, only manuscript books.

Predictably, the amount of correspondence and documents increased. After 1200 more scribes translated literature from ancient Greek and medieval Arabic into Latin, spreading knowledge of the ancient world among the elites of Europe. Papyrus was brittle; rag paper was not. Bureaucrats demanded rag paper, and rag paper justified the employment of more bureaucrats.

Since more people were reading (or trying to), there was more demand for glass lenses to correct poor eyesight. In 1268 Roger Bacon described reading spectacles for the farsighted. In 1451 Nicholas of Cusa described spectacles for the nearsighted. A probable first location for the manufacture of spectacles was Venice. The Venetians, having learned glassmaking from Byzantium, were noted for their glass products.

In 1289 block-printed books similar to those used in China appeared in Ravenna, Italy. But printers used this method only for works of less than a hundred pages.

By the fifteenth century scribes hand-copied works on medicine and science. Specialized publishers marketed them.[26]

While most people were innumerate, there were more merchants who needed to keep accounts and calculate. In the trading world of the Indian Ocean, merchants of many ethnic origins moved between Africa, the Near East, India, and Southeast Asia. By the sixth century A.D. the Indians invented signs for the numbers one to nine. In the ninth century they added a sign for zero, which became a place holder in a system of positional notation. The Arabs adopted these signs and transmitted them to Europe.

In A.D. 1202 in Italy Leonardo Fibonacci advocated the use of "Arabic" (actually Indian) numerals and positional notation. During the commercial boom of the thirteenth century, when more merchants needed to keep accounts, these numerals spread rapidly. By the fifteenth century Arabic numerals were widely used in Europe, replacing Latin numerals. Bureaucrats were using them to calculate and record revenues and expenditures.[27]

Transportation

The people of the Netherlands were the first Europeans to develop skills in draining wetlands and using the water in canals for transport. In the thirteenth century human haulers were used to tow boats and barges upstream in the Low Countries. They installed the first pound lock at Vreeswick in 1373. By this time 85 percent of the transport of the Low Countries went by river or canal. The canal system was also a deterrent to invasion by land.

In the twelfth century northern Italy began to develop a system of canals. During the period 1179–1209 the Milanese built the Naviglio Grande Canal. At this time Milan had at least two hundred thousand inhabitants. It was not linked to the sea by a navigable river. To gain access to the Ticino, a tributary of the Po, the canals had to drop eighty feet. In the fifteenth century the Milanese used locks to solve the problem.[28]

The great Chinese contribution to world transportation was the compass. In the first century A.D. the Chinese may have used lodestones in navigation. By 1086 they were using a magnetized needle floating in water. This was available in the West by 1180. European sailors improved it by mounting it dry on a pivot and adding a windrose of directions to which it might point. Windroses had been available in the Mediterranean since ancient times.

The main advantage of the compass was that it could give direction when atmospheric conditions were foggy or cloudy and no celestial bodies or coastal markers were visible. Previously the only device available in such circumstances was the lead line for sounding the bottom. At the end of the thirteenth century, when the compass and windrose were in use, ships began to cross the Mediterranean even in winter, when the skies were cloudy. It became possible to make two trips a year between Italy and the Levant ports.

In this period the Chinese built sailing ships so seaworthy that they could go as far south as Indonesia and as far west as Africa. These ships had watertight compartments, separated by bulkheads, in their hulls. They were equipped with axial rudders attached to a rear bulkhead (junks, which could not travel such great distances, were flat-bottomed and had no fixed keel or sternpost).

Europeans gradually acquired the expertise to build oceangoing ships. In the twelfth and thirteenth centuries, encouraged by the great increase in commercial activity, northern shipbuilders created a revolutionary new ship called the cog. It was skeleton-built, meaning that its ribs were set up before its hull. The hull was clinker-built (with overlapping planks) for durability in rough seas, especially the North Sea. The cog was set well down in the water for stability and had plenty of freeboard to ward off high waves. Its keel was deep, and it had an axial rudder attached to its sternpost to prevent it from drifting downwind. It was rather tubby, its cargo capacity being generous. However, the cog had only one square sail, which could be trimmed to various angles, and consequently it was less maneuverable than Mediterranean ships using lateen sails.

Technological Improvements, 1300–1500

Communication

In Europe manuscript books were still not affordable because of the great labor involved in producing them. In Lombardy in the late fourteenth and early fifteenth centuries the price of a medical book equaled the cost of living for an average person for three months. The price of a law book equaled the cost of living for one year and four months.[29]

Why did Gutenberg introduce printing with movable type when and where he did? Almost surely he did not intend to meet the needs of common folk. Initially printers did not even print books for university students. Prior to 1484 they set up printing presses only in centers of business, banking, and government.[30]

It may be significant that Johannes Gutenberg, the inventor of printing with movable type, lived in Mainz. Mainz was a Rhineland town on the urban axis of Europe between the Low Countries, its northern terminus, and northern Italy, its southern terminus. It was one of the most important free cities and commercial centers of the middle Rhine, competing with Strasbourg upriver and Cologne downriver. Here on August 22, 1450, Gutenberg signed a contract with Johan Fust, a lawyer, who loaned him money to produce a certain invention.

By profession, Gutenberg was a goldsmith with hands-on knowledge of the properties of various common metals. His father was a prominent official of Mainz who had worked in its mint. A device for stamping coins at this time was the screwpress, so Gutenberg probably learned about it at the mint of Mainz. By 1438 Johan was experimenting secretly with different metals in order to adapt this kind of press for printing on paper.

Gutenberg found much of the technology he needed already available: paper, the press itself (which was also used on grapes and olives), and printer's ink. What he invented was movable type made of metal. It was called movable because each piece contained only one sign and could be moved from one type frame to another. Instead of the five thousand characters needed to print basic Chinese, only the twenty-six letters of the alphabet, ten numbers, and some punctuation and diacritical marks were needed to print European texts.

As a goldsmith, Gutenberg knew how to cut a punch (die) of soft metals such as brass or bronze. Artisans used punches as hallmarks, in making coins, or in inscribing cast bronze bells. The punch would create a hollow reverse image in a lead matrix. Then molten metal could be poured repeatedly into the matrix to generate many identical copies of the design. The process of pouring liquid metal into a mold was known as casting, and it was one of the oldest metallurgical techniques, going back to the Bronze Age. This was an improvement over cutting a letter repeatedly into a wood block, since each copy of such wood-block letters would be a little bit different.

Gutenberg found that an alloy of lead, tin, and antimony melted at low temperatures and solidified without distortion of form. Tin prevented rapid oxidation of the lead. Antimony gave the alloy durability. When combined, their melting point was only 240 degrees Celsius, and when poured in a mold the alloy set instantly. This alloy proved to be a durable choice.[31]

Unfortunately, Gutenberg was unable to pay his debt to Fust. In 1455 Fust sued him for the loan plus interest and acquired the press. In 1456 someone used this press to print the Bible for the first time. Gutenberg died in 1468 at about the age of seventy, neither rich nor famous. But the press, operated by Peter Schoffer, lived on. Around 1475 Schoffer began to make dies of steel and matrices of copper, metals that continued to be used for this purpose until the nineteenth century.

Printing was the first mass-production industry: a printer could do in one day what a scribe could do in one year.[32] It was possible to make every copy of a text identical.

In order to make money, printers had to sell works of a general nature to those who could afford them. In 1464 they found their first great commercial success in northern Italy. Florence became the center of the printing trade, followed by Milan and Venice. It was here that books of literature and philosophy were in greatest demand, for northern Italy was an early center of Renaissance humanism. Here rich and powerful individuals liked to read Greek and Latin writings about public affairs.

Between 1450 and 1500 at least a thousand printers published about thirty thousand titles in a total of nine to twelve million copies. These are now referred to as *incunabula* (publications "in the cradle"— appearing in the first fifty years of printing with movable type). They added up to more books than the monks and scribes of the whole medieval era had produced. Elites in cities bought most of these books.

The Islamic world did not adopt printing with movable type. Why? According to the ulema (Islamic religious authorities), the Koran had to be written by hand. In 1485 the Ottoman sultan forbade the printing press and printed works for Moslems in his empire. This ban lasted until 1835. The Ottoman rulers did not want Christian or political literature in Arabic or Turkish circulating in their domain, because it might cause unrest.[33]

Transportation

The other great European achievement of the fifteenth century was the creation of a full-rigged ship capable of navigation anywhere on the globe. It was skeleton-built (preferred because a boat so built could be larger than before. Its hull planks were joined edge to edge (the carvel method) to offer less resistance to the water. Some ships had planks both inside and outside the ribs. The new ships had the rounded lines, the sternpost axial rudder, and the straight keel of the cog. Their distinctive feature was their rigging, which was distributed between three masts. The foremast and main mast were rigged in square sails to catch winds astern, and the mizzen (rear) mast had a lateen sail to maneuver and to catch winds abeam. In order to reduce the toil of raising and lowering a large sail, the sails in the rigging tended to become smaller and more numerous. Soon full-rigged ships sailed between northern Europe and the Mediterranean and became the dominant oceangoing vessels. The caravel (a kind of full-rigged ship) became more important than the caravan.

Before the full-rigged ship was developed, the warships that ruled the Mediterranean were galleys. They were long and narrow and powered by oarsmen. They were fast and maneuverable in quiet waters. They could carry warriors with hand weapons and later firearms, but they were too unstable to carry cannon. Galleys were of no use on oceans.

The rounded full-rigged ship was stable enough to carry cannon, which replaced soldiers. It became a kind of mobile castle. Such a ship was oceangoing. It could carry more food and water than the galley and so could stay at sea for a longer period.

It was in the fifteenth century that sailors traveling between the Canary Islands off Africa and the Iberian Peninsula learned the pattern of prevailing winds and currents of the central Atlantic Ocean. It was easy to sail from Iberia to the Canaries, since the winds came from the stern, but it was almost impossible to return directly to Iberia. The maneuver used to solve this problem was the volta, or turn: instead of sailing northeast straight to Iberia, mariners sailed northwest in a curving course until they reached the zone of westerly (west to east) winds. Then they turned eastward toward Iberia.

Columbus and other explorers discovered that by first sailing southwest to the Canaries and then catching the northeast trade winds (east to west) they could cross the Atlantic, curve to the north, and return by the westerlies (west to east).

Navigation requires two kinds of knowledge: knowledge of position and knowledge of direction. To determine north-south position one can measure the distance of the polestar from the horizon. Determining east-west position is much more difficult.

At night navigators used the pointer stars of the Little Dipper to determine midnight. The position of Kochab in relation to Polaris was measured with a device called a nocturnal, which had a scale showing divisions of time. Its error, however, was plus or minus fifteen minutes. In the daytime mariners put a pin in the center of the ship's compass. When the shadow fell on due north it was inferred that the hour was noon. This method had an error of fifteen to twenty minutes. It was of little use in determining longitude.

As in ancient times, medieval European sailors navigated mainly by the stars and dead reckoning. The stars gave them their north-south position, and dead reckoning revealed how far they had traveled since their last position. The compass could reveal their direction at any time of day and in all atmospheric conditions. So if they knew the latitude of their destination, sailors proceeded to that latitude and continued to sail on it until they arrived.

In 1492 Columbus set sail in a full-rigged ship westward across an ocean. In his time most people regarded such an act as foolhardy, if not suicidal. However, Columbus, familiar as he was with Atlantic winds and currents, knew that success was possible.

Why the Decline in Chinese Inventiveness?

In the thirteenth century the Chinese were at their peak of inventiveness, leading the world in mechanics, metallurgy, explosives, agronomy, hydraulics, printing, and other technologies. They had a large army and a navy, skilled in both offensive and defensive warfare. But after the fourteenth century Chinese technology improved very little. Why?

We can eliminate a number of possible explanations for the virtual end of Chinese inventiveness. It cannot be blamed on variance in commercial activity, since such activity was not correlated with inventiveness.

From the point of view of the government, China's main problem lay on the other side of its inner Asian frontier. Never again, thought the bureaucrats, must the dirty, smelly Mongol horde be allowed to return. This was probably why in the fifteenth century the Ming rulers stopped naval construction and discouraged maritime trade: They did not expect enemies to arrive by sea, and indeed until the nineteenth century no threats came from that direction. Instead they invested heavily in the construction of the Great Wall and other defenses on its northeast frontier.

Kang Chao has suggested that the rapid growth of the Chinese population, from 100 million in 1500 to 330 million in 1800, created such a labor surplus that it discouraged inventors from creating new labor-saving technologies.[34] There were no improvements of importance in Chinese agricultural technology after 1313. But population growth does not necessarily prevent technological progress. Some scholars think that in the eighteenth century European population growth contributed to the Industrial Revolution.

I suggest that the decline of Chinese technical inventiveness was linked, ironically, to the rise of meritocracy in the civil service. In the late tenth century, when the civil service examinations were opened to all boys regardless of birth, and numerous provincial schools prepared candidates for those examinations, the best and the brightest flocked toward this opportunity and were co-opted by the ruling class. It would seem likely that fewer bright boys became artisans; such careers involved low-prestige manual work. Paradoxically, the government, by adopting a just and rational civil service recruitment policy, may have drained the best brains from below.

Did technological inventiveness increase in Europe during the fifteenth century? Yes. By the 1380s blast furnaces and cast iron, which had first appeared in China, became widely available in Europe. From then on Europeans could mass-produce guns. In another technological direction, in the early fifteenth century they were able to change continuous rotary motion to reciprocal (back and forth) motion and vice versa with a crank and connecting rod (found earlier in China). This is an essential part of railroad locomotives, automobiles, and sewing machines today.

In the fifteenth century the Chinese were probably unaware of the new departures in Europe. This was unfortunate for them. The printing press of Gutenberg and full-rigged ships represented major breakthroughs in world history.

Notes

1. C.U. Hammer et al., "Greenland Ice Sheet Evidence of Post-Glacial Volcanism and Its Climatic Impact," pp. 230–35 (the Crete Index); G.A. Zielinski et al., "Record of Volcanism Since 7000 B.C. from the G1SP2 Greenland Ice Core and Implications for the Volcano-Climate System," p. 949 (the Summit index).

2. H.H. Lamb, "Volcanic Dust in the Atmosphere, with a Chronology and Assessment of Its Meterological Significance"; Clifford F. Mass and David A. Portman, "Major Volcanic Eruptions and Climate: A Critical Evaluation." All population statistics in this chapter are from Colin McEvedy and Richard Jones, *Atlas of World Population History.*

3. Karl W. Butzer, *Quaternary Stratigraphy and Climate in the Near East,* p. 123.

4. Albert Hourani, *The History of the Arab Peoples,* p. 23.

5. M.R. Rampino et al., eds., "Introduction," *Climate: History, Periodicity, and Predictability,* pp. 37–46.

6. Bernard Lewis, *The Middle East: A Brief History of the Last 2000 Years,* p. 80; F.A. Hassan and B.R. Strecki, "Nile Floods and Climactic Change."

7. Andrew Watson, *Agricultural Innovation in the Early Islamic World.*

8. William H. Te Brake, *Medieval Frontier: Culture and Ecology in Rijnland,* p. 138.

9. Mary K. Matossian, *Poisons of the Past,* ch. 1.

10. Lewit, *Agricultural Production,* p. 37.

11. Bert Brunekreef et al., "Home Dampness and Respiratory Morbidity in Children"; R.E. Dales et al., "Respiratory Health Effects of Home Dampness and Molds Among Children"; "Adverse Health Effects in Adults Exposed to Home Dampness and Molds"; Lyanne Dijkstra et al., "Respiratory Health Effects of the Indoor Environment in a Population of Dutch Children"; S.D. Platt et al., "Damp Housing, Mould Growth, and Symptomatic Health State"; W. Smoragiewicz et al., "Trichothecene Mycotoxins in the Dust of Ventilating Systems of Buildings."

12. Marianne Kyriakos, "Builder Agrees to Rid Condos of Toxic Mold," *Washington Post,* October 8, 1994, pp. E1, E11. Robyn Meredith, "Infants' Lung Bleeding Traced to Toxic Mold," *New York Times,* January 24, 1997, p. A8.

13. Francesca Bray, *Science and Civilization in China,* vol. 6, part 2, *Agriculture,* pp. 492–93; Mark Elwin, *The Pattern of the Chinese Past,* pp. 122–29.

14. Fang Jin-qi and Guo Liu, "Relationship Between Climactic Change and the Nomadic Southward Migration in Eastern Asia During Historical Times"; Fang Jin Qi and Pao-Kuan Wang, "On the Relationship Between Winter Thunder and the Climatic Change in China in the Past 2200 Years"; Joel D. Gunn, "Global Change and Regional Biocultural Diversity," p. 95; K.R. Brief et al., "A 1400–year Tree-Ring Record of Summer Temperatures in Fennoscandia."

15. Graham Twigg, *The Black Death;* Mary Matossian, "Did Mycotoxins Play a Role in Bubonic Plague Epidemics?"; Michael Dols, *The Black Death in the Middle East;* John K. Fairbank, *China: A New History,* p. 124.

16. Pierre Alexandre, *Le Climat en Europe au moyen age, 1000–1425;* M. Lyons, "Weather, Famine, Pestilence and Plague in Ireland, 900–1500."

17. William C. Brice, ed., *The Environmental History of the Near and Middle East Since the Last Ice Age,* p. 98.

18. Eliyahu Ashtor, *Levant Trade in the Later Middle Ages,* pp. 200–10, 433, 512.

19. Robert Temple, *The Genius of China,* pp. 111–12.

20. John W. Chaffee, *The Thorny Gates of Learning in Sung China: A Social History of Examinations,* pp. 15–16.

21. R.W. Bulliet, *The Camel and the Wheel;* William McNeill, "The Eccentricity of Wheels, or European Transportation in Historical Perspective."

22. Hilde Gauthier-Pilters, *The Camel: Its Evolution, Ecology, Behavior, and Relationship to Man,* pp. 115–19.

23. Albert C. Leighton, *Transport and Communication in Early Medieval Europe, A.D. 500–1100,* pp. 42–59.

24. Steven Ozment, *The Age of Reform, 1250–1550,* p. 199.

25. Jeremy Griffiths and Derek Pearsall, *Book Production and Publishing in Britain, 1375–1475,* pp. 11, 396.

26. A. Murray, *Reason and Society in the Middle Ages,* pp. 168–200.

27. James E. Vance, *Capturing the Horizon: The Historical Geography of Transportation Since the Sixteenth Century,* pp. 40–46.

28. George H. Putnam, *Books and Their Makers During the Middle Ages,* pp. 234–39, 290.

THE CHINESE MILLENNIUM   87

29. Carlo M. Cipolla, *Before the Industrial Revolution: European Society and Economy, 1000–1700,* 2d ed., p. 178.

30. Robert Raymond, *Out of the Fiery Furnace,* pp. 105–6.

31. Anthony Feldman and Peter Ford, *Scientists and Inventors,* p. 17.

32. Lewis W. Spitz, *The Protestant Reformation, 1517–1559,* p. 53; Edith Simon, *The Reformation,* p. 13.

33. Toby E. Huff, *The Rise of Early Modern Science: Islam, China, and the West,* pp. 225–26.

34. Kang Chao, *Men and Land in Chinese History: An Economic Analysis.*

6 REASONED DISSENT

Printing, Universities, and Transport

*Thou hast most traitorously corrupted the youth of the realm in
erecting a grammar-school, and whereas, before, our forefathers
had no other books but the score and tally, thou hast caused
printing to be used, and, contrary to the king, his crown and
dignity, thou has built a paper mill.*

—William Shakespeare, *King Henry VI,* part 2

What is reasoned dissent? Why is it important?

To dissent is to advance an opinion, especially in matters of law,
religion, and politics, that is different from the prevailing view. Most
people realize that not all dissenting opinions are correct and that majority opinions aren't necessarily correct, either. For any discussion to
occur, the participants must recognize that no one has a monopoly on
the truth. We know that everyone has blind spots and sees things in a
manner colored by distorted perceptions, emotions, and desires.

But the strong and consistent dissenter, even if humble, has natural
enemies. When powerful people see themselves threatened by a dissenting opinion, they try to suppress it. When they believe that an
irrational belief system is to their advantage, they defend it.

But some members of the political elite may eagerly accept an inconvenient innovation when they encounter it. The farsighted few,
such as Francis Bacon (1561–1626), realize that knowledge itself is
power. Since some of this inconvenient new knowledge does translate
into power, elites may tolerate it.

The founding of universities in the high medieval period (1100–
1300) made reasoned dissent possible. In 1450 Gutenberg's invention

of printing with movable type made the wide distribution of dissenting literature inevitable.

Medieval Universities and Reasoned Dissent

The evidence from world history suggests that before the sixteenth century intellectual discovery was unusual and sporadic. Political elites needed clerics to legitimize them, and clerics demanded a monopoly on intellectual and spiritual authority to legitimize themselves. As a result, they were defenders of orthodoxy. They called dissenters "heretics" and persecuted them. Unless the innovators amused them, neither elite group was friendly to intellectual innovations.

Many intelligent people became learned by studying on their own. But to make sustained progress, scholars and scientists needed autonomous intellectual communities. They needed neutral ground on which they could communicate with each other freely. Such communities required long-term funding and political protection.

During the high medieval period in Europe only the Roman Church had the resources to do such a thing. Fortunately, the Church founded and developed higher educational institutions for the training of priests, and by the fourteenth century some of these institutions had become mature universities.

In the same period the Church developed the law of corporations, which gave universities the right to regulate themselves under the supervision of the Church. This made dissent on important (and unimportant) matters possible.[1]

By the end of the medieval period professors had come to think that the love of learning *(amor sciendi)* bound them together. They believed that they had the responsibility to increase knowledge. They believed that a professor should be ready to defend his important assertions in public. He should be open to all objections to his argument.[2]

European scholars, cooperating with Arab and Greek scholars in Spain, Sicily, and northern Italy, had for the first time translated into Latin important ancient works. These works included the surviving mathematical and scientific literature of ancient Greek and medieval Arab writers, such as Aristotle's biological observations, Euclid's geometry, al-Khwarizmi's algebra, Ptolemy's astronomy, and the medical writings of Hippocrates, Galen, and Avicenna.

Fortunately, students and teachers of mathematics, natural philosophy (natural sciences), and medicine escaped from the oversight of the theological faculties.[3] This division of labor served to reduce conflicts and provide freedom for those with no great interest in matters of faith and morals.

Medieval European science was not empirical; it consisted of disputes over theories. Nor was it experimental; scholars were under the spell of the recently recovered writings of ancient Greeks and Arabs and did not subject these theories to experimental testing. Natural scientists could not progress until they became skeptical about ancient authorities, especially Aristotle and Ptolemy.

As Francis Bacon said, truth emerges more readily from error than from confusion. It was helpful to have ancient authorities whose views could be analyzed and criticized. Scholars could detect their errors and test their theories.

In the Islamic world and China, as Toby Huff has shown, the state and Moslem authorities *(ulema)* did not establish permanently funded institutions of higher learning. The *ulema* of the Islamic world and the mandarins (scholar-gentry) of China felt threatened by any idea that might challenge their authority.[4]

Consequently, outside of Europe critical thinkers did not publicly investigate politics, economics, and religion until the twentieth century. But in fifteenth-century Europe men such as Lorenzo Valla and Desiderius Erasmus thought critically about religion and religious texts and discussed them. Discussion remained a privilege of the Latin-reading elite.

Printing with Movable Type

Even after the invention of phonetic writing in 3500 B.C. most human communication had been oral. In ancient Athens probably no more than 5 percent of the population could read.[5]

During the Dark Ages of Europe (actually the "wet ages") (c. 500–1000), when knowledge of Latin declined, most of the secular elite became illiterate. Only the better-trained members of the Christian clergy could still read Latin. The minds of the common people did not "darken" in this period; they had always been "dark" and remained so.

How did reasoned dissent break out of the universities and spread like an epidemic over Europe?

In 1450 Johannes Gutenberg invented printing with movable type. More accurately, he assembled a new technology. He already had available the screwpress, used in the Roman Empire to press grapes. He had rag paper, invented in China fifteen hundred years previously. He also had printer's ink, made of lampblack and linseed oil.

Using Gutenberg's technology, a printer was able to accomplish more in a week than a manuscript copyist could do in a year. Printing was the first mass-production industry. Many printers made good money, and some grew rich. Since their scandalous publications sold best, they of course favored freedom of the press.

Of course Gutenberg's best customer was the Church. In 1450 most of the literates in Europe were members of the clergy. Gutenberg's first major publication was probably a great folio Bible, which the clergy intended to place on a lectern and read in public. But soon merchants were demanding printed works. By 1471 the most important trading towns on the urban axis of Europe (Cologne, Mainz, Strasbourg, Basel) had a printing press, as did nearby Rome, Venice, and Paris. The Church wanted every parish to own a copy of the Bible. The early printers also produced prayer books, simple sermons, and woodblock prints on religious subjects. Unfortunately, Gutenberg went bankrupt before his idea spread.

In the first fifty years of printing, 1450–1500, printers produced ten million copies of forty thousand different titles (the incunabula). It would have taken a copyist a thousand years to do the same.

Printing apparently gave a decisive boost to Protestant reformers. Between 1500 and 1517, when the Reformation began, printers published ten million printed volumes. Between 1517 and 1520 Martin Luther wrote thirty treatises, of which three hundred thousand copies were printed. By 1550 printers had published about a hundred and fifty thousand titles in sixty million volumes.[6]

Printing was a form of external information storage, relieving the burden on biological memory.[7] People could store information not only as words but also in maps, charts, tables, and illustrations. Using an edited and corrected proof sheet, a printer could reproduce thousands of perfect copies.

Consequently, people lost fewer creative masterpieces, discoveries, and new ideas. Knowledge became more cumulative. In 1543 printers saved the heliocentric theory of Copernicus from oblivion. In 1610 printers distributed *The Starry Messenger,* a record of Galileo's telescopic observations of the heavenly bodies. It was a smash hit, even among the Roman clergy.

As inexpensive books and pamphlets became available in cities, the motivation to learn to read tended to increase. A positive feedback relationship developed: the more and the cheaper the printed material, the greater the number of people who learned to read. The greater the number of literates, the lower the per-unit cost of printing. The lower the price of books, the greater the number of people who learned to read.

There was no necessary limitation to the market for books. People constantly wrote new ones. The population was steadily growing. Books often wore out or became out-of-date, so they had to be reedited and replaced.

The small size of the standard quarto printed book (about the size of a contemporary hardcover) made it easier to hide than a folio manuscript volume. A book was easy to smuggle across international borders. A border guard usually could not read Latin, and if his palm was crossed with silver, he might decide that one copy of one little book could do no harm. On the other side of the border, another printer could reset that one little book and sell a thousand copies. How could anyone stop this? Censorship always failed. While medieval scholars had made reasoned dissent possible, printers made tolerance of reasoned dissent inevitable.

Another consequence of printing was change in language itself. In 1450 elites were using Latin as an international language. To be literate meant to be able to read Latin; a grammar school was a place to study Latin grammar. So a large proportion of early books were in Latin. A popular vernacular dialect, that of Tuscany, was not yet standardized as Italian.

A printer working in a city could not hope to profit from printing a book written in a provincial dialect. Many different dialects were spoken in the countryside and were not written and read in the capital. Moreover, most of the people who could afford the early books were members of the elite. After several generations the elite dialect, as a result of frequent use by printers, became a standard vernacular language, with grammars and dictionaries. This was a necessity, given the economics of printing.

Today a joke among linguists is that a dialect differs from a language in that a language has an army and navy. One might add that a national language has not only an army and navy but also detachments of teachers, lexicographers, grammarians, and typesetters to defend it. It was no easy task to subdue the power of provincial dialects, founded in intimacy and sentiment. However, only people with a knowledge of the "standard" language (English, French, German, etc.) might belong to the elite, and those who could not speak it were recognized as "vulgar" as soon as they opened their mouth. The musical *My Fair Lady* illustrated this truth. As a standardized vernacular tongue spread, more people entered the world of reasoned dissent.

It was safer to disagree with an author than with a teacher. The reader of a book was able to think things over and form his or her own opinion. In private, people could think logically without being interrupted by others' illogical and irrelevant remarks.

The invention of printing altered lifestyles because in order to read and write a person had to have privacy. In the medieval period, private life took place everywhere and therefore nowhere. When people left home they did so in groups; solitary wandering was thought to be a sign of insanity. However, in fourteenth- and fifteenth-century Tuscany, a center of the Renaissance, the master of the house often had a private study. By the end of the seventeenth century educated people with a taste for solitude were no longer thought strange.[8]

Aristocrats, preferring life in their country estates during the warm season, took care to provide themselves with private libraries. Their children could learn independently or with the help of a tutor or governess. But usually English aristocrats dispatched their sons to boarding schools to learn how to read and write in Latin and to become familiar with the Greco-Roman classics. By the seventeenth century a gentleman by definition was educated in the classics, and a lady was at least literate.

Urban common people who could read could get an education without going to school. Books mapped the world of the privileged, a world that was mostly invisible to others. They provided vicarious experience of travel to distant lands. They suggested possible new activities, such as collecting plants, writing poetry, and looking at the night sky with a telescope. Consequently, books served to liberate the abilities and talents of many who would otherwise have been unaware of what they were missing.

Printing probably had little influence upon peasants. This was apparently true of France. Most peasants in France could not speak French, much less read it. As Eugen Weber has shown, only in the second half of the nineteenth century did the majority of French peasants learn standard French.[9]

In seventeenth-century England literate property owners began to hold more offices in local government. They assessed property for taxes and kept tax records. They acted as law enforcement officers, clerks, churchwardens, and justices of the peace.[10]

Printing also facilitated the internalization of moral values. People still learned moral values from the examples and words of parents and priests. However, the availability of printed Bibles and other works on ethics and religion enabled the more reflective individuals of society to sort out and prioritize their values. This may have made it easier to develop a character, or psychic gyroscope.

Such a character did not depend on social support to function properly. A person with definite principles was less vulnerable to irrational social pressure. Character was also "portable" to foreign lands, where settlements were more isolated and positive social support was lacking.

In the eighteenth century in England and France, some printed materials clearly tended to weaken authority and social discipline. Commoners began to challenge the notion that aristocrats had "better blood" than others. Journalists could publicize the vulnerabilities and vices of powerful individuals (drunkenness, sexual promiscuity, brutality, and sexual abuse of servants). Writers of fiction could satirize the entire social order.

Writers, teachers, and publishers developed a common economic interest in freedom of the press. A critical thinker could speak more freely in an anonymous pamphlet than to a street gathering, where the danger of arrest was serious.

Printing made the Bible widely available, with two different kinds of result. One response was to believe more intensely in the literal truth of the Bible, which was seen as the word of God dictated to the writer. To be sure, it contained grammatical errors and anachronistic references, but some people felt they could explain them away. Such a frame of mind we call today "fundamentalism."

However, there was another response to the accessible Bible: skepticism. Skeptics took grammatical errors and anachronistic references seriously. They became attentive to internal contradictions. They thought that perhaps the Bible was neither the word of God nor even divinely inspired. It might be a collection of literature written by human —all too human—beings.

Literacy and education (mostly self-education) enabled commoners to climb the social ladder. Literacy and education became signs of gentility for political elites in Europe. In China this had been true for a thousand years.

In contrast, from 1485 until the early nineteenth century the Ottoman sultans would not let printing presses or printed matter circulate among the Moslem populations under their rule (in the Balkans, the Near East, and North Africa). The Moslem clergy and the Ottoman elite did their best to prevent the spread of "dangerous ideas" among their flocks. They did not even want the Koran to be printed.[11]

In China, as mentioned in Chapter 5, it was impractical to print with movable type in view of the nature of the writing system. Simple inertia, if not the desire of the literate elite to practice intellectual birth control, was an obstacle to reform. Today computer designers find the Chinese keyboard a nightmare. In mainland China reformers have simplified written Chinese to five thousand characters. Still, a keyboard with five thousand keys would occupy a whole kitchen tabletop.[12]

Urban Development and Transportation Technology

Between 1450 and 1750 the greatest lay centers of cultural creativity were cities such as London, Paris, and Florence. University towns remote from big cities might also become cradles of ideas—for example, the ideas of Martin Luther, of Wittenberg University, and Isaac Newton, of Cambridge University. But after 1564, when the pope confirmed the decisions of the Council of Trent which launched the Counter-Reformation, some scientists in the cities of Italy, Spain, and Portugal stopped doing research or migrated north. This lasted until the late eighteenth century.

After the invention of printing with movable type, scholars could communicate with each other more efficiently over long distances. However, to increase their progress they also needed face-to-face intellectual interaction with people in many towns and cities. The more efficient the travel between college towns and cities, the better for scholars.

Early modern transportation technologies were simple. They included sailing, being towed on canal barges, and road travel by horse and carriage. Wind in the sails of ships was free. Currents that moved boats downriver operated by gravity, which was also free. The smell of the dung of horses pulling carriages and of mules towing canal barges was unpleasant, but the dung was biodegradable. These technologies may not have been very efficient, but they were free of major negative side effects. Later, with improvements in infrastructure, these technologies worked better.

The community of reasoned dissent preferred to live in towns, the better to interact with each other. However, the supply of food and fuel limited the size of town populations. The colder the winters, the more serious the problem. Traction animals bringing wood to cities required food, as did woodcutters and drivers.

In Europe the cost of land transport was 4 to 5 kilograms per ton; the cost of river or canal transport was 0.9 kg, and that of sea transport was 0.3 to 0.4 kg. The provisioning of a city with fuel required that it be located at the water's edge.[13]

Italian cities might hold hundreds of thousands of people. The region's winters were relatively mild. This may serve to explain the prosperity and early advent of the Renaissance in Italy.

Soon shivering folk clear-cut the woods near their homes. In the Netherlands, where wood had always been scarce, the Dutch burned .peat, which they transported to their cities by river and canal. English cities resorted to coal.

The cities with the greatest potential for growth were seaports, inland cities on the main trade routes of Europe's urban axis (such as Basel), or cities on navigable inland waterways.[14]

Inland waterways in western Europe were very important. In the seventeenth century the Dutch canal system proved quite efficient. Canal barges carrying up to thirty passengers had timetables and ran frequently. A boy riding a tow horse towed them upstream at about seven kilometers an hour. From the interior these barges also brought peat fuel to the coast.

In the seventeenth century the French, realizing that their rivers flowed in three directions (north, west, and south), undertook to connect them with canals at their watersheds.[15] The central government built most canals. In 1642 the Breare Canal linked the Loire River with the Seine River; in 1681 the Languedoc Canal joined the Bay of Biscay on the Atlantic with the Mediterranean Sea.

In the eighteenth century both public officials and private entrepreneurs were improving roads in western Europe. In 1716 the French government established the first national highway department. In 1747

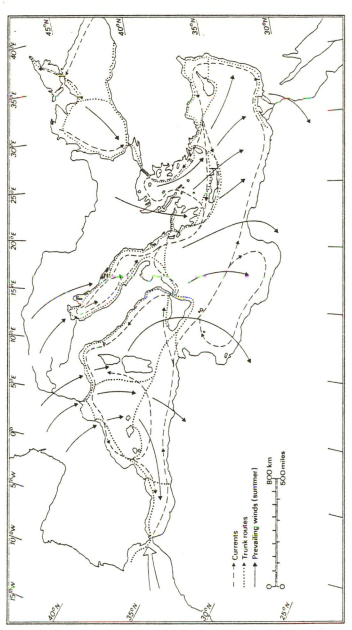

Figure 9. **Currents, prevailing summer winds, and trunk routes in the Mediterranean Sea in the medieval period.** This map shows how water routes hugged the coasts. There was relatively little traffic along the south shore (North Africa). Only after reconquering the north shore of the sea was it possible for Christian crusaders to reach the Holy Land directly and later to renew their supplies. The prevailing summer winds made it possible for an oared ship to travel upstream on the Nile. Note the triangular shape of the Nile Delta. (Reprinted with permission from John H. Pryor, *Geography, Technology, and War* [Cambridge: Cambridge University Press, 1988], p. 14.)

it established an engineering school, the School of Bridges and Highways. Private entrepreneurs constructed Britain's roads and bridges, making them more convenient for traders.[16]

As the network of passable roads grew, people could move personal correspondence and printed matter around more quickly. Gentlemen in their manors sent and received timely information about politics and business. They could travel more and thus were able to widen their range of social contacts. Unable to endure the vermin-ridden inns of the time, most gentlemen travelers stayed at the homes of friends. In this way communication networks became denser and more extensive.

In the eighteenth century two cities, London and Paris, became centers not only of government and trade but also of intellectual development. For lay intellectuals, rich and poor, these were exciting places. Rich young men could enjoy sophisticated plays, attend balls, and court heiresses. In the 1660s some of the rich and powerful became patrons of scientists. They sponsored national academies of science. Until his execution in 1792, Louis XVI of France was an enthusiastic amateur scientist.

Prior to 1789 most dissenters were themselves members of elites. For many the new conversation, often adversarial, was fun. Science as discussed among gentlemen was a great form of entertainment. A scientist demonstrating the effects of static electricity amazed upper-class people. So the party went on.

Notes

1. Toby E. Huff, *The Rise of Modern Science: Islam, China, and the West*, pp. 119–48.
2. Helde de Ridder-Symoens, *A History of the University in Europe*, vol. 1, pp. 23–33.
3. Edward Grant, "Science and the Medieval University," pp. 68–102; John Gascoigne, "A Reappraisal of the Role of the Universities in the Scientific Revolution."
4. Huff, *Rise of Modern Science*, pp. 360–64.
5. William V. Harris, *Ancient Literacy*, p. 325.
6. Lewis W. Spitz, *The Protestant Reformation, 1517–1559*, p. 90.
7. The principal works on the consequences of the invention of printing with movable type are: Elizabeth L. Eisenstein, *The Printing Press as an Agent of Change: Communications and Cultural Transformations in Early Modern Europe;* Craig E. Harline, *Pamphlets, Printing and Political Culture in the Early Dutch Republic;* S.H. Steinberg, *Five Hundred Years of Printing*, 3d ed.
8. Philippe Aries and Georges Duby, gen. eds., Georges Duby, vol. ed., *A*

History of Private Life, vol. 2, *Revelations of the Medieval World,* pp. 530–38, 561–65.

9. Eugen Weber, *Peasants into Frenchmen: The Modernization of Rural France, 1870–1914;* David Bell, " 'Lingua Populi, Lingua Dei': Language, Religion, and the Origins of the French Revolution."

10. Carl Bridenbaugh, *Vexed and Troubled Englishmen, 1590–1642,* pp. 42–50.

11. Huff, *Rise of Modern Science,* p. 225.

12. *Wall Street Journal,* February 21, 1996.

13. Paul Bairoch, *Cities and Economic Development: From the Dawn of History to the Present,* p. 227.

14. Ad van der Woude et al., *Urbanization in History: A Process of Dynamic Interactions,* pp. 8–12, 141–42; Jan de Vries, *European Urbanization, 1500–1800,* pp. 156–57.

15. Jan de Vries, *Barges and Capitalism: Passenger Transportation in the Dutch Economy, 1632–1839.*

16. James E. Vance, *Capturing the Horizon: The Historical Geography of Transportation Since the Transportation Revolution in the Sixteenth Century,* p. 54.

7 PROTESTANT MARITIME POLITICAL CULTURE

The Breakthrough to Freedom

The Lord showed me, so that I did see clearly, that he did not dwell in these temples which men had commanded and set up, but in people's hearts . . . his people were his temple, and he dwelt in them.

—George Fox

In the early modern era (1450–1750) a new political culture emerged in England and the Dutch Republic. This culture recognized civil rights for all citizens, usually propertied males, and instituted government that represented all citizens. Also, merchants and other commoners participated in the decision-making process. This political culture developed only in Protestant states. There was a strong element of anti-hierarchical thinking among Protestants, but especially among radical Protestants such as Baptists and Quakers. In these societies political organizations were decentralized, but powerful just the same. Their leaders showed a new way to build power, from the ground up.

Nowhere else in the world were there other political cultures like this one. All governments today that guarantee civil rights and have representative bodies are following the example of seventeenth-century England and the Dutch Republic. Protestant maritime political culture was unique and represented a breakthrough in world history.

This culture was maritime in that it appeared only in countries that traded along sea routes. (Switzerland was an exception, but it had a well-developed commerce by land.) The focus of the Protestant states was the North Sea–Black Sea trading area. These were states in which commerce was well established; there were many rich merchants in the cities. But the same could be said of the Catholic world of the northwest Mediterranean.

Various elements in the new political culture had medieval precedents. Beginning in the twelfth century prosperous cities had tried, with much success, to throw off the rule of noble lords and manage their own affairs. In the thirteenth century the Catholic Church developed the law of corporations, which permitted guilds, cities, and universities to have autonomy and regulate their own affairs.[1]

After negotiating with their overlords, the cities paid them taxes, usually in cash. Some merchants loaned money to kings and nobles. This money was essential to wage war. Consequently cities had bargaining power.

Moreover, mercantile wealth was movable. If pressed too hard for money by lords, merchants could take their money and go elsewhere.[2] But urban freedoms did not extend throughout medieval kingdoms, especially in areas with little commercial activity.

The Contrast with Medieval Feudal Monarchies

Let us use medieval monarchies as a model to make clear the difference between them and Protestant maritime political culture. Rich and titled great families were dominant minorities in medieval feudal kingdoms. The royal family was the greatest among them. All these families had clients and client families for whom they had done favors and who were expected to do favors in return. This system was called patronage. Kings in fact did not have absolute power. Their personal resources were too limited for them to maintain a standing army or a royal police force. They also could not afford a large bureaucracy.

The king was like a spider in the center of a network of patron-client relations. The greater the king's resources, the more patronage he could dispense. This was the only way he could control anyone beyond his family and court: nobles, city corporations, cathedral chapters (all canons [clerical personnel] of a collegiate church or cathedral, who acted as a community).[3] In late medieval societies, according to Joseph Strayer,[4] local aristocrats controlled the raising and spending of money within their territory. It was difficult for the king to persuade these aristocrats to carry out his commissions.

The king's officials were inefficient by our standards. They did not take a census, which could serve as the basis for rational taxation. They did not keep assessments of property up to date. Indeed, they did not keep most government records methodically or file them logically. There was an annual budget, but often no data on the size of the army or the trade balance. Each department of government became a small principality with fixed routines.

Bureaucrats were frequently at odds with the great aristocrats, who attempted to make policy but were often ignorant, selfish, and impulsive. The lords voted taxes on staples, which hurt the poor, but not on luxuries for themselves. In France they voted themselves exemption from the *taille,* the most important land tax.

In late-fifteenth-century England and France, kings responded to rebellious aristocratic policy-making councils by assigning to them three to twelve professional councilors to guide everyday operations. Soon the king's professional councilors became de facto policy makers, and the aristocratic amateurs lost influence. To control aristocrats on their local turf, the king, against much opposition, started a ministry of the interior.

With some notable exceptions, most medieval kings were not particularly honorable, just, or kind. But they were, compared with later rulers, quite weak. There were no absolute monarchies or enlightened despots in medieval Europe.

In the period 1350–1480, when there was a decline of population and of tax revenues, kings began to call representative assemblies of the richest citizens and most important corporations of the realm. In Italy, Spain, France, England, and Germany these assemblies debated and voted. Their most important role was to give kings the right to levy new taxes. But in northwestern Europe politically active citizens came to believe that representative assemblies (parliaments) should approve all important laws and do so publicly.[5]

The proportion of the population represented in those late medieval assemblies was very small—1 to 5 percent. Only in a few places, such as Tyrol, Friesland, Denmark, and Sweden, were peasants—and then only prosperous, market-oriented peasants—represented. In the Netherlands, since commerce outweighed agriculture in the economy, wealthy merchants were dominant in the Estates General (the parliament) of the whole country.

Continental Political Culture

During the sixteenth century, after the invention of gunpowder weapons, wars grew more and more expensive. Only large, wealthy states could afford the necessary defenses and offensive weapons. The number of independent states declined, and the size of many surviving states increased.[6]

In order to survive in a more competitive world, these larger states had to keep increasing their military (or naval) power. Raising money to pay for it was the most difficult problem. The rich people in parliament often voted themselves exemptions from taxation. So most of their taxes were indirect. It was easy to collect customs on foreign trade coming through the main ports. The salt tax, often a state monopoly, was a very important source of income on the Continent. In central Europe governments taxed mines and collected tolls on the Rhine and the sound at Copenhagen. The Russian government taxed vodka and luxuries imported by the nobility.[7]

Protestant maritime political culture can be better understood if one compares it to continental political culture. The latter prevailed on most of the European continent, including Russia, Germany, France, and Spain. Continental political culture was similar to that of imperial China.

The principal characteristics of states with continental political culture were: (1) an economy in which agriculture was dominant and commerce relatively undeveloped, with the landed nobility being wealthier than the merchants by far; (2) a geographic position that made the country very vulnerable to attack by land, less so by sea, and so forced rulers to lay emphasis on developing their armies; (3) a top-down hierarchy of political control, with a large portion of conflicts resolved by command rather than by negotiation, bargaining, and compromise, and in which the ruler was above the law and a source of law; (4) paid professional bureaucrats who did most of the work of government, both in the capital and in the countryside; and (5) a charismatic ruler and royal family, which gave the state legitimacy.

Protestant Maritime Political Culture

The states in which Protestant maritime political culture developed, by contrast, had these characteristics: (1) an economy in which commerce was well developed, if not dominant over agriculture; this was a result of the development of the full-rigged ship, which made oceanic travel possible and allowed many men to grow rich with no help from their government; (2) a geographic position favorable for commerce, usually maritime, that made defense relatively cheap and allowed rulers to invest more in their navies than in their armies; (3) a political system in which merchants shared power with the landed aristocracy and in which participants usually resolved conflicts by negotiation, bargaining, and compromise; (4) a minimum of government bureaucrats, with unpaid volunteers doing much of the work of local government and some of the work of central government; and (5) a greater participation of citizens in decision making, and therefore a more legitimate-appearing government.

England and the Dutch Republic were financially strong because their wealthiest citizens, represented in parliaments, consented to pay their taxes. Many actually did so. In England the landed aristocracy co-opted the merchants.

In the Dutch Republic the merchants limited the activities of the aristocracy. The Dutch parliament, the Estates General, conducted foreign policy, but there was no sovereign federal government of the Netherlands. The Stadtholder (chief executive officer) served as head of all the armed forces in time of war. Each of the seven provinces controlled its own domestic affairs; there was no uniform system of taxes and laws.

Oligarchies of merchant families controlled the cities. The most powerful province was Holland, a league of eighteen city-republics. The cities sent delegates to The Hague for meetings of parliament.

The population of the Dutch Republic was the most literate and best-informed in Europe, and its press was the freest in the world.

An Example: The Society of Friends

In England an example of pure Protestant maritime political culture was the Society of Friends (Quakers).[8] This religious organization was national but very decentralized. It held meetings to decide business matters, like those of town governments in many parts of England and New England.

George Fox, the founder of the Society of Friends, excelled in attracting and organizing people into self-regulated communities. These communities were animated at least to some extent by universal spiritual and moral concerns. This was in contrast to a familistic society, in which morality consisted mainly of maintaining and extending the influence of one's own family.

In the mid-seventeenth century Fox gathered around him principally simple people, artisans and farmers, but he also attracted some of the gentry. Initially his followers called themselves Seekers, since they found some moral issues problematic and sought to know God's will. They were also good listeners, hoping to learn from each other what they could not gain by individual insight.

Then they began to call themselves the Society of Friends. People joined the Society voluntarily, and the Society accepted them voluntarily. A Quaker meeting was not coterminous with the population of a piece of territory, like a parish. It was selective. Just as individuals chose the Society, the Society chose its members. The Society censured members for bad behavior. The meeting disowned anyone who consistently did not live like a Quaker. As a persecuted group, the Society was very much concerned that all its members should bring it credit. The free-thinking Quakers behaved in a disciplined way.

Following the example of Fox, the Friends were honest, trustworthy in business, thrifty, and careful how they spent their time. One became a Friend not by accepting a doctrine so much as by following a pattern of behavior.

Quaker meetinghouses were plain; simplicity was their chief aesthetic value. Wood benches in rows were arranged to form a hollow square. Altar, pulpit, and religious images were absent. The walls were bare; not even a cross appeared. Quakers themselves dressed plainly, avoiding bright colors. They wanted nothing to distract them from serious thinking.

Quaker services usually began in silence. The silence might remain unbroken during the whole hour of worship. When people spoke, they were expected to speak in response to what God was telling them.

Quakers believed in the spiritual equality of men and women. Quaker marriages were supposed to be true partnerships. In most Protestant groups, women listened silently in church services, but Quaker women could speak out, or "minister," during meetings for worship. In some cases Quaker women met separately from men for worship and business.

As a teenager George Fox became involved in religious discussions with adults. Soon he became dissatisfied with how the parish priest answered his questions. George used the familiar *thou* and *thee* with the priest and other "betters" instead of the respectful *you.* He would not observe the conventions of his time by taking off his hat to his superiors and bowing as a sign of respect.

He did not even regard the Bible, as interpreted by the local priest, as the ultimate religious authority. In his search for answers to moral and spiritual problems George Fox learned to rely on what he called the Holy Spirit speaking to his conscience. This is why his "betters" regarded him as a radical. Men who claim that they talk directly with God are a threat to both sacred and secular authority.

The young George Fox was apprenticed to a shoemaker and small businessman and soon excelled as a business manager. Unlike his competitors, he refused to bargain; rather, he charged everyone the same price, a price he believed to be fair. Charging a fixed price later became the practice of the members of the Society of Friends.

Fox was restless: he did not really know what he sought, but he knew it was not to be found in his native village. With family support, at the age of nineteen he set off traveling around England. During this period he began to call existing church buildings "steeple-houses," since he believed the true Church was a spiritual community of living members. God, he would say, did not live in temples made by human hands but in human hearts. Quakers held "meetings" in "meetinghouses."

In doing this Fox, like many other radical Protestants, was calling attention to the emptiness of mere ritual and symbol when nominal Christians remained unregenerate in their heart and lifestyle. According to Rightson, even in reformed parishes of the early seventeenth century the truly godly were in a minority. Many who attended church arrived late, slept in their seats, whispered, joked, and left early.[9] Such parishioners were not very serious about the imitation of Christ on weekdays, either. The village alehouse was often the true community center.

George Fox avoided both the steeple-house and the alehouse. After going to London and visiting some priests he had heard were worth knowing, he came home, still uncertain what to do. One spring morning in 1646 he had an "opening" from God that education at Oxford and Cambridge was not enough to qualify men to be ministers of God. At the time Anglican priests normally received such an education. Fox believed that everyone has an inner light, and that simple people could receive a revelation from God.

Like other religious radicals of his time, Fox believed in continuous revelation: that the truths in the Bible were not final. In interpreting the Bible he did not accept the authority of biblical scholars (such as Luther) but rather the collective judgment of people who led Christian lives.[10]

Although only a youth, he began to draw a following. Physically Fox was attractive; he had a powerful frame, flashing blue-gray eyes, and long, curly hair. He also had a deep, strong speaking voice, with which he could attract a crowd. Since he went about in all kinds of weather he wore the leather clothes of a workingman.

By the beginning of 1655 the organization was thriving. There were about one hundred meetings of Friends. Fox switched from leather clothes to middle-class clothes made of gray cloth. In 1657 he attracted to his community Isaac Pennington, eldest son of the Lord Mayor of London. He later converted William Penn, the son of an admiral, who led the Quaker migration to the New World.

Since Fox was a pacifist, he would not participate in the English civil war (1642–1649). In 1654 he wrote to Oliver Cromwell, England's Puritan dictator, that his weapons were spiritual, not "carnal," meaning that he did not believe in using the sword or gun.

In 1665, five years after the monarchy was restored, Fox was imprisoned in Scarborough Castle, where he shamed soldiers for beating him. "If thou art so brave," he said, "why dost thou strike someone whom thou knowest will not hit back?"

Fox believed in racial tolerance. In 1657 he pleaded for improvement in the lot of slaves in the British colonies. Negroes and Indians, he affirmed, were children of God. He did not call for the abolition of slavery, however; other Quakers did that in the next century.[11]

Friends got in trouble because they, like Fox, did not observe the rules of deference to their social betters. They used *thou* and *thee* instead of the more respectful *you*. When they met someone of a higher social class they kept their hats on. For this they might suffer confiscation of property, imprisonment, and whippings. According to Lawrence Stone, the hat and the whip (representing authority, power) were key symbols in English society. The hat was taken on and off to emphasize differences in rank and authority. The quiet refusal of Friends to remove their headgear was a challenge to the ruling class.

A common excuse for persecuting Quakers was the fact that they refused to swear oaths, citing the New Testament. They claimed that they always spoke the truth. To swear an oath would imply that when not under oath they did not always speak the truth. They would not even swear an oath of loyalty to the king.

When Friends got in trouble with local authorities, George Fox and his friend Margaret Fell, a woman of gentry origin who later married Fox, sometimes went straight to the king. Their tactic was "to speak truth to power," which meant taking the risk of telling powerful people they were wrong. To the surprise of many, Friends sometimes got away with it. Smart rulers had an aversion to flatterers.

Like an English parish, each Quaker meeting took care of its own business. The meeting encouraged all members to participate in decision making, and this gave the decisions authority.[12]

However, Quaker business meetings had peculiarities. They made decisions not by majority rule but by unanimous agreement. The clerk, leader of the meeting for the year, stated what he or she thought was the consensus, or "sense of the meeting." If no one dissented, then the matter was resolved. If someone dissented stubbornly, the decision was postponed. If time did not solve the problem, the dissenter might withdraw from the Society of Friends.

Quakers rarely went to the universities because they were not welcome there. They attended elementary and secondary schools of their own. By the end of the eighteenth century the whole Society, with rare exceptions, was literate.

How Did Protestant Maritime Political Culture Emerge?

Why did this new political culture emerge in the early modern era (c. 1450–1750) and not some other time? Why did it emerge in England and the Dutch Republic, and not in some other place?

As for location, the geographic factors are fairly obvious. The English and Dutch lived close to the sea and were intensely involved in commerce. Both were able to increase their national wealth in this way.

Both had advantages in defending themselves. Britain was an island and required no standing army. The British navy was the country's sword and shield. The defense of Britain was inexpensive.

The Dutch were separated from their Catholic neighbors in present-day Belgium by the Maas and Waal Rivers, which run east-west. This blocked the movement of armies from the south. By the sixteenth century the northern Netherlands was a dense cluster of fortresses, walled towns, canals, dikes, and rivers. In the emergency of 1672, when faced with the dangerous invasion of a large French army, the Dutch decided to open their dikes. This made enemy military movements difficult and costly.[13]

The British and Dutch had access to the North Sea–Baltic Sea trading area and the Atlantic Ocean. The British planted colonies in the New World; the Dutch learned early how to sail directly to the Spice Islands (the Moluccas, in Southeast Asia). They colonized what is now Indonesia and traded as far north as Japan. They had early success in the "rich trades"—in luxury goods valuable enough to carry over long distances.

In the population history of early modern Europe, the British and Dutch were fortunate. The Dutch were little affected by the Black Death of 1348–1350: their urban population continued to grow between 1350 and 1500. The plague also had little effect on British population growth.[14] In the first half of the seventeenth century the population increased in Britain and the Dutch Republic, while in Spain, Italy, Germany, Austria, and Scandinavia it remained stagnant or declined.[15]

It is unlikely that the climate in these two lucky countries was better than it was in neighboring, less fortunate countries. What distinguished them was their intense commercial activity. Their people could choose from a greater variety of foods and among foods from varying sources. They were, therefore, less likely to ingest a fatal dose of a single toxin from spoiled food.

The British and Dutch governments protected property rights in their domains. Their representative governments (representing no more than 5 percent of the population, however) and the recognition of other civil rights served to prevent attacks on property.[16] Compared to other European states, Britain and the Dutch Republic were more urbanized and more accustomed to deferring to the needs of merchants. The large cities were accustomed to self-government.

In this period there was a revolution in military technology, the gunpowder revolution. Most European states were struggling to pay for new weapons and defensive works they needed. Neither the English nor the Dutch suffered from a financial crisis in this period. The reason was that in these populations those who had the greatest ability to pay were active participants in national decision making. They invested heavily in state loans and so were large state creditors.[17] They were, therefore, opposed to tax evasion and government default on loans.

The Protestant reformers played a subversive role against institutional authority. In England the aristocrats declared the established church as "Anglican" and declared the king and not the pope as its head. The Dutch organized the Dutch Reformed Church, which no longer considered the pope its head. Protestant sects such as the Quakers, Baptists, and Congregationalists were even more antihierarchical. They did not defer to the leaders of the "reformed" churches.[18]

Advantages of Protestant Maritime Political Culture

This culture suited migrant individuals and nuclear families, who often could not rely on local approval and disapproval to guide and support their behavior. In strange lands other people might be hostile or indifferent. It was better for migrants and colonists to be guided by an internal system of values.

Under normal conditions, this political culture allowed information to flow freely throughout the religious community, for the more dominant members were less concerned about hanging on to their positions, and the less dominant saw no great advantage in concealing information from others. Sharing economic information was mutually advantageous. For example, since Quakers were receptive to innovation in general, they welcomed new industrial technologies, scientific discoveries, and insights.

Protestant maritime political culture is unique in world history. Since its birth in northwestern Europe it has been widely dispersed. The foundations of freedom were commercial and industrial growth, the participation of wealthy commoners in political decision making, and the antihierarchical tendencies in the Protestant Reformation. People saw that decentralized government could be well financed and secure. Observers saw that political power could be built from the bottom up as well as from the top down. Kings did not become Quakers, but they perceived that radical Protestants were good taxpayers and were well behaved.

Thus representative government and civil rights were born out of two necessities: (1) the need of feudal kings to raise money for military purposes; (2) the need of commoners to be secure in their property rights from attacks by kings and aristocrats at home and abroad. Wealthy commoners obtained rights and freedoms by paying more taxes and loaning money to the state. They also got a share in major political decision making, a new source of pride.

Conclusion

In this chapter I have argued that a favorable maritime location, changes in communication technology (printing with movable type), changes in transportation technology (the full-rigged ship), and the tradition of urban self-government favored the political breakthroughs in Britain and the Dutch Republic that I have labeled Protestant maritime political culture.

Notes

1. Toby E. Huff, *The Rise of Early Modern Science*, pp. 149–201.
2. Philip T. Hoffman and Kathryn Norberg, *Fiscal Crisis, Liberty, and Representative Government*, p. 309.
3. H.G. Koenigsberger, *Medieval Europe, 400–1500*, pp. 42–44.
4. Joseph Strayer, *On the Medieval Origins of the Modern State*, pp. 62–88; John R. Hale, *Renaissance Europe: Individual and Society, 1480–1520*, pp. 161–65.
5. A.R. Myers, *Parliaments and Estates in Europe to 1789*, pp. 24–30.
6. Charles Tilly, *The Formation of Nation States in Central Europe*, p. 15.
7. Bernard Guenee, *States and Rulers in Later Medieval Europe*, pp. 99–109.
8. H. Larry Angle, *First Among Friends;* Emerson Wilde, *Voice of the Lord;* George Fox, *The Journal of George Fox*.
9. Keith Rightson, *English Society, 1580–1680*, p. 213; Hugh Barbour, *The Quakers in Puritan England*, pp. 6–10.
10. William C. Braithwaite, *The Beginnings of Quakerism*, 2d ed., pp. 12–25; Christopher Hill, *The World Turned Upside Down*, pp. 76, 84, 123, 300.
11. Lawrence Stone, *The Crisis of the Aristocracy, 1558–1641*, pp. 34–35.
12. Wallace Notestein, *The English People in the Era of Colonization, 1603–1630*, pp. 228–41.
13. Jonathan Israel, *The Dutch Republic: Its Rise, Greatness, and Fall, 1479–1806*, pp. 12, 131.
14. Ibid., p. 14.
15. Colin McEvedy and Richard Jones, *Atlas of World Population History*.
16. Douglass North, *The Paradox of Freedom*, pp. 7–8
17. Hoffman and Norberg, *Fiscal Crisis*, pp. 306–9.
18. William Bouwsma, "Liberty in the Renaissance and Reformation."

8 THE SCIENTIFIC REVOLUTION OF THE SEVENTEENTH CENTURY

*I do not know what I may appear to the world; but to myself I
seem to have been only like a boy playing on the seashore, and
diverting myself in only now and then finding a smoother pebble
or a prettier shell than ordinary, whilst the great ocean of truth
lay undiscovered before me.*

—Isaac Newton (1642–1727)

The preceding two chapters described the social context from which
modern science emerged. The key innovations were the universities,
the printing press, and decentralized, self-regulating government.

Copernicus

The first scientific revolution began in Catholic Europe with the work
of a Pole, Nicolaus Copernicus (1473–1543). In the seventeenth century the focus of scientific activity shifted from Italy (home of Galileo)
to Protestant northwestern Europe, especially to England and the
Dutch Republic. The new science was limited to research in physics
and astronomy, but it held the promise of discoveries in other areas.

According to Steven Shapin, in England scientific thinking became
associated with gentlemanly behavior, political liberty, and Protestant-
ism.[1] Most scientists were gentlemen, and gentlemen were supposed to
tell the truth to other gentlemen (except when serving the government).
They thought that only financially independent people like themselves
could be relied upon to tell the truth, while those who were financially
dependent might lie for some personal gain. English gentlemen be-

112

lieved they were more likely to tell the truth than Italian gentlemen, who, they thought, were deceitful.

Gradually, as the urban public of northwestern Europe became literate and schooled, scientific thinking became more familiar, gained respect, and began to permeate the thinking of the educated. An unprecedented intellectual revolution unfolded.

During the early sixteenth century scientists had overcome some of the obstacles that prevented scientific progress. Enlightened by the artist's theory of perspective, they realized that distant objects looked smaller than they actually were. Consequently, stars and planets might be larger than they appeared.

Like mapmakers, scientists had learned to represent space impersonally, using longitude and latitude as coordinates. They used impersonal space as the abstract framework for physical events.[2] This was different from the personalized symbolic space of medieval people.

Superstition and fantasy were not the only enemies of science. So was common sense. Many people thought the early scientists to be strange because they used logic to cast doubt upon the evidence of their senses. Scientists were less likely than others to trust appearances.

Nicolaus Copernicus believed that the sun and not the earth was the center of the solar system. To reach this conclusion he had to be able to distinguish the real center of the solar system from the apparent center of gravity. When he succeeded in doing this by a leap of the imagination, he was able to switch from a geocentric model of the solar system to a heliocentric model.[3]

Copernicus was a Pole, the son of a wealthy merchant. After his father's early death his uncle, a prince and bishop, took care of him. He lived in Italy from 1496 to 1505, studying medicine and canon law.

In Italy scholars knew that one of the ancients, Aristarchus, had suggested that the earth revolved around the sun. In 1440 an Italian, Nicholas of Cusa, had made the same suggestion.

Beginning in 1512 Copernicus tried to work out heliocentric theory in full mathematical detail. However, he was afraid to publish it. In the last year of his life he gave in to his friends and let them arrange for its publication. In 1543, when he lay on his deathbed, they gave him a bound copy of his book, entitled *On the Revolutions of Celestial Bodies*. Only a few hundred copies were printed; a second edition came out in 1566 in Basel, Switzerland.[4]

Kepler

The next important astronomer was Johannes Kepler (1571–1630), who was born in Germany, the son of a professional soldier. His grandfather had been mayor of their small town. Kepler's family could afford to send him to college, where he showed brilliance in mathematics. He at first accepted medieval cosmology, in which earthly realities constantly changed but heavenly realities did not. A celestial event changed his mind.

In 1572 the Danish astronomer Tycho Brahe observed a supernova, a fixed star that suddenly gained in brightness. This supernova was the first a European had recorded since 125 B.C. In 1604 Kepler himself observed another supernova. When sighted by observers in different locations, the supernova did not change position. Therefore, it could not be near the earth. Kepler concluded that supernovas were far beyond the supposedly unchangeable starry realm of Aristotle (384–322 B.C.). Most medieval scholars accepted Aristotle's views.

So Kepler knew that both heavenly and terrestrial realities changed. From then on he could consider the heavens and the earth as part of one variable realm. Kepler went on to assign for the first time a physical cause to the movement of a heavenly body. Instead of attributing the movement of the sun, planets, and stars to spiritual forces, he proposed that the causes of motion were the same both in the heavens and on earth. The force that kept the earth and planets in motion was the magnetism of the sun. He inferred that physics and astronomy had the same laws. Kepler realized that the force of the sun's pull was in inverse relation to the distance of a planet from the sun. That is to say, the greater the distance of a planet from the sun, the less the strength of the sun's gravity. However, since calculus did not exist at the time, he lacked the mathematical knowledge to quantify that relation.

Kepler finally rejected the medieval assumption that heavenly bodies always moved in circles. Using the precise observations of Tycho Brahe, he discovered that the only model that could fit the observed facts of planetary motion was the ellipse. In this respect he was ahead of Galileo.

When he had worked out the pattern of movement of the sun and planets, Kepler said, "I contemplate its beauty in incredible and ravishing delight." He realized that planets did not move at the same speed. Intuitively he perceived that two antagonistic forces were acting upon them in a tug-of-war, with different results. Kepler understood one of those forces (gravity) but he didn't understand the other, inertia. He knew that objects at rest tend to remain at rest, but he didn't realize that objects in motion tend to remain in motion. It took Newton to get that straight and to create a conceptual system that took all known facts into account.

Galileo

In 1610, while Kepler was still alive, Galileo (1564–1642) burst onto the scene like a supernova. He published *The Starry Messenger,* a report of what he had seen through a telescope that he had built for himself and turned upward toward the sky.[5]

Galileo got the idea for his telescope from a Dutch example and then improved upon it.[6] Italy had once been the center for lens grinding: Italian experts had been making eyeglasses since about 1280. However, by 1608 the Dutch Republic had become the lens grinding center of Europe.

The principle of the telescope can be understood by examining eyeglasses for nearsighted and farsighted people. A concave lens corrects nearsightedness. For a person of normal vision, such a lens makes a distant tower look smaller, but clear. A convex lens corrects farsightedness.

If a person of normal vision places a convex lens out in front of a concave lens, a distant tower remains clear and reassumes normal size. If one moves the convex lens away from the eye, the tower gets larger: It is magnified. If one continues to move the convex lens away, at some point the tower becomes a blur. So the first telescope consisted of a concave lens and a convex lens held at a certain distance from each other. Telescope makers adjusted that distance so as to achieve maximum magnification with clarity.

Galileo was able to create a telescope with a magnifying power of about thirty times normal. He observed that the Milky Way was made up of many separate stars; that the sun had spots; that Jupiter had four moons; that Venus went through phases, like the earth's moon; and much else.

Since Galileo wrote *The Starry Messenger* in Latin, an international language in his time, he became well known among educated people in Europe. In 1611 he received a warm welcome at the papal court in

Rome, for he did not propose any revolutionary theories to account for what he saw. This was discreet behavior for Galileo.

By that time Galileo had secretly accepted Copernican theory. Now he had some evidence of his own to support it. In his time people imagined that if the earth moved, it would lose the moon: Galileo observed that Jupiter moved and its four moons stayed in their orbits. So maybe the earth, like Jupiter, was able to move and at the same time keep control of its moon.

Another question was what could cause the phases of Venus. What else could it be, Galileo reasoned, except the sun? The moon, by analogy, went through phases depending on its relationship to the sun. The earth reflected the light of the sun onto the dark part of the moon, which glowed dimly. The earth's shine was reflected sunshine. The earth was not on fire; after sunset all was dark. So the earth behaved like a planet.

These observations did not prove the heliocentric theory directly. They were analogies that suggested the theory was true.

Since the sun had spots it was not a perfect body, as the Greeks had believed. Galileo followed individual spots around the sun and concluded that the sun rotated on its axis every twenty-seven days.

In 1610, when Galileo became famous, he was forty-six. On what trajectory was he propelled? From where did he start?

He was the son of a fairly affluent musician of a patrician family distinguished in medicine and public affairs. From his youth he wanted to learn nature's principles and put them to practical uses. He became adept at making mechanical toys, a skill that helped him later to make scientific instruments.

His father sent him to medical school at the University of Pisa, but he didn't like it. Instead, he persuaded his father to hire him a tutor in mathematics. After four years he had learned enough to be accepted as a junior professor of mathematics at the University of Pisa.

Using only algebra and geometry, Galileo began to study the behavior of falling bodies. This had applications for gunnery. It was impractical to measure the behavior of cannon balls (they moved so fast), but he could roll balls slowly down an inclined plane. He could make the slope very gentle, minimizing the effect of gravity, and then measure the speed.

In this way Galileo could demonstrate that the total distance a body covered increased as a square of the time it took to cover that distance. He concluded that the laws of nature were mathematical.

He also showed that two forces could simultaneously influence the movement of a body. If a cannonball was shot horizontally forward, it encountered another force, gravity, that constantly forced it downward at an accelerated speed. The two forces working together, horizontally and vertically, caused the cannonball to form a parabolic curve. Galileo was turning gunnery into a science.

He showed that the rotating earth (as described by Copernicus) would not leave behind it everything not firmly nailed down. The downward pull of earth's gravity did the job.

Galileo attracted lots of students but antagonized other faculty members. In 1592 he moved to the University of Padua, in Venetian territory. From there he corresponded with Kepler, who also accepted Copernican theory. Kepler generously offered to help Galileo, but this was help Galileo could not use. Kepler had some fantastic ideas and, alas, Kepler was a Protestant. Galileo needed Catholic help.

Galileo became the best lens grinder of his time. He built many telescopes. Some Venetians would eagerly climb to the top of towers to look far out to sea through one of his telescopes and try to catch sight of ships otherwise invisible. Galileo sent his telescopes all over Europe so that others could confirm his observations in the sky.

The Venetians awarded him a lifetime appointment at the University of Padua and a big increase in salary. However, he preferred to return to his beloved Florence to become mathematician and philosopher to the Grand Duke of Tuscany and chief mathematician at the University of Pisa.

In 1613, in his "Letter on Sunspots," he defended the Copernican system in print for the first time. Then he got bolder. In 1615 he wrote the "Letter to Christina" in which he said that the investigation of nature was the business of scientists. The business of theologians was to reconcile scientific facts with the language of the Bible, for the Bible, as the clergy knew, was a work on faith and morals, not science. Unfortunately, biblical writers used commonsense language, such as saying that the sun "rose" and "set," that reflected apparent realities. Apparent realities, Galileo and others argued, were not always real.

This affirmation of the difference between science and religion may not seem shocking today, but in 1615 it was both shocking and dangerous. True, Galileo left moral issues to the Church: He did not try to change the advice the Church gave the people. However, the Church based its advice on a complex philosophical system that the clergy were reluctant to revise.

In 1616 the pope put *De Revolutionibus* by Copernicus on the Index, a list of forbidden books, where it remained until 1835. He forbade Galileo to teach the theory. It was not that Copernicus or Galileo had challenged Christian orthodoxy. The problem was that Galileo, like Luther, was challenging the authority of the Church, which considered all learning its domain. Galileo was trying to set aside the study of nature as the turf of the scientist.

Galileo lay low for a time. However, in 1623 he said that the Church had no authority on any matter that people could investigate directly. Specifically, what he called the "Book of Nature" was written in mathematical language and could be deciphered only by those who knew mathematics.

By 1632 tempers had cooled and the current pope, Urban VIII, allowed Galileo to publish a second book, *Dialogue of the Two Chief World Systems*. The pope thought Galileo understood that he should not advocate the Copernican theory as an established truth. Galileo obeyed in letter but not in spirit. He created an imaginary dialogue in which the advocate of the Copernican theory made the opposition leader (Simplicio) look ridiculous. Unfortunately, Simplicio strongly resembled Pope Urban VIII.

The pope was not amused. He ordered the publication of this work halted, and he ordered Galileo to come to Rome to be tried for heresy before the Inquisition. The friends and enemies of Galileo argued and conspired behind the scenes. His enemies won.

But why did the Church bear down on Galileo? The following of the scientist was limited to the small world of Italian intellectuals. Most other people had no interest in what Galileo had to say. He did not attack princes or complain about social injustice.

However, Galileo was feisty. He loved a good argument. His logic was simple and clear, and he was very sarcastic. That made him fun to listen to and read, but it also made him enemies, both in academe and the Church. People like this are likely to get in trouble even today.

In 1633 Catholic scientists had a stunning setback. The Church condemned the astronomer-physicist Galileo Galilei for teaching the theory of Copernicus, that is, that the earth and planets revolved around the sun. Under threat of being burned for heresy, Galileo recanted his views. The pope banned all of Galileo's writings, past and future, and placed him under house arrest, forbidden to teach.

The old man was not quite finished. In spite of oncoming blindness

Galileo finished his final work, a summary of physics. No printer in Italy would dare to touch it: The pope was too powerful. However, a French diplomat visited him secretly. This diplomat would take it north to another country, a country where printers were willing to publish dangerous thoughts.

Galileo was in a weaker position than was Luther, who had started the Protestant Reformation. Luther fought about an issue the masses of urban Germans could understand: financial exploitation by the Church. He also had a German prince protecting him. He was far to the north of the center of papal power. However, Galileo did not have a popular issue or a powerful protector. He lived close to the center of papal influence. In the end he turned to a new constituency: the scientists and educated laymen of Protestant northern Europe.

In 1635 the Dutch published a Latin edition of Galileo's last work. Thus educated people in northwest Europe knew what the Italian stargazer and scientist had said. Still under house arrest and by this time blind, Galileo died in 1642, the year Newton was born.[7]

In Galileo's time northwestern Europe was on a commercial roll, while Italy was losing its economic preeminence. We see this in the downward trend of Italian exports.[8] Along with the shift in economic power to the northwest was a shift in political power in favor of the Protestant nations, mainly the Dutch Republic and England.

In 1650 there were about eleven million Italians, compared with two million Dutch and five million English. However, the Protestant countries were well organized, well funded, and well defended by sea. Italy was still disunited.[9]

When economic and political power moved to northwestern Europe, so did intellectual activity. Like the Japanese and Americans today, the ambitious English and Dutch entrepreneurs were interested in any scientific discovery or invention that they could use to their advantage. The Dutch were making telescopes, microscopes, clocks, and other scientific instruments.

Neither the Dutch nor English Protestant clergy managed to get a cultural monopoly in their respective domains. Publishers had a lot of freedom. They defended it because there was money to be made from controversy. Political elites concluded that most scientists were godly folk who did not stir up the common people. They loved law and order. All they asked for was autonomy in the study of nature.

The Catholic Church that condemned Galileo for heresy was a

church on the defensive. It had reformed itself, but the Protestants had not returned to the fold. It had argued its case patiently, reasonably, but the Protestants were not convinced. When it came to war with neighboring states during 1659–1713, the great Catholic protagonist, Spain, was the loser. Net gain went to Protestant powers (Britain and the Dutch Republic) and France (a liberal, ostensibly Catholic, state).

Galileo had some competent Italian contemporaries, especially his student, Evangelista Torricelli (1608–1647). Torricelli invented the barometer. He discovered that the height of a mercury column in a glass tube (about thirty inches) reflected air pressure on earth. It also varied from day to day, showing that air pressure did, too. However, no other Italian physicist of genius appeared until the time of Alessandro Volta (1745–1827). The Spanish and Portuguese produced no scientist of note until Ramón y Cajal (1852–1934).

The Dutch Republic

Great scientists began to appear in northwest Europe. During the seventeenth century the small Dutch Republic (population two million) produced many fine examples, especially Christian Huygens (1629–1695) and Antonie van Leeuwenhoek (1632–1723).

The Dutch were active in the life insurance business. This was well known to Huygens, a Dutch patrician who spent much of his time in Paris. He published the first formal book on probability theory, applying it to work out life expectancy tables. Realizing that navigators needed a more accurate clock to calculate longitude, in 1656 Huygens invented the pendulum clock. It was very accurate on land, but because of the effects of the pitching and tossing of the ship, it was not accurate at sea.[10]

Van Leeuwenhoek was a modest man with very little schooling. He owned a drapery shop and began to grind magnifying glasses to inspect cloth more closely. He made a single lens that could magnify nearly two hundred times.

Then he developed a passion for peering through his microscope at small things, including insects, microorganisms, protozoa, bacteria, spermatozoa, and capillaries. He found that maggots did not arise spontaneously from rotting meat, or fleas from sand and dust. Instead, these tiny creatures reproduced themselves from eggs laid by the female and fertilized by the male. He peered, drew what he saw, and theorized little. His discoveries made him world-famous, and his restraint in theorizing kept him out of trouble.[11]

Harvey and Descartes

The Dutch did not monopolize science after Galileo. Two other men, William Harvey (1578–1657) and René Descartes (1596–1650), were at least equal in stature to Huygens and Van Leeuwenhoek.

William Harvey was an English physician with a passion for scientific research. He studied medicine at the University of Padua and was impressed by Galileo's scientific methods. In England he was a successful practitioner and became court physician to Kings James I and Charles I. However, his great achievement was to demonstrate how the blood circulates. This was not easy in view of the impossibility of observing blood circulation directly.[12]

Since the time of the Roman physician Galen, doctors believed that blood oscillated back and forth in the vessels. Harvey, by dissecting the valves of the heart, discovered that blood could flow only one way. He also calculated that in one hour the heart pumped out a quantity of blood that was three times the weight of a human being. It seemed impossible that the body could form blood and break it down at such at rate. It had to be the same blood, always flowing in one direction in a closed system. Blood circulated; the heart pumped it.

Harvey published his discovery in 1628. At first other physicians ridiculed him, and his practice declined. However, by the time he was old, physicians generally accepted his theory.[13]

The Frenchman Descartes supported Harvey. However, he was a mathematician and philosopher, not an applied scientist. He received a Jesuit education and obediently rejected Copernican theory. But Descartes chose to spend most of his adult life in Holland. Here he was able to combine algebra and geometry, to the great enrichment of both. Descartes realized that every point on a plane can be represented by an ordered system of two numbers and that every curve represents an equation. Today this is called analytic geometry. It paved the way for the invention of calculus.

Descartes was also famous for his ideas about body and mind. Inspired by Harvey, he was able to see the human body as a kind of machine. But where was the human soul? He decided it was outside the body and independent of it. So defined, the soul interacted with the body by means of a small structure attached to the brain called the pineal gland. The relation of mind to body was like that of a "ghost" to a "machine." This concept lingered in popular thinking for three centuries.

The greatest scientist of the early modern era, if not of all time, was the Englishman Isaac Newton (1642–1727). Galileo, Harvey, and Descartes had combined mathematics with scientific investigation. Newton went on to invent calculus, which made possible even more important discoveries in astronomy and physics.

Newton

Newton's career coincided with the shift of economic dominance from the Netherlands to England. While the English were organizing an empire, Newton was organizing scientific knowledge. After Newton the English maintained economic dominance and produced more distinguished scientists.

At the core of Newton's great synthesis, *Mathematical Principles of Natural Philosophy* (1687), was the concept of the universe as an interactive system. All bodies in it interacted gravitationally in a predictable way. Educated people immediately recognized Newton's work as a masterpiece.

Newton was born in 1642 in rural Lincolnshire. He came from a moderately prosperous landowning family. His father died before he was born, and his mother remarried when he was three. She handed him over to her mother to raise. When he was ten his stepfather died and his mother returned to him. On the advice of the boy's uncle, a Cambridge faculty member, in 1661 she sent him to Cambridge.

During 1665 and 1666, when Cambridge was closed on account of the bubonic plague in the area, Newton stayed at home and began the studies that would lead him to invent calculus. In 1669 he published a work that showed the progress he had made. Without the use of calculus he would not have been able to construct his synthesis of physics and astronomy.

In 1669 Cambridge University granted Newton tenure as a professor of mathematics. Most of the time he led a solitary life, having no interest in women, and he was extremely absentminded and sensitive to criticism. Over a period of five years an acquaintance at Cambridge heard Newton laugh only once. Newton had loaned an acquaintance a copy of Euclid's *Geometry*. The borrower asked what use the study of geometry would be to him. This question made Newton "very merry." Apparently he wondered how could anyone ask such a stupid question.

Newton published *Mathematical Principles of Natural Philosophy* in 1687. At this time the phrase "natural science" did not exist; "natural philosophy" was used instead. Newton's work brought together the relevant discoveries of Copernicus, Kepler, Galileo, and lesser lights. Newton took from Kepler the elliptical model for planetary orbits and the theory that the moon influences the tides on earth. He determined that the force of gravitation was inversely related to the square of the distance between two objects. (Kepler had known it was some function of the distance, but not specifically the square.) Moreover, every particle in the universe attracts every other particle with a force that is directly proportional to the product of their masses. But Newton said it in a way that assumed the laws of nature were mathematical and with words that indicated what should be measured.

Newton codified from Galileo's findings three laws of motion. The first stated the principle of inertia: Not only do objects at rest tend to remain so, but objects in motion remain in motion at a constant speed so long as outside forces are not involved. His second law defined a force in terms of mass and acceleration. The mass of a body represented its resistance to acceleration. His third law stated that for every action there was an equal and opposite reaction. This is the principle behind rocket propulsion: to escape earth's gravity by directing a force downward.

Newton clinched the Copernican theory in 1687. He argued that two bodies rotated around their common center of mass. Since there was a huge disparity in the masses of the earth and the sun, their common center of mass had to lie near the center of the sun. Hence the earth necessarily revolved around the sun.[14]

Newton showed that his principles were the basis of Kepler's three laws of planetary motion. He quantified Kepler's laws more precisely.

After 1687, when Newton was famous, someone asked him how he discovered the law of universal gravitation. "By thinking on it continually," he said. He might have created his synthesis even if Galileo had not smuggled his last book out of Italy. However, Galileo's final "crime" had symbolic significance: It represented the transfer of scientific leadership from the Catholic to the Protestant world.

Except for van Leeuwenhoek, who observed but did not theorize, all these early scientists obtained some higher education. We find among them no peasants (who were 80 to 90 percent of the population), no practicing clergy, and no women. All had enough money to spend a great deal of time engaged in their passionate quest.[15]

The scientific revolution of the seventeenth century was a breakthrough in world history. Its earliest practical applications had military significance. Galileo's work was important in the development of ballistics.

The new astronomy aided navigators. Yes, many European political leaders thought, knowledge *(scientia)* really *is* power. What else would scientists discover?

Had there been no realm of reasoned dissent in Europe, no freedom of the press, no high value placed on honesty, it is difficult to imagine how modern science could have put down roots. Had there been no political elites that could discern the potential value of science and were willing to provide financial support to scientists, it is difficult to imagine how scientific knowledge could have become cumulative.

Notes

1. Steven Shapin, *A Social History of Truth: Civility and Science in Seventeenth-Century England,* especially pp. 69 and 118.

2. Robert D. Sack, *Human Territoriality: Its Theory and History,* p. 85.

3. Hans Blumenberg, *The Genesis of the Copernican World,* pp. 249, 433.

4. There are two recent histories of astronomy: Timothy Ferris, *Coming of Age in the Milky Way* (see especially pp. 66 and 81), and Rocky Kolb, *Blind Watchers of the Sky.* For the biographies of Copernicus and the other scientists discussed here, Isaac Asimov, *Asimov's Biographical Encyclopedia of Science and Technology,* 2d ed., is indispensable.

5. Sympathetic biographies of Galileo include Giorgio de Santillana, *The Crime of Galileo,* and Ludovico Geymonat, *Galileo Galilei.* Critical of Galileo is Jerome J. Langford, *Galileo, Science and the Church,* rev. ed.

6. Henry C. King, *The History of the Telescope,* pp. 27–30; Albert van Helden, *The Invention of the Telescope.*

7. "Galileo Galilei," *Dictionary of Scientific Biography,* Charles C. Gillispie, ed.

8. Carlo Cipolla, *Before the Industrial Revolution: European Society and Economy, 1000–1700,* pp. 185–92, 257–74.

9. Colin McEvedy and Richard Jones, *Atlas of World Population History,* pp. 43, 65, 107.

10. Dirk J. Struik, *The Land of Stevin and Huygens: A Sketch of Science and Technology in the Dutch Republic During the Golden Century.*

11. Abraham Schierbeek, *Measuring the Invisible World: The Life and Works of Anton van Leeuwenhoek.*

12. I. Bernard Cohen, *Revolution in Science,* pp. 175–89.

13. Antonio R. Damasio, *Descartes' Error.*

14. The standard biography of Newton is Richard S. Westfall, *Never at Rest: A Biography of Isaac Newton.* See also Gale E. Christianson, *In the Presence of the Creator*; Rupert Hall, *The Revolution in Science, 1500–1750,* 2d ed., p. 118.

15. Peter Burke, *The Italian Renaissance: Culture and Society in Italy,* 2d ed., p. 283; Margaret Jacob, *The Cultural Meaning of the Scientific Revolution,* p. 25.

9 THE POPULATION EXPLOSION

1700 to 1900

> *Population, when unchecked, increases in a geometrical ratio. Subsistence increases only in an arithmetical ratio. A slight acquaintance with numbers will show the immensity of the first power in comparison with the second.*
>
> —Thomas Malthus

The population explosion in Europe and China that began in the early eighteenth century was a breakthrough of a different kind. People wanted to have children, but they did not intend to create such a dramatic increase in the population. This explosion brought benefits to some, poverty and ill health to many more.

We know more about the course of this growth in China and Europe than anywhere else in the world. It continues today worldwide, but we will end our study in 1900, when practitioners of scientific medicine began to reduce mortality rates.

Between 1700 and 1800 the population of all Europe (including European Russia) rose by 50 percent, while that of China rose 113 percent. Between 1800 and 1900 the population of Europe increased 116 percent, while that of China rose by 41 percent There was little immigration into these regions.[1]

The population explosion was part of a major change in human ecology. From 1700 to 1900 population growth in both Europe and China formed a J-curve, showing exponential growth. This development influenced economies, technologies, politics, warfare, migration, and creativity. But its origins are a puzzle.

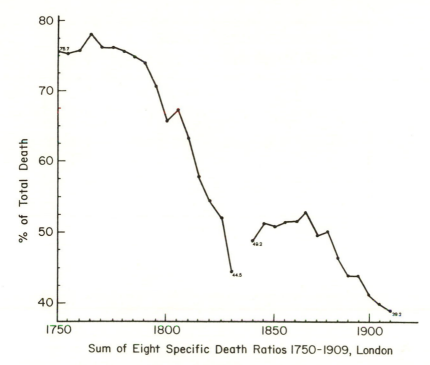

Sum of Eight Specific Death Ratios 1750-1909, London

Figure 10. **Mortality in London, 1750–1909, as expressed in the sum of the specific death ratios of the eight biggest killer diseases.** The first national vital rates (including London) were reported in 1840. The first census in London was in 1800. It is impossible to calculate death rates per thousand population before 1840. However, for the period 1750–1837 we can make estimates of the annual variance in mortality by using the bills of mortality in London, broken down by supposed cause of death. The bills were drawn from parish records. I calculated the sum of the specific death ratios of the eight biggest killer diseases for the 1750–1837 data and spliced them to the official death ratios, 1840–1909. (From Mary K. Matossian, "Death in London, 1750–1909." Reprinted from *The Journal of Interdisciplinary History* 16 [1987], p. 187, with the permission of the editors of *The Journal of Interdisciplinary History* and The MIT Press, Cambridge, Massachusetts. © 1985 by the Massachusetts Institute of Technology and the editors of *The Journal of Interdisciplinary History*.)

Origins of the Population Explosion

In 1900 physicians and public health officers still did not know how to clean up an urban water supply. The building of sewers often did little to improve health because the raw sewage was dumped in the local river.

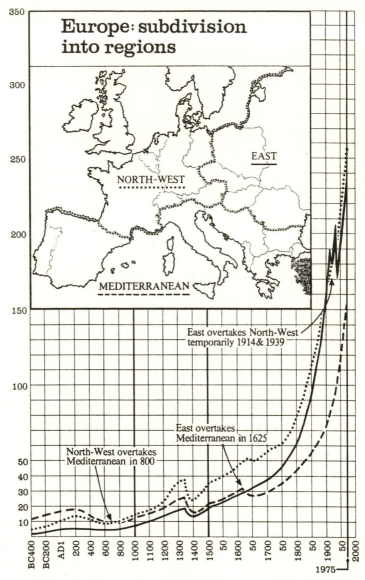

Figure 11. **Population growth in Europe, 400 B.C. to A.D. 1975.** Note the J-curve of growth that began about 1750. The population of the northwestern part of Europe may have overtaken that of the Mediterranean area as early as A.D. 800. Given their faster population growth, England and the Low Countries were able to dominate international commerce. The more commerce, the less mortality, and the faster the population growth. (From Colin McEvedy and Richard Jones, *Atlas of World Population History* [Harmondsworth, UK: Penguin Books, 1978], p. 28. Reprinted by permission from the authors.)

Medical treatments were mostly palliative, and doctors could not prevent or cure most infectious diseases (though a major exception was smallpox, which could be prevented).[2]

Did climatic changes influence the occurrence of infectious diseases? A measure of annual changes in Eurasian temperatures, especially those of Europe, can be found in Greenland ice cores, which indicate levels of volcanism. Usually the smaller the amount of volcanism, the warmer the temperature (see Figs. 2 and 3).

I am also going to consider other possible contributing causes of population trends: dietary change, changes in transportation technology, and variation in commercial activity. These causal factors, I believe, influenced population growth mainly by influencing the quality of the food that a given population consumed. Particularly damaging to food quality were natural fungal toxins. Climatic change influenced the amounts in which these toxins were present in food. Trading activity in a town, by varying the sources of food consumed, served to reduce the intake of a single toxin.

Climatic Change

During the seventeenth century in Eurasia temperatures tended to be colder than usual. Populations grew a little or declined a little. The people of England, France, and the Dutch Republic were especially fortunate. In spite of the cold, wet, and stormy weather of the first half of the seventeenth century the populations of these countries increased, while those of Spain, Italy, and Germany decreased. This was associated with an increase in trade in the first three countries mentioned and a decrease in trade in the second group. Climatic conditions in both areas were much the same.

We know something about Chinese temperatures since 1500 because of studies of Chinese annals and Tibetan tree rings.[3] These studies indicate that in the eighteenth century temperatures in China rose earlier than they did in Europe. Despite climatic adversity during the nineteenth century, the population of China continued to rise.

Dietary Change

A majority of studies of the history of diet are concerned with Europe. They are descriptive or narrative in character and do not marshal support of any hypothesis on population history.

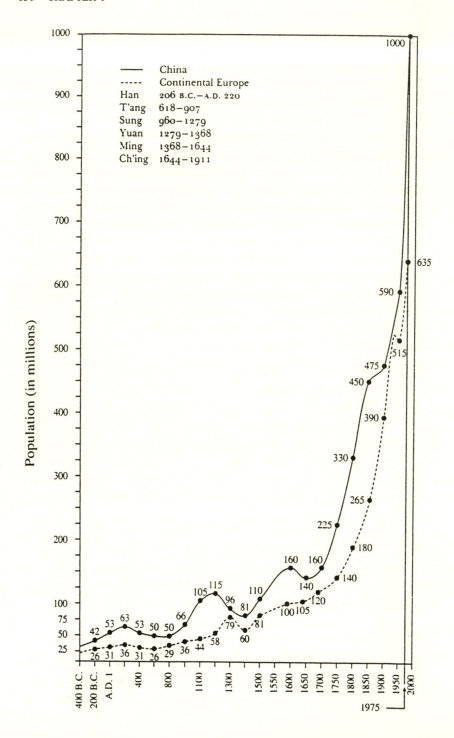

During the eighteenth century in Europe bread was indeed the staff of life. In Paris the average adult ate a pound of dark bread (mostly rye) a day; in the countryside, two to three pounds were consumed. Bread was the least expensive form of calories. According to Fernand Braudel, no more than 4 percent of the European population ate white wheat bread, which was a rich man's food.

Meat cost eleven times as much per calorie as did bread; eggs cost six times as much; butter and oil, three times. Most people spent about half their income for cereals.[4] As the population grew, food prices moved higher. In the 1790s, real wages declined sharply. This situation put pressure on the poor to try unfamiliar but cheap foods such as potatoes. By growing potatoes farmers could produce two to three times as much starch per acre as they could with rye. Moreover, potatoes could grow in poor soils at lower temperatures. In England and Wales potato consumption rose from 0.25 potato per capita per day in 1775 to 0.62 potato per capita per day in 1838.[5]

In 1815 France produced 1.6 million metric tons of potatoes, and the average French person ate 44 pounds of potatoes a year. By mid-century this was up to 176 pounds a year.

After 1820 the price of wheat in Europe declined. White wheat bread was coming within the reach of the common people. Since white bread was less likely to contain mycotoxins than dark bread (contaminants tended to be sifted out during the refining of flour), this may have served to reduce mortality. By 1900 the price of wheat in London had fallen to one third that of 1800, while real wages had increased.[6]

In most parts of Europe mortality declined, accounting for most of the population growth. Wrigley and Schofield put greater weight on fertility increase, but the vital rates for 1541–1840 that they reconstruct from parish records are seriously in error and in any case do not support their hypothesis. Wrigley and Schofield commit the blunder of failing to correct their sample of parishes for wealth. Apparently they

Figure 12. **Population growth in China, 400 B.C. to A.D. 1975.** Apparently the population of China exceeded that of Europe throughout this period. The Chinese population began its takeoff around 1700, earlier than Europe by fifty years. (From Paul S. Ropp, ed., *Heritage of China* [Berkeley: University of California Press, 1990], p. 227. It is a modification of a graph that first appeared in Colin McEvedy and Richard Jones, *Atlas of World Population History* [Harmondsworth: Penguin, 1978]. Reprinted by permission of University of California Press. © 1990 by The Regents of the University of California.)

did not consult any genealogists, who could have explained to them why this was important. English genealogists know that before the recording of vital events became compulsory, such recording was mainly a means of transferring property efficiently from one generation to another. Consequently, the wealthier an individual, the more likely he was to keep a record of vital events in his family. The common people, having little or no property to pass on, had little incentive to keep a continuous record of vital events.

With the best of intentions Wrigley and Schofield chose to study the best-recorded parishes of England and Wales. But parishes chosen in this way could not be representative of the population of England and Wales. Their study has a bias toward representing the more fortunate individuals in the population.[7]

Transportation and Trade

Improvements in transportation technology, as noted in Chapter 6, were associated with the growth of cities. They were also associated with the growth of trade and industry.[8] Trade in turn, may have influenced food quality, and food quality may have influenced mortality rates.

The mechanism connecting improved food quality with the growth of trade may have been as follows. The greater the amount of trade, the more diverse the sources of food, and the more diverse the fungal poisons in grain. When citizens obtained their food from many different sources (not necessarily changing the various kinds of food they ate), they were likely to consume less of any one fungal toxin. Fresh foods from nearby markets might contain no toxins at all. If people had to rely entirely on locally grown food, instead of food from diverse sources, they were more likely to get a large dose of a particular toxin.

Furthermore, with the development of railroads and steamships, especially after 1850, merchants could move food faster from the place of its production to the place where consumers waited for it. The faster the transport of food, the fresher it is. The better the system of all-season roads, canals, steamships, and railroads, the more rapid the technological improvement and economic growth, and the better the food quality. In the nineteenth century cities were able to grow, for the first time, by significant natural increase and were not wholly dependent on immigration. In short, better food quality and declining death rates were tied to overall economic activity.

European Mortality Decline in the Nineteenth Century

The three countries for which we have national statistics by 1790 were France, Sweden, and Norway. The years 1790 to 1844 showed the steepest mortality decline. In this period the same can be said for the city of London.[9]

What caused this sudden decline? Let us consider the greatest killer of the time, tuberculosis (also known as consumption or phthisis). Some medical historians think that tuberculosis peaked in the late eighteenth and early nineteenth centuries. After 1850 it appears that tuberculosis, without medical intervention, declined in western Europe and the United States. This was a mystery, for during the nineteenth century nobody knew of a cure for tuberculosis.[10]

Tuberculosis is characterized by a deficiency of T-helper cells, an essential part of the immune system. While the poor of London were eating more potatoes and less cheap cereals, tuberculosis declined sharply.

Potatoes did not contain any insidious fungal poisons. When attacked by fungi, the tubers became so repulsive that no one would eat them. By contrast, people did eat spoiled grain, and some of the poisons found in such contaminated cereals weakened the human immune system and made people more vulnerable to infectious diseases.

During the period 1750–1834 Salaman's index of potato availability predicted, for London, 80 percent of the variance in the specific death ratio of children from birth to two years. In addition, the index predicted 60 percent of the variance of the specific death ratio from "consumption" (probably tuberculosis).[11]

From 1875 to 1914 there were seven European countries that collected statistics on mortality, grain production, and potato production. We can use them to estimate relationships between diet and mortality. In six of these countries a high production of potatoes in relation to grain production can be correlated with a lower death rate. This suggests that eating potatoes was healthier than eating cereals.

In the seventh country, Sweden, the relationship between potato production and mortality was reversed: the more potatoes, the higher the mortality rate. This may have been because the Swedes used potatoes

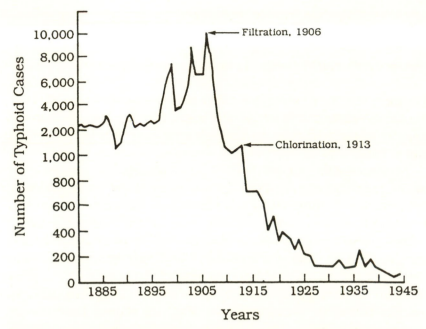

Figure 13. **The number of typhoid cases in Philadelphia, 1880–1945.** Typhoid is a waterborne disease. The construction of sewers in the last decades of the nineteenth century failed to reduce typhoid mortality. Sewers often leaked, contaminating wells. They transported untreated sewage to the nearest river, from which the people took water for drinking and laundry. From 1885 to 1905, the number of typhoid cases actually increased. (Reprinted with permission from Ervan Garrison, *A History of Engineering and Technology* [Boca Raton, FL: CRC Press, 1991], p. 180. © 1991 by CRC Press, Boca Raton, Florida.)

not so much for food but for distilling alcoholic beverages, and it made a difference whether one ate potatoes or drank them: Alcoholism was a severe problem in Sweden in the first half of the nineteenth century.[12]

When white wheat bread became more affordable, this was correlated with mortality decline. In northwest Europe (England, France, Sweden, Germany, and the Netherlands) the cheaper the grain, the lower the death rate. More people could eat white wheat bread instead of dark wheat and rye, and fewer people had to eat contaminated grain. In addition, people were consuming more calories per capita.

In many parts of central and eastern Europe (Austria, Hungary, and Russia) where the principal affordable alternative to rye bread was potatoes, the higher the rye prices, the lower the mortality.

European Fertility Decline, 1875–1914

Modern rubber contraceptives were not generally available before 1914 and then only in England, Germany, and Holland. Even birth control information was difficult to obtain. Nevertheless, after 1875 fertility declined in the eight countries that kept usable records on diet and fertility.

In addition, fertility declined at about the same rate as mortality. The correlation between the two was unusual: $r^2 = .93$. This had not been true in the countries that kept national statistics before 1875— England, Sweden, and France.[13]

After 1945 Western demographers, thinking that mortality decline caused fertility decline, predicted that if modern public health measures were taken in poor countries then both mortality and fertility would decline. They talked of a natural "demographic transition." This was an overly optimistic expectation. After 1945 mortality declined, as predicted, but fertility remained the same or increased. Then the population explosion that had begun in eighteenth-century Europe and China spread over most of the globe.[14]

Demographers did not consider the possibility that in late-nineteenth-century Europe a third variable might have influenced both mortality and fertility decline. This third variable, which I shall discuss shortly, may have been largely responsible for the correlation between the fertility and mortality rates. Consequently, in spite of postwar national economic growth many of the less well-off in poverty-stricken countries remained poor.

How did Western demographers go wrong? Perhaps it was because they did not know that there was an important change in European diet in the age before mass contraceptive use.

By 1875 Europeans had settled on new staples: potatoes, white wheat bread and other baked products. Both potatoes and white bread are low in zinc, an element that is necessary for reproduction to occur. A serving of white wheat bread contains 0.15 mg of zinc; a boiled potato, only 0.23 mg. Fruits and vegetables are no better sources. Zinc comes mainly from whole grains, dairy products, meat, and fish (especially oysters).

Zinc does not accumulate in the body and so must form a part of the weekly food intake. Adults and adolescents need to ingest 15 mg of zinc a day for normal functioning. Thus if a woman did not get enough zinc, she might bear no offspring, even if her husband often ate meat for lunch in a restaurant.

There was probably another causal factor involved as well. During the 1860s and 1870s entrepreneurs in Switzerland and Hungary established new mechanical roller mills. These mills spread to England and the rest of Europe. The whiter flour that these mills produced was even more deficient in zinc than earlier white flours. But the whiter flour contained lesser amounts of fungal poisons, which formed in the grain husks. This could account for the close correlation of fertility and mortality in the years 1875–1914. The third variable to which I referred earlier may have been the percentage of roller-mill flour production out of all flour production.

The development of certain countries is also revealing. At about the time of the French Revolution (1789), fertility in France began to decline—much earlier than in the rest of Europe. This coincided with an increase in white bread consumption in France. The soldier-patriots of Napoleon's armies demanded white bread and got it. In the nineteenth century upwardly mobile French became embarrassed if caught eating dark bread. Moreover, in the early nineteenth century the amount of potatoes in the French diet was rapidly increasing.

Then there was the case of Ireland. The Irish were notorious for their dependence on potatoes. Their zinc came from dairy products. Predictably, the Irish had low mortality and normal fertility.

Another interesting case is that of nonmarital fertility. After 1875 marital fertility and nonmarital fertility declined together. This may have been because unwed mothers and married women of the same social class had a similar diet. There is no evidence that sexual behavior changed significantly. Ironically, this change of diet made illicit sex safer, because it was less likely to result in a pregnancy.

Between 1875 and 1914 fertility decline was a blessing in western and central Europe. The most important consequence was that the standard of living increased there. On account of this and other factors, the restiveness among workers that Marx and Engels had observed in 1848 declined.

China's Population Explosion

In order to explain the Chinese population explosion it is tempting to point to dietary change. It is true that by the eighteenth century the Chinese were growing corn, sweet potatoes, Irish potatoes, and peanuts —all new crops originating in the Americas.[15] The trouble with this hypothesis is that the Chinese dietary staples remained the same: wheat in the north and rice in the south. The new crops provided only some nutritional supplements. In 1700 there were 150 million Chinese, compared to 120 million Europeans. The difference of 30 million was far less than it is today (about 600 million). What can account for this?

The climate of China warmed early in the eighteenth century, several decades before the climate of Europe did. From 1691 to 1750 it was consistently warm in China.[16] These facts suggest that at the beginning of the population explosion in Europe warmer conditions (beginning after 1742) were a major causal factor. However, the period 1751–1880 was mostly cold, in China as in Europe. China was especially chilly between 1775 and 1825; temperatures were lower then than they were at any other time in the period 1450–1900. In spite of this, from 1750 to 1900 the Chinese population continued its rapid growth, as did the European population.

There were no major changes in Chinese infrastructure between 1700 and 1900. In 1700 China already had an excellent system of roads and canals. It built no railroads until the end of the nineteenth century. During the nineteenth century, in spite of a falling standard of living, the Chinese continued to reproduce rapidly. Little work has been done on Chinese economic history for the nineteenth century, when relevant records were abundant. Chinese "isolation" from world trade is a fact, but one that is often misinterpreted. Perhaps future research will show that domestic commerce in China remained intense. If so, there may have been a continued diversification of natural toxins in the Chinese diet, and China's mortality rate would have remained low enough to permit continued population growth.

Conclusion

The course of the population explosion in Eurasia may be broken down into the following sequence:

1. Population growth in both Europe and China began in the early eighteenth century. Winters in this century remained generally cold, but summers were warmer. The population began to grow, causing a rise in food prices. Then the poor sought cheaper alternative foods; Europeans favored potatoes. Thus, in Europe high grain prices forced the introduction of new foods into the diet.

2. In the nineteenth century European entrepreneurs who introduced more turnpikes, canals, and steam technology into the transportation system increased the volume of trade and enlarged food markets.
In China the intensified use of old technology was also influential. It
served to delocalize the diet of trading cities. With the diversification
of toxins came a decline in mortality.

3. From the 1860s on, European entrepreneurs introduced roller-
mill technology in the processing of grain. The flour produced in this
way continued to have reduced levels of fungal poisons but contained
even less zinc. So fertility and mortality moved downward together.

Economic historians now agree that in Western Europe the population explosion was a necessary but not sufficient cause of the Industrial
Revolution. Not every country with a rapidly growing population pro-
ceeds to industrialize. The Chinese did not industrialize until 1950, a
century after population growth forced most of them to live in terrible
poverty.

Notes

1. Colin McEvedy and Richard Jones, *Atlas of World Population History,*
pp. 18, 171.
2. Ervan Garrison, *A History of Engineering and Technology,* pp. 177–80;
see especially graph on p. 180. J.P. Goubert, *The Conquest of Water: The Advent
of Health in the Industrial Age,* p. 245, admits that in France there was no decline
in diarrhea and enteritis until 1906, and that in 1933 typhoid fever was still
widespread.
3. X.D. Wu, "Dendroclimatic Studies in China," pp. 4–49.
4. Fernand Braudel, *Civilization and Capitalism, 15th to 18th Century,* vol.
1, *The Structures of Everyday Life,* p. 137.
5. Redcliffe N. Salaman, *The History and Social Influence of the Potato,* p. 613.
6. R. Perren, *The Meat Trade in Britain, 1840–1914;* D.J. Oddy, *The Making
of the Modern British Diet;* E.J.T. Collins, "Dietary Change and Cereal Consumption in Britain in the Nineteenth Century"; Roger Price, *The Modernization of
Rural France;* F. Meyer, "Evolution de l'alimentation des français, 1781–1972."
7. E.A. Wrigley and R.S. Schofield, *The Population History of England,
1541–1871.*
8. Rick Sjostak, *The Role of Transportation in the Industrial Revolution.*
9. B.R. Mitchell, *European Historical Statistics, 1750–1975,* 2d ed.; Mary K.
Matossian, "Death in London, 1750–1909."
10. Scott D. Holmberg, "The Rise of Tuberculosis in America Before 1820";
F.B. Smith, *The Retreat of Tuberculosis, 1850–1950;* L.G. Wilson, in "The Historical Decline of Tuberculosis in Europe and America," believes that segregation
of tuberculosis patients caused the decline of tuberculosis in England.

11. Matossian, "Death in London," and John Bunnell Davis in his 1817 book, *A Cursory Inquiry into Some of the Principal Causes of Mortality Among Children,* pp. 9–10, deplores the fact that poor children were eating "large quantities of bad potatoes and vegetables half boiled." He advises mothers to give children cold baths, to avoid warm nurseries, and never to allow a nurse to chew the food of the child. For the index of potato availability, see data in Redcliffe Salaman, *The History and Social Influence of the Potato,* p. 613.

12. Gunnar Fridlizius, "Sex Differential Mortality and Socio-Economic Change: Sweden, 1750–1910," p. 263.

13. Mary K. Matossian, "Fertility Decline in Europe, 1875–1913: Was Zinc Deficiency the Cause?"

14. See McEvedy and Jones, *Atlas of World Population History, passim.*

15. Lloyd F. Eastman, *Family, Fields and Ancestors: Constancy and Change in China's Social and Economic History, 1550–1949;* Albert Feuerwerker, "Chinese Economic History in Comparative Perspective."

16. J. Zhang and Thomas J. Crowley, "Historical Climatic Records in China and the Reconstruction of Past Climates"; Wu "Dendroclimatic Studies," pp. 4–49; Chiachen Chang and Zhiguang Lin, *The Climate of China,* p. 295.

10 THE INDUSTRIAL REVOLUTION IN BRITAIN

*To found a great empire for the sole purpose of raising up a
people of customers, may at first appear a project fit only for a
nation of shopkeepers. It is, however, a project altogether unfit
for a nation of shopkeepers, but extremely fit for a nation whose
government is influenced by shopkeepers.*

—Adam Smith

It is one thing to describe the Industrial Revolution, which began in
late-eighteenth-century Britain. It is another to explain how it began.

From the perspective of world history, economic growth and technological innovation did not necessarily occur together. Economic
growth at times occurred in the absence of technological innovation.
Using existing technologies more extensively, merchants could maintain economic growth by increasing the volume of trade. That was in
accordance with the principle of specialization with complementarity.

Even when a technology is possible and desirable, no one may see
fit to develop it. A notorious case was Faraday's discovery in 1831 of
the principle of the electric dynamo, which was little utilized for fifty
years even though entrepreneurs knew about it. Now large dynamos
provide the current to light our buildings, run our electric appliances,
and operate our computers.

Two economic historians, Crafts and Harley, estimated the annual
industrial growth in England. English industrial output increased tenfold
between 1743 and 1850, from an index of 2.63 in 1743 to 21.20 in 1850
$(1913 = 100)$.[1] The growth process was gradual, not explosive. It depended upon the use of new technologies that intensified resource use.

Certain regions in England, notably Lancastershire, led the way. By the early nineteenth century other regions in western Europe had also become centers of innovation: the Rhineland, Alsace, Flanders, Swiss alpine areas, Salerno, and Moscow-Ivanovo. Industrial growth was not a coordinated national effort.

During the first wave of technological innovation, mechanics with a hands-on knowledge of machines made small improvements in them. James Watt of Scotland was an artisan who made and sold calculating instruments. He is deservedly famous for improving the steam engine, but others without scientific training, such as George Stephenson, also made important contributions.

The Search for Explanations

Many scholars have proposed plausible theories to explain the first Industrial Revolution (c. 1780–1870), but all these theories have proved disappointing. The first Industrial Revolution was not driven by overseas commerce, as Floud and McCloskey discovered.[2] Nor was it driven primarily by an abundant supply of cheap labor; sustained population growth occurred many times in the past without an Industrial Revolution. In fact, in the case of printing with movable type, invented in 1450, there was a labor *shortage* at the time: Gutenberg sought a means to replace scarce labor.

It is true that in Great Britain population growth and industrial growth moved upward together. On a world history scale, this burst of population growth was extraordinary. Did it have any causal connection with the Industrial Revolution?

By about 1600 Great Britain had become a great commercial power. It achieved dominance in European commerce by 1700. The British navy ruled the seas, facilitating commerce abroad. By 1769, when Watt made his famous invention, many British businessmen were rich, savvy, and ambitious.

Moreover, Britain already had large and advanced communication and transportation systems, that is, infrastructure. This infrastructure included print shops, canals, all-weather roads, bridges, vehicles, and ships. Road improvements made possible regular postal service.

The British political elite approved patent law, believing that they might profit if inventors could obtain fair rewards for the achievements. British courts enforced British commercial laws. In contrast, the

Chinese had no coherent body of laws. Law was simply the emperor's will. There was no patent law. Chinese bureaucrats hesitated to approve new commercial ventures; they demanded bribes from merchants. Merchants could join the power elite only if they succeeded in passing the civil service examinations. So many Chinese merchant families migrated to Southeast Asia. In this way the government of China lost many of its wealthiest taxpayers.

The British, unlike the Chinese, had a tradition of representative government. Parliament served as a check on royal power. By 1688 the British power elite recognized some civil rights, especially property rights, which protected businessmen. Since the thirteenth century the power elite had co-opted great merchants by giving them representation in the House of Commons. Merchants did not have to get a higher education and join the civil service in order to get ahead.

I think it worthwhile to consider the Industrial Revolution as an extension of two earlier cultural trends: the development of Protestant maritime political culture and the rise of modern science. British elites preferred economic freedom (as opposed to government regulation), religious freedom (rather than papal regulation), and intellectual freedom (as opposed to censorship). The British political elite (peers and gentry) did not resist industrial development; indeed, many profited from it. They used their economic freedom to diversify their investments, shifting their wealth from land to banking and finance, exploiting the mines on their estates, and building bridges and canals. Families with venture capital were interested in technological innovations made by artisans, mechanics, and engineers.

Key Inventions in the First Industrial Revolution

Blacksmiths did not build the new machines of the Industrial Revolution. In 1709 a British Quaker ironmaster, Abraham Darby (1678–1717), was responsible for the first successful European use of coke for smelting iron. Coke is a residue (chiefly carbon) of coal that has been previously heated with limited access to air. Coke replaced charcoal, which is a residue (chiefly carbon) of wood that had been previously so heated. England was becoming poor in wood, but it remained rich in coal.

Coal mines, like other mines, tended to become flooded by the seepage of groundwater into them. So in 1712 Thomas Newcomen, an

English engineer (1663–1729), invented a steam engine for pumping out the water. It used low-pressure steam from burning coal to drive a piston. This was the device that James Watt later improved.

As a boy Watt showed talent in mathematics. His father, a shipbuilder and businessman, helped him. Watt received no secondary or higher education; such education was mainly the privilege of a gentleman. Like most other inventors who created the new technology of the first Industrial Revolution, Watt was an artisan with no formal training in scientific theory. He used handicraft methods to build his machines.

Life for Watt was difficult at first. He suffered from migraine headaches followed by depressions. He needed ten hours of sleep a night. He lost his wife, who died young after bearing six children.

In 1765 Watt studied Newcomen's engine and then constructed one that was four times as fuel-efficient. Instead of one cylinder, this engine had two. The cylinder with the piston contained boiling hot water, and the other cylinder was kept cool (60 degrees Fahrenheit) to condense the steam.

Watt attached the top of the piston to a beam that lifted water from a flooded mine. Steam pressure from the boiler pushed the piston up; then water cooled the empty cylinder, created suction (a vacuum), and pulled the piston down. More efficient condensation created more suction for less fuel.[3] Whereas the Newcomen engine consumed 8.4 kilograms of coal an hour, Watt's engine burned only 2.9 kilograms.[4] He patented his improved engine in 1769.

In 1774 Watt moved from Glasgow (where he designed and manufactured scientific instruments) to Birmingham and went into partnership with Matthew Boulton, a manufacturer of metal products. Boulton was a born promoter. He once wrote to Catherine the Great, "I sell what the whole world wants: power." He married first one heiress, and after her accidental death, he married her sister, thus inheriting the whole fortune.[5]

Watt's engine produced reciprocal movement. Boulton realized that if the engine could produce rotary movement, it could be used to run other machines. The obvious solution, a rod and crank, had been invented in China in the second century B.C. It reached western Europe in the fifteenth century. It had recently been patented in England; this patent was to expire in 1794.

So in 1781 Watt invented and patented a "sun and planet" pair of gears as a substitute for the rod and crank. The next year he created a double-acting piston, which was both pushed and pulled by steam (the Chinese had invented it in the fourth century B.C.). In 1788 he added a centrifugal governor that made the machine self-regulating. The oscillation of the beam switched the steam and water on and off at the right times in the cycle. This device was novel in Britain.

Otto Mayr, after studying self-regulating mechanical devices from ancient times through 1800, noted that from 1600 on, with one exception, all inventors of self-regulating devices lived in northwestern Europe.[6] Moreover, after the population expansion began there was a sharp increase in the invention of self-regulating devices. As Mayr observed, there was an association between the creation of new self-regulating devices and thinking about self-regulation in economic systems. To this I would add that both occurred within a context of self-regulating political culture.

The most important champion of economic self-regulation was Adam Smith (1723–1790), whose work *The Wealth of Nations* was published in 1776. Smith believed that an "invisible hand" regulated the activities of self-seeking individuals in a free market, creating both harmony and growth. This "invisible hand" consisted of the automatic feedback mechanisms of supply and demand. They controlled wages and prices, keeping the economic system in balance.[7]

Adam Smith and James Watt were reared in a self-regulating political culture. They were both Scots, and they knew each other. While Adam Smith translated the idea of self-regulation into economic theory, Watt translated it into technology. Powered by coal, Watt's steam engine was the first of the modern prime movers, taking energy as it occurred in nature and utilizing it to drive machinery. James Watt was the first engineer to find a way to measure the efficiency of his creation. He could measure the ratio of the quantity of heat energy taken up to the mechanical energy obtained. The heat energy he measured by the weight of the coal burned; the mechanical energy output he measured in "horsepower" units, one horsepower being the maximum weight an average horse could lift over a pulley. Fuel economy, not speed, was the main concern of eighteenth-century engineers. However, after 1800 coal mine owners needed a new kind of machine: one with enough power to pull coal cars on rails from mine to wharf. To be practical, such an engine had to pull coal cars faster than horses, which walked at four to five miles an hour. Atmospheric pressure and low-pressure engines, such as Watt's creations, weren't good enough.[8]

Richard Trevithick, a mining engineer, built the first locomotive. His steam engine generated a maximum pressure of 145 pounds per square inch, compared to a maximum of 5 pounds in Watt's engines. Trevithick had to use stronger metals than those used by Watt in order to withstand the higher pressure. However, George Stephenson (1781–1848) got the credit for building the first commercially successful locomotive. Stephenson made his key discovery around 1815, while working the steam pump of a coal mine. In order to silence the loud hissing sound of escaping steam from his stationary engine, he allowed the waste steam to escape through a narrow pipe by way of the chimney. This reinforced the draft in the furnace, enabling the engine to go faster.

Stephenson came from an even more humble background than that of James Watt. His father operated the steam engine that pumped a coal mine. George had little schooling until his son Robert was ready for school; then he studied Robert's books.[9] As a boy George Stephenson made clay models of steam engines. Soon he was tinkering with the engine his father operated. When steam blinded his father in an accident, to support him George went to work full time on the steam pump. In the early nineteenth century colliery owners were still using horses to pull coal on wooden rails. One mine owner, Lord Ravensworth, and his partners commissioned Stephenson to build a steam locomotive to replace the horses. In 1814 Stephenson did so; his first machine could go four miles an hour, about the same speed as the horses. He continued to tinker and in 1818 got the speed up to six miles an hour. Then he got his big chance. In 1821 Parliament authorized construction of the Stockton and Darlington Railroad, the first in the world. The authorization did not specify whether horses or locomotives should pull the cars. When Stephenson heard about this he sought out a Quaker, Edward Pease (1767–1858). The Quakers, or Society of Friends, were noted for honesty and strict business ethics. Stephenson told Pease that he thought he could build a locomotive that could pull a ninety-ton load at fifteen miles an hour. Then Pease inspected Stephenson's engine at the Killingworth mine.

Pease was a country wool merchant and banker in the county of Durham in northeast England. In a time when water transport was far cheaper than land transport and canal building was the rage, Pease, after seeing Stephenson's locomotive, became interested in it. His first project was to link the coal mines near Stockton with the town of Darlington on the Tees River, a distance of twenty-seven miles.[10]

Pease raised the necessary capital from other Quaker businessmen related to him by blood or marriage. At first Lord Darlington opposed the project because of the damage that might be done to his fox coverts, and the House of Commons refused to approve the project. So the line was resurveyed to avoid the fox coverts as much as possible, and Parliament gave its approval in 1820.

In the beginning the entrepreneurs left open the possibility that the coal could be transported by horse-drawn trams along railroad tracks, for the crude and unreliable stationary steam engines then available would not have been much improvement over these trams. However, in 1823 Pease provided the bulk of the capital for Robert Stephenson (George's son) to manufacture improved locomotives.

The Stockton and Darlington Railroad opened in 1825, and by 1830 it was a huge success. Between 1839 and 1841 the annual dividend was 15 percent. Edward Pease grew rich but continued to live in a modest Quaker way. He cultivated fruit trees of many kinds, served good wines to his guests, and worried because his children were losing their Quaker discipline.

George Stephenson moved to Liverpool and became principal engineer of the project to link Liverpool and Manchester by rail. Some promoters were still uncertain about the practicality of steam locomotives. They thought it would be more efficient to transport goods on the rails by means of twenty-one stationary steam engines fixed at intervals along the track.

To settle the issue the promoters offered a prize of five hundred pounds sterling for the best locomotive that could maintain a minimum speed of ten miles an hour. They held the contest just outside Liverpool on October 8, 1829. Four engines competed; three broke down. *The Rocket,* built by George Stephenson and his son Robert, attained an average speed of fifteen miles an hour when loaded, and a maximum speed of thirty-five miles an hour when unencumbered.

The Liverpool and Manchester Railroad opened officially on June 14, 1830. Crowds stood watching as a procession with eight Stephenson engines went by. Soon twelve hundred people a day rode the line. To the surprise of the promoters the profits from passenger traffic exceeded those from freight. People had fun riding on trains. During its first eight years the Liverpool-Manchester line sold five million passenger tickets.

The railroads of England speeded up urbanization. This permitted a larger segment of the population to move from the country to the city and reduced the costs of doing business. Trains brought fresh vegetables, fruit, meat, and milk to the cities. Before the existence of railroads, farmers could not market fresh milk more than 15 miles from the dairy. By the 1870s, they could market it from 150 miles away.[11]

Railroads widened markets while reducing transport costs. This was of decisive importance in the economic development of France, Germany, Russia, the United States, and Canada. Railroads made possible a greater volume of exports. Railroad construction and operation stimulated the coal and iron industries.[12]

James Watt and George Stephenson were two among hundreds of inventors at work in western Europe during the period 1750–1850. During this time the number of inventions patented each year increased twenty times.[13] Most inventors were artisans using handicraft methods. Competing with each other, they created a new set of technologies.

These new technologies had three important characteristics. First, they involved the substitution of mechanical devices for human skills. With the application of these devices, change was especially rapid and intense in the textile industry, where machines now did the spinning, weaving, and fulling.

Second, they substituted coal-generated steam power for human, animal, and water power. Before Watt's invention the English had many industrial uses for coal, but with the steam engine they were able to utilize it more fully.

Third, the innovations made it cheaper and faster to obtain and process raw materials, especially in the metallurgical and chemical industries.[14] In the 1780s many ironmasters began to use and improve on the methods of smelting with coke pioneered by the Darby family. The price of pig iron declined from twelve pounds a ton in 1728 to six pounds in 1802.

While the new technologies developed and spread, for a long time most of the economy did not change. Artisans continued to use handicraft methods. Entrepreneurs built the modernized industries in a few enclaves distant from each other. Well into the nineteenth century British manufacturers used water power along with steam power. Between 1740 and 1780 growth in the supply of labor and capital invested in production was greater than growth in productivity. Even where they were used, the new industrial technologies were not yet very effective.

All through the eighteenth and nineteenth centuries the British increased their productivity by improving their transportation system. As Rick Sjostak has argued, this served to increase regional specialization with complementarity, facilitate the emergence of new industries, increase the scale of production from household to factory, and stimulate further technological innovation.[15]

It should not be thought that the Industrial Revolution brought about "mass production" as it is understood today. Machine parts were not interchangeable, for precision machine tools for making them did not exist before 1850. High-quality steel for machine parts was not available, either. Hence quality control was poor, and it was hard to predict the performance of a machine in advance.[16]

When freed by the railroads from the need to be located near running water, industrialists built factories in towns near the raw materials they needed. By 1840 almost half the English population lived in towns, compared to one third in the rest of western Europe. Only one fourth of the English population was engaged in agriculture and mining, compared to over one half in the rest of western Europe.

The English were able to expand agricultural production after 1750 by more widespread use of existing techniques and minor inventions. By 1850 they started to import food, for agriculture was not an activity in which they had a competitive edge. The supply of cheap food from the New World was increasing.

Those who profited most from the first Industrial Revolution were members of established trading families. Such families had the advantage of accumulated capital and business skill. When they became wealthy they could pay the fees to send their sons to Oxford and Cambridge Universities. These universities turned out gentlemen; they were gateways to co-option. They did not become active scientific centers until the second half of the nineteenth century.

Progress in Chemistry and Physics

During the years from 1750 to 1850, given the level of scientific and technological knowledge, it was possible to make discoveries and invent with only a small amount of intellectual capital and cash. The investigative technology of science was relatively cheap. Inventors did not need university degrees because they could learn for themselves from experience, books, and conversations.

When James Watt went to Cornwall to install steam engines in the tin mines, he befriended an exuberant young man called Humphry Davy. Watt, who had not abandoned completely his original calling as a maker of calculating instruments, sold some to Davy.

Davy was an unlikely scientific leader. He was born in poverty, the son of a woodcarver. While serving as apprentice to a pharmacist he began to teach himself chemistry the dangerous way: by unsupervised experiments. When several of his reactions led to explosions, the pharmacist fired him. However, he charmed his way into another job, with a physician, and engaged in more thrilling experiments: breathing unknown gases.

In 1800 Davy wrote a report about the effects of breathing nitrous oxide, or laughing gas. For some years thereafter recreational sniffing of this gas was fashionable. Davy's report—together with his good looks and charm—enabled him to get a job as lecturer at the Royal Institution in London. This was an establishment for scientific research and teaching. About forty years later nitrous oxide became the first chemical anesthetic.

In 1800 Davy learned that an Italian physics professor, Alessandro Volta (1745–1827), had produced a steady electric current by building the forerunner of a modern battery. Looking more deeply into the matter, Davy showed that Volta's battery depended on a chemical process, the oxidation of zinc.

With this understanding, Davy built a stronger battery. He used the battery to run currents through solutions of metal-containing materials and then through the molten materials themselves. On October 6, 1807, he ran a current through molten potash (potassium carbonate, a salt), liberating little shining globules of metal (potassium). These globules recombined with the oxygen in the water, in the process releasing hydrogen gas, which burst into a lavender flame. Davy danced for joy.

Through this process, called electrolysis, within two years Davy discovered six new elements: potassium, sodium, barium, strontium, calcium, and magnesium. Moreover, he also contributed a new theoretical insight. His successful use of electric current to split a chemical compound suggested that chemical combination might be the product of electrical attraction.

In 1813 Davy took on as a laboratory assistant a poor bookbinder's apprentice, Michael Faraday. Faraday became his protégé. Eventually the protégé outshone his mentor: Faraday became an even greater ex-

perimental scientist. Sad to say, Davy was bitter and jealous, and regarded Faraday as his nemesis.

In those days there was no clear division between chemistry and
physics. In addition to chemical experiments Faraday explored electricity and magnetism. Fifty years later the findings from his experiments made possible a second Industrial Revolution.

The first Industrial Revolution, which provided opportunities for the
sons of mechanics and businessmen, had also opened new possibilities
to scientists. It seemed plausible that some scientific discoveries would
have industrial or military applications. Consequently, people of power
and wealth in England were willing to finance the research of Davy,
Faraday, and others.

The work of Volta, Davy, and Faraday was part of a new wave of
discovery in the physical sciences. At this time scientists knew nothing
about the structure of matter (atoms, molecules). They knew little about
electricity and magnetism. They did not know that chemical changes
could produce electricity or that electricity and magnetism were related.

The next breakthrough came from Denmark. Hans Christian Ørsted,
a Danish physics professor, used electric current to produce magnetic
attraction (the deflection of a magnetized needle). Faraday then attempted to reverse this procedure. He wanted to use magnetic attraction to produce electric current. He wound a coil of wire around a
segment of an iron ring and attached the wire to a battery. In this way
he knew that he could make the iron ring temporarily magnetic. Then
he coiled wire around a segment of a second iron ring. He attached this
coil to a galvanometer, a device for detecting small amounts of electric
current. Faraday wondered if temporary magnetism in the first coil
would set up an electric current in the second coil.

The experiment did not turn out as expected. When Faraday turned
on the current in the first coil, it did not set up a steady current in the
second coil. Instead, the needle in the galvanometer jerked and then
registered nothing. When he turned the current off, the needle jerked
again. In between jerks the needle registered nothing. Faraday had
shown that a steady current does not induce a steady current. However,
the process of turning the current on and off did have an effect.

Faraday was puzzled. Yet he did not stop. He next showed that he
could induce an electric current with a permanent magnet (like a
lodestone). However, the magnet could not remain stationary—it had
to move.

In a subsequent experiment in 1831, Faraday used a permanent horseshoe magnet with divided poles. The space between the poles was a magnetic field. He set a copper disc rotating so that its edge passed between the two poles. This created an electric current in the disc. The current could be led off by a wire and put to use. In the laboratory Faraday had created the first crude electric generator.

This was probably the most important electrical discovery in history and a great turning point in the development of the physical sciences. Before Faraday the chemical battery was the only means of creating a steady current. After Faraday it was possible to create a large amount of electric current cheaply by attaching the copper wheel or its equivalent to some device that would keep it moving in a magnetic field. Both steam and water power later proved to be efficient for this purpose.

William Gladstone, when he was head of Britain's treasury, asked Faraday what good electricity was. Faraday replied, "One day, sir, you may tax it."

Faraday had a counterpart in America, Joseph Henry (1797–1878). Henry, the son of a day laborer, began as poor as Davy. He rose to become a mathematics and science teacher. He did the same experiments as Faraday but was a little late in reporting them. Henry also advised Morse on how to build the telegraph.

Henry's own invention was the electric motor. In 1831 he published a report describing one. This device was the opposite of the electric generator in that it converted an electric current to mechanical force (a rotating wheel) and not vice versa. For this and other achievements in 1846 Henry was elected the first secretary of the newly formed Smithsonian Institution. He became the most important American scientist after Benjamin Franklin, founding the National Academy of Sciences.

Steam Presses and Telegraphs

Given the growth of urban populations hungry for entertainment, by the end of the eighteenth century publishers were seeking ways to increase speed and volume in printing. At the time the printer had to drive the printing process manually.

In 1814 the publishers of the *Times* of London were the first to use a steam-driven press. Two Germans, Koenig and Bauer, had invented it two years before. It achieved a speed of 1,100 sheets an hour, compared with the previous maximum of 250 sheets an hour. Other mechanical improvements and the use of rolls of paper improved the performance of cylinder presses so that by 1865 they could print 12,000 complete newspapers an hour.

In the first half of the nineteenth century inventors developed several methods for making paper from wood pulp, which was cheaper than rags. The performance of presses improved. By 1893 it was possible to print 96,000 eight-page copies of the *New York World* per hour. Now even the poor could afford newspapers.

Improvements in telecommunication were linked with improvements in transportation. Railroad builders in the 1830s had an urgent need for efficient telecommunication. At that time stationary engines, called winding engines, were placed near the top of a steep grade. By attaching a strong cable to a train, the operators of the stationary engines could help propel the train up a grade. However, they needed to communicate with the train engineers at speeds exceeding that of the train itself.

The solution was the telegraph, a device that sent electric signals through wire. Electrical energy is related to light, so telegraph messages could move at the speed of light by day and night and in all kinds of weather.

Michael Faraday and Joseph Henry had already discovered the principles that were needed for building a telegraph. Telegraph inventors in England, the United States, France, and Germany went to work simultaneously, and it is difficult to say who deserves the greatest credit.

However, it is agreed that an American, Samuel F.B. Morse, was the inventor of Morse code, used in telegraphy.[17] This was a binary code, a type first used by the ancient Greeks. Binary codes had the advantage of being relatively free of noise and interference. In the case of the telegraph, operators made the fast-moving signal carrier (an electric current) carry messages simply by interrupting it in a patterned way.

Morse was born in 1791 in Charleston, Massachusetts, the son of a minister of modest means but excellent social connections. His father sent him to Yale, where he learned about electricity. However, Morse was a mediocre scholar and was more interested in painting. So his father sent him to England for training, and on Morse's return he was able to make a living painting portraits. At the age of forty-one he became the first American professor of sculpture and painting at what is now the City University of New York.

In 1832, just a year after Faraday's famous experiment, Morse got the idea for the telegraph from a fellow passenger on a transatlantic ship. Back in America he contacted a friend, who introduced him to Joseph Henry, then a professor at Princeton. Henry told Morse how to get the necessary electric voltage to transmit a current over a long distance. He said it could be done by using a battery of many cells and by increasing the number of turns in the wire wrapped around an electromagnet.

With this advice Morse built a telegraph apparatus, took out a patent, and applied for financing from Congress. He got it, and in 1844 workmen completed a pole telegraph line from Washington to Baltimore. The normal operating speed was twenty to twenty-five words a minute. In 1847 the government sold the line to private entrepreneurs, and in 1865 various private telegraph companies merged as the Western Union Telegraph Company. Similar developments occurred in Britain, France, and Germany.

Although the telegraph was intended mainly for use with railroads, people found many other uses for it. The telegraph ended the isolation of police and firemen in different districts of a city. From 1859 until the installation of telephones and radios, the telegraph was the key to the control of fires and crime in major cities. For example, in 1845 John Tawell, after killing his mistress in the English village of Slough, disguised himself as a Quaker and took a train to London. The Slough police telegraphed his description to the police in London, and they arrested Tawell on arrival. Better means of transportation had enabled the criminal to leave the scene of the crime faster, but better methods of communication had enabled the police to catch him.

In the United States newspaper publishers and stockbrokers found the telegraph very useful. In 1848 they formed the Associated Press to pool telegraph expenses. In 1855 entrepreneurs laid telegraph cables across the Mediterranean Sea and the Black Sea. In 1861 they completed the American transcontinental telegraph line. In 1866 the first news from Europe crossed the Atlantic to America by marine cable.

These developments initiated a new era of mass communications. Messages could move over long distances at the speed of light, for it was electrons that moved, not people or paper.

The telegraph was a great asset in the projection of British power to overseas colonies.[18] It provided early warnings of political unrest in these possessions. It provided information about local markets to central stock exchanges. No wonder the telegraph caught on quickly. It was not just a way of sending sad tidings to a family; it made rich people richer, and powerful people more powerful.

Conclusion

The Industrial Revolution was the third breakthrough in world history in which the British participated. The other breakthroughs were representative government and the scientific revolution. Clearly, the first two developments influenced the third. By developing representative government England's political elite co-opted the merchants. The latter invested in the government by loaning it money, which the government repaid on time. This business behavior served to keep the government business-friendly.

In the first half of the nineteenth century modern science began to influence technological innovation. The telegraph was one of its early contributions.

Notes

1. N.F.R. Crafts and C.K. Harley, "Output Growth and the British Industrial Revolution: A Restatement of the Crafts-Harley View."

2. Joel Mokyr, *The Economics of the Industrial Revolution,* pp. 4–5; Mokyr, *The Lever of Riches;* Roderick Floud and Donald McCloskey, *The Economic History of Britain Since 1700,* vol. 1, pp. 8, 158.

3. Mokyr, *The Economics of the Industrial Revolution,* pp. 4–5; Mokyr, *The Lever of Riches;* Floud and McCloskey, *The Economic History of Britain Since 1700,* vol. 1, pp. 8, 158.

4. D.S.L. Cardwell, *Turning Points in Western Technology,* p. 67; Bertrand Gille, *The History of Techniques,* vol. 1, p. 687.

5. H.W. Dickinson, *Matthew Boulton.*

6. Otto Mayr, *Authority, Liberty and Automatic Machinery in Early Modern Europe.*

7. Rudolf Lowe, "Adam Smith's System of Equilibrium Growth," pp. 72–73.

8. Charles Singer, *A History of Technology,* vol. 4, p. 680; Dickinson, *James Watt,* pp. 23, 119, 160, 199.

9. Samuel Smiles, *The Life of George Stephenson and His Son Robert Stephenson, passim.*

10. M.W. Kirby, *Men of Business and Politics: The Rise and Fall of the Quaker Pease Dynasty of North-East England, 1700–1943, passim.*

11. David Grigg, *The Dynamics of Agricultural Change,* p. 140.

12. Alfred D. Chandler, *The Railroads.*

13. Phyllis Deane, *The First Industrial Revolution,* 2d ed., p. 135.

14. J.D. Bernal, *Science in History,* p. 429.

15. Rick Sjostak, *The Role of Transportation in the Industrial Revolution.*

16. Bernal, *Science in History,* p. 427.

17. Carleton Mabee, *The American Leonardo: A Life of Samuel F.B. Morse,* pp. 1–5.

18. Daniel R. Headrick, *The Tools of Empire: Technology and European Imperialism in the Nineteenth Century;* Headrick, *Telecommunication and International Politics, 1851–1945.*

11 SOCIAL CONTROL SINCE 1789

*The brain is not an organ of thinking but an organ of survival,
like claws and fangs. It is made in such a way as to make us
accept as truth that which is only advantage. It is an exceptional,
almost pathological constitution one has, if one follows thoughts
logically through, regardless of consequences. Such people make
martyrs, apostles, or scientists, and mostly end on the stake or in
a chair, electric or academic.*

—Albert Szent-Gyorgi

This chapter will cover innovations in social control in Europe after
1789. These innovations were not revolutionary. Indeed, they were
designed to prevent revolutions.

Prior to 1789 in Europe religion had sufficed to keep the lid on
public discontent. But in Paris and London a growing number of young
single men went unchurched. Many became religious skeptics. These
were the most dangerous urban elements.[1]

So after 1789 other methods were needed. By keeping the common
people quiet, soft social controls enabled the rich to get richer and the
strong stronger. The common people saw many innovations, such as
welfare legislation, as benevolent. They were grateful to the powerful
people who introduced them.

Political Cultures and Literacy

Should the common people be taught to read? Many city people already did. The number varied from one family structure to another,
from one church to another, and from one political culture to another.

It may be recalled that by the early modern era there were two major political cultures. The continental type was found all over Eurasia, including much of Europe. The Protestant maritime type was found only in northwestern Europe and its colonies.

These two cultures, in turn, were associated with characteristic family structures. Continental political culture was associated with two kinds of three-generation families, the joint family and the stem family. The joint family included one or more married brothers who divided their inheritance equally. Paternal authority was strong and maternal authority was weak. In societies in which joint families were dominant, political structures tended to be authoritarian (see Fig. 14).

The stem family was also three-generation and authoritarian. But the father gave most of the inheritance to one son, who stayed at home, and lesser amounts to the other sons, who had to go out in the world and seek their fortunes. In such a society men were especially competitive. The stem family was dominant in Germany, Ireland, Scotland, Sweden, Norway, Switzerland, Japan, and Korea.

In Eurasia family structures did not follow linguistic lines. In Russia, China, and India the joint family was dominant; in Germany, Japan, and Korea it was the stem family.

Protestant maritime political culture was associated with the absolute nuclear family. This was a two-generation family in which the parents had complete freedom in the distribution of their estate: children might inherit either equally or unequally. The mother's position was strong, almost equal to that of the father.

The absolute nuclear family was often associated with radical Protestants—Congregationalists, Quakers, Baptists—and was dominant in England, the Netherlands, and Denmark. It was associated with representative and decentralized political structures.

Titled British aristocrats and other very rich people usually maintained a stem family, in which primogeniture in inheritance was common. The eldest son inherited the principal country estate and the family title (baron, marquess, earl, duke). The other sons inherited lesser amounts and had to go out to seek their fortune.

According to the hypothesis of Immanuel Todd, the political ideology of a people is the intellectual embodiment of its family structure. The fundamental values that govern its family relations are transposed into its political relations.[2]

For example, Communism was most successful in places where the

158

Figure 14. Family types in Europe, main anthropological regions. Todd's "exogenous community family" is more commonly known as the joint family. His "authoritarian family" is more commonly known as the stem family. (Reprinted with permission from Emmanuel Todd, *The Explanation of Ideology*, trans. David Garrioch [Oxford, UK: Basil Blackwell, 1985], Map 2.)

joint family was dominant: Russia, Yugoslavia, China, and Vietnam. Communist regimes sought to replace family patriarchs with Communist Party leaders. In such countries people tend to see liberty as anarchy and to prefer a strongman as ruler. They are comfortable with unequal, bureaucratic relationships and with a vertically integrated society.

Where the stem family is dominant the people make a strong claim to autonomy or superiority over their neighbors. They focus on their own uniqueness and their differences from others. They have a strong sense of their own history and tend toward prejudice against foreigners (for example, as in Germany, Japan, and Korea).

In the Anglo-Saxon world the absolute nuclear family stresses liberty but not equality. It gives the strongest support of all family forms to individualism and feminism. The government associated with this family type tends to be decentralized, with high participation of citizens.

In interpreting the Islamic world, another social scientist, Mary Maxwell, notes that where polygyny is allowed, the higher the rank of a man, the more wives he maintains. Reproductive inequality is associated with economic and political inequality, and thus absolutism.[3]

Todd thinks that the weak position of women in the Islamic world has been a disadvantage for all, since women, being illiterate themselves, traditionally played no role in teaching small children to read, write, etc. In the Muslim world, sub-Saharan Africa, and north India, where women usually marry before the age of twenty and have a very weak position in the family, literacy rates are lowest.[4]

In early modern Europe, Protestant countries had higher literacy rates than Catholic countries. Chartier found that in a given French city, Protestant professional men owned on the average three times the number of books as did Catholic professional men.[5] In Protestant countries male owners of small property, who usually were literate, could keep records and as volunteers held offices in representative local government. This reduced the cost of government.

Did a more literate population tend to increase political stability? Perhaps not. Lawrence Stone discovered that in England (1642), France (1789), and Russia (1917) when 50 percent of males, or 70 percent of young adult males, were literate, a revolution occurred.[6] Such readers were likely to read politically subversive literature.

Richard Curtis says that information, like food, creates negentropy (an increased capacity for spontaneous change), while ignorance creates entropy (decreased capacity for spontaneous change).[7] Literacy is a vital tool for obtaining needed information. While television screens now provide information to illiterates, such people still have trouble finding work in a predominantly literate society. Since they can't read street names, they even have trouble driving a taxi around a city. Literacy is a necessity of urban life.

The elites finally realized this. They apparently intended to spread literacy and to create "good" literature to appeal to literates. A little knowledge of the *wrong* kind was a dangerous thing. It was necessary to teach the people, through newspapers and other print media, the *right* kind of knowledge and keep them convinced it was true.

The French Revolution of 1789: Origins and Consequences

According to older texts, modern European history began with the French Revolution of 1789. Today most historians still consider it an event of major importance. Jack Goldstone believes that the population explosion that began in 1743 was an important causal factor.[8] I agree.

After spilling the blood of hundreds of thousands, the French revolutionaries failed to establish democracy in France or any other place in Europe. By "democracy" I mean a system in which all free adult males have the right to vote for their political representatives. This should be distinguished from "representative government," found in the ancient Mediterranean and medieval Europe. All free male citizens of a representative government could vote, and a man was recognized as a citizen usually only after he acquired a certain amount of property.

It seems important to point out that the French Revolution of 1789 was in part a symptom of ecological stress. Too many peasants were competing for the use of scarce arable land. Too many youths were competing for niches in urban society. This happened at a time when France was having difficulty competing with Britain and was compelled to reform its fiscal system.

During a period of warm, dry weather from 1743 to 1768 steady population growth in France began. Prices and land rents rose far faster than wages. More children were born and survived infancy, and so by the 1780s more ambitious young men than usual were trying to make their way in the world. In particular, there were too many men who wanted army commissions and not enough commissions to satisfy them. Noncommissioned officers could not get promoted, and their loyalty weakened. For the king, this was a dangerous development.

By 1789 the democratic idea was circulating actively in northern and eastern French cities, where, as noted earlier, 70 percent of young adult males were literate. Also popular was liberalism (belief in political and civil liberties for individuals). Radicals used these ideas to justify revolutionary violence. They apparently thought that true liberty was never granted, and could only be taken.

The leaders of the French Revolution wanted to change the political culture of the country from continental to Protestant maritime. They admired the governments of England and the United States. In general, the higher up a man was on the French social ladder, the more intense was his desire for radical change in government. However, the radicals failed, and first Napoleon, then the restored monarchy, reestablished continental political culture. The first lasting democratic French government was finally operational only in 1875.

At the same time there was revolutionary violence in neighboring countries. The years 1770–1789 were years of bad weather and economic depression. In 1786 the Norwegian peasants revolted; in 1788 the Norwegian nobles revolted; in 1789 there were constitutional reforms in Norway-Sweden. From 1781 to 1787 the Dutch revolted to get back their town and parish liberties from the Stadtholder. In 1789 the Belgians revolted against Austrian rule. In 1792 there was a revolutionary coup in Geneva, Switzerland. So the French Revolution was part of a wave of disturbances in western Europe, all of which may have been related to increasing population pressure on scarce resources.

These disturbances ended with the fifteen-year Napoleonic era (1799–1815), in which French aggressive tendencies initially directed upward toward authority were directed sideways toward foreigners. French soldiers came to see themselves as patriotic citizens, not killers for the sake of glory and loot. Between 1791 and 1815 about 1.3 million Frenchmen died in military campaigns.

Since the French army treated the people they conquered with arrogance, it was only natural that their subjects should develop anti-French attitudes. However, the Austrian, German, Polish, and Italian rulers, thoroughly frightened by their ordeal with the French, were also afraid of the nationalism of their own subjects. They associated nationalism with demands for civil liberties, representative government, and democracy. So in the first half of the nineteenth century the conservatives of Europe suppressed nationalism, liberalism, and democracy.

With the increase in restless young men in the cities, the ruling elite needed large urban police forces. In London, which had relied on amateurs, in 1829 the government began to recruit and train police professionals. Within a few decades the London police obtained telegraphs to connect police stations, instituted photography for mug shots, and knew the value of fingerprinting, discovered by Francis Galton. However, coercion, while necessary as a fallback defense, was an expensive and inefficient form of social control. From the beginning of civilization in the Near East, elites also used soft social controls. These were still the most important tactic in the nineteenth century.

Nationalism

Consciousness of nationality may be traced back to medieval Europe, but the term *nationalism* is appropriate only after the French Revolution of 1789. The idea of nationalism might be briefly summed up as "every state a nation and every nation a state." That is, every ethnic group should have its own state.

The word *nationality* began to appear in various European languages between 1815 and 1848, about the same time as mass newspapers and railroads.

In the middle of the nineteenth century the conservative political elites of Germany wanted to increase their power by unifying the various states of German-speakers. Italian elites were trying to do the same thing. So they encouraged nationalist sentiment to attract popular support for themselves. Nationalist sentiment helped them unify these states. This achievement impressed conservatives everywhere, who thought that perhaps they too could make use of nationalism.

Nationalism, like all political ideologies, contained a number of useful fictions.[9] In fact, since the early Middle Ages families and village communities were the basic units of society, not tribes or nations. Nineteenth-century political elites developed the notion of fictive tribes: that all persons of the same nationality were descendants of the same ancestors.

Supposedly the speakers of a single vernacular language were fellow nationals. One could ignore the genealogies of these individuals, their class or occupational status, their dialects, and even their religious affiliations. Given a common language, they could develop a political communication community. A feedback loop could be established between officials and citizens. In this way the ruling elite could systematically cultivate the loyalty of the people to the government.

Using fictive tribalism, bureaucrats manufactured traditions for the masses, creating public ceremonies, monuments, patriotic songs, and patriotic postage stamps.[10] They made banners and heraldic devices, formerly the insignia of noble families and clans, into national symbols, which schoolchildren had to salute. They depicted the territory of the nation, formerly the patrimony of the dynasty, as the homeland of the people.

Citizens tended to shift their loyalty from the person of the ruler to "the nation." They celebrated memorial feasts formerly dedicated to deceased royal and noble ancestors as memorial holidays for national heroes. Historians rose to the occasion and molded a vision of "the nation's" past to contemporary political needs.

The hostile actions of foreign governments, well publicized in the mass media, served to intensify popular nationalist feeling and direct it sideways instead of upward.

Nationalism was revolutionary at first because it served to unite common people speaking different dialects. This made it possible to unite them against any political elite that excluded them from power. Linguistic and cultural diversity had kept the people in chains; homogeneity and the new communication community liberated them.[11]

Democracy

In the early nineteenth century the political elite extended the vote first to all white males with a minimum of property, and in the late nineteenth century even to those without property. The people did not take the right to vote for themselves; rather, the political elite granted it to them when it suited them.

The elite permitted the formation of popular political parties. This made it possible for individuals who were not born wealthy to make a career in politics. By encouraging radicals to become "proactive" in this way, the established elite attracted many potential rebel leaders and co-opted them.

Political elites knew that it was risky to extend suffrage to the common people, for the representatives they elected might seek to confiscate the estates of the rich through progressive taxation. So it was important that the newly franchised voters should become "responsible citizens." Western European governments made elementary education free and compulsory. The printed mass media continued the education of the common people.

Systematic Co-option

Belatedly, European elites realized the value of recruiting the gifted and talented for the civil service. As the Chinese elite had recognized a thousand years before, co-option not only strengthened the forces of the ruler but also reduced the number of potential leaders of popular rebellions.

Of course co-option had always existed informally, affecting at least a few outstanding individuals. The outbreak of the French Revolution in 1789 set off the movement toward systematic co-option. Five years later, in 1794, the Prussian royal government declared that government posts were to be filled on the basis of merit. The higher posts could be attained only by men who had university degrees and had passed examinations. At first only Prussian aristocrats could satisfy these requirements. However, after observing Napoleon's success, Prussian rulers made it easier for nonaristocrats to compete for the civil service.

Napoleon I of France, who ruled from 1799 to 1815, started the policy of permitting careers "open to talents" both in the army and the civil government. His successors spread the practice of recruitment by school degrees and examinations. There were a few scholarships for the brightest (such as Louis Pasteur), but in most cases parents had to pay school tuition above the elementary level. Consequently careers were open mainly to middle-class talent.

The British aristocracy moved more slowly. Fearing the corruption of British officials in India, in 1833 they began to use examinations in selecting such officials. Beginning in 1855 aspirants for the British domestic civil service also had to take examinations to fill the growing number of positions. This helped the middle class to obtain more government positions.

By 1870 the traditional social myth of Europe was changing. When monarchs became unpopular, the political elite tried to shift popular loyalty to positive abstractions: Britannia, the Fatherland, Mother Russia, la patrie. How could the common people rebel against an abstraction?

The elite encouraged the people to be loyal to a piece of familiar real estate, their country. The territorial imperative, or turf defense, seemed to be a common instinct not only of humans but also of many other animals. How could the people decline to fight for their home turf? The political elite could cast themselves as protectors of the country against foreign enemies, thus justifying the unequal distribution of power and wealth within the country.

Social Control After 1918

There is a lot of information about particular instruments of social control after 1918, but I am not aware of any overall study. The following is an agenda of topics to investigate.

1. *Distractions.* Distraction is any form of entertainment that serves to divert the attention of the public from their discontents to pleasurable imaginary or vicarious experiences. After 1918 this form of social control became more important than sermons and speeches. The new entertainment media were radio, motion pictures, recordings of popular music, television, spectator sports, and computer games. Men have made great fortunes in these new businesses.

I do not want to suggest that political elites deliberately organized these distractions as a means of social control. There was probably no conspiracy involved. As I see it, there was money to be made in the entertainment business, and this business happened to serve as a means of social control.

2. *Safety nets.* First in England and Germany, then in France, the United States, and the Soviet Union, and then all over Europe, welfare legislation gave the public a safety net in case of unemployment, serious illness, disabilities, and old age. These have been effective bulwarks against political revolution. But recently, even though Social Security and Medicare threw the U.S. budget into deficit, these concessions have been difficult to withdraw.

3. *Even more systematic co-option.* Each country developed a public school system, and college scholarships were easier to get. Education became the great ladder. Most young people with academic and social skills had a chance to climb the ladder.

4. *Electronic surveillance technology.* After 1945 listening devices became increasingly sophisticated. There is no protection from these

devices outdoors, in noisy restaurants, or at crowded public gatherings. Anyone can buy and conceal a small listening and recording device on his or her person. Consequently the content and circumstances of secret political conversations have changed.

5. *Electronic data bases.* Since the appearance of computers, government and credit agencies have compiled huge data bases providing information about almost everyone. Personal privacy is dwindling.

6. *Public relations and advertising.* The psychological manipulation of masses of people has become a profession. In politics we have "spin control." In business we have not just advertisements but marketing programs. For people more isolated and lower down on the social scale we have televangelists, radio talk shows, advocates of "spiritual growth," and alternative forms of "healing." Formerly priests spoke with one voice; now we hear many voices calling our names. How diverse the messages!

Conclusion

The French Revolution demonstrated to Western political elites and their challengers that existing means of social control, especially clerical activity, had become inadequate. Governments increased their police forces and gave them more training. In the nineteenth century new police devices—the mug shot, fingerprints, telegraphs, and telephones —became available.

After about 1870 conservatives adopted as their own two radical innovations: nationalism and democracy. They made concessions, setting up safety nets for the unfortunate and expanding educational systems. They fostered the development of a gigantic entertainment and public relations sector in the economy. Are these part of the solution or part of the problem?

Notes

1. Owen Chadwick, *The Secularization of the European Mind in the Nineteenth Century,* pp. 94, 125.
2. Immanuel Todd, *The Explanation of Ideology.*
3. Mary Maxwell, *Morality Among Nations: An Evolutionary View,* pp. 133–36.
4. Immanuel Todd, *The Causes of Progress,* pp. 14, 37, 64, 76.
5. Roger Chartier, ed., *A History of Private Life: Passions of the Renaissance,* pp. 130–32.

6. Lawrence Stone, "Literacy and Education in England, 1640–1900."

7. Richard K. Curtis, *Evolution or Extinction,* p. 224.

8. Jack Goldstone, *Revolution and Rebellion in the Early Modern World,* pp. 179–348.; Simon Schama, *Citizens: A Chronicle of the French Revolution;* William Doyle, *Origins of the French Revolution,* 2d ed.; T.C.W. Blanning, *The French Revolution; Aristocrats Versus Bourgeois?;* Donald M.G. Sutherland, *France, 1789–1815: Revolution and Counterrevolution;* Lynn Hunt, *Politics, Culture and Class in the French Revolution.*

9. The best demythologizers of European nationalism are Ernest Gellner, *Nations and Nationalism,* and Eric Hobsbawm and T. Ranger, eds., *The Invention of Tradition,* pp. 263–79.

10. Hobsbawm and Ranger, eds., *The Invention of Tradition.*

11. David Bell, "Lingua Populi, Lingua Dei."

12 DARWIN'S DANGEROUS IDEA

*[The great synthesizer] is a kind of lens or gathering point
through which thought gathers, is reorganized, and radiates
outward again in new forms.*

—Loren Eisley

Charles Darwin (1809–1882), like Isaac Newton, was a great synthesizer of materials already available. However, his work was controversial from the beginning and remains so today.[1] Darwin was the first scientist to reach major conclusions that were incompatible with the religious orthodoxy of his time—and to publish them.

Charles Darwin was an unlikely revolutionary. He was affluent, genteel, happily married, the father of a large family, and shy. From the time he formulated the principle of natural selection (1838) until his death (1882) he was tormented by a mysterious illness. It appears that he was a man obsessed with an insight and terrified of the anger and rejection it was sure to evoke if he published it.

When Darwin was born, scientists accepted the fact of evolution: that the structures of living things changed through time. Darwin sought to explain the fact of evolution by discerning a mechanism for it. Herbert Spencer called Darwin's theory "the survival of the fittest," but that is not exactly what Darwin meant.

Darwin believed that in a given environment living things competed with each other for the resources available. The creatures that survived long enough to reproduce most successfully were those that were the best-designed. Survival alone was not enough.

Darwin called his fundamental mechanism of evolution "natural selection": that is, selection of the best individuals and species by the workings of nature, not by the will of an anthropomorphic god. The mechanism worked automatically. In nature there were no commanders or controllers, only opportunities and constraints.

Darwin never explained the origin of species; it took geneticists to do that. Instead Darwin demonstrated why some random variations of a species tend to flourish, while others do not.

The Importance of Geology

Darwin's dangerous idea was built on a foundation of rock: the science of geology. Once the Industrial Revolution was launched, canal builders and miners began to detect patterns of successive rock strata. Geologists, by studying these patterns, helped entrepreneurs to plan additional canals and locate new seams of coal and minerals.

In so doing, geologists discovered fossils of animals and plants that no longer existed. From the rock strata patterns and the level of deposit of the fossils, geologists constructed a chronology that could apply to all known parts of the world. Rocks, plants, and animals had a history that scientists first called "natural history." This process was later called "evolution."[2]

Natural history contradicted the account of creation in the Bible and the Koran. One could not believe in evolution and at the same time believe that God literally created everything in a week.

An important early geologist was the Scot James Hutton (1726–1797), who first made money as a chemical manufacturer and then retired to pursue his hobby, the study of rocks. He was fortunate to live in Edinburgh, the most important center of science and medicine in Britain. Hutton's mind was unencumbered by belief in the literal truth of the Bible. He did not accept the authority of the Church in scientific matters.[3] This was not unusual among educated men of the eighteenth century.

Then Hutton became interested in volcanoes. There was nothing in the Bible about the role of volcanoes in creation, but that didn't bother him. No one before Hutton suspected the volcanic origin of a widespread kind of rock now called igneous ("fiery"). Other geologists thought most rocks were sedimentary, the result of deposits in water. Hutton was responsible for creating the present threefold classification of rocks: igneous, metamorphic, and sedimentary.

This keen observer traveled through much of western Europe. He saw huge granite boulders in the valleys of Switzerland, and he doubted that rivers had transported them there. He saw glaciers and wondered if they had pushed the boulders out of the mountains. He studied the processes of erosion, sedimentation, and elevation of the ocean floor. He believed that ocean floor elevation was responsible for the findings of the fossils of marine animals on mountains.

Hutton did not believe in terrestrial catastrophes of supernatural origin such as the biblical Flood of Noah's time. The processes that geologists could observe in the present, said Hutton, had also been at work in the past. Scientific laws applied through time uniformly because natural processes operated through time uniformly. This belief is called uniformitarianism.

Today scientists think that natural catastrophes did occur in the past, causing mass extinctions of species. But they see no supernatural forces at work in such catastrophes. Hutton's contribution was to exclude from the science of geology any consideration of supernatural forces and to shift attention to gradual natural processes.

Hutton published his major work, *The Theory of Earth,* in 1788. After the French Revolution of 1789, English political conservatives feared a revolution in Britain. So they dismissed scientific theories that might undermine traditional religious beliefs.

This is understandable if one realizes that aristocrats relied upon the clergy to do the work of controlling the common people. The aristocrats distrusted any notion, even about rocks, that "rocked the boat." So for forty years most educated Englishmen were not familiar with Hutton's ideas. The man who changed this was a lawyer and amateur scientist, Charles Lyell (1797–1875). His comprehensive two-volume work *Principles of Geology* was first published in 1830–1831 and appeared in many subsequent editions.[4] It influenced Charles Darwin, who became a personal friend of the author, for it provided a nonbiblical account of the development of rocks and stressed the uniform character of natural processes through time. It is difficult to imagine how Darwin could have conceived of his theory of evolution without this foundation.

Evolutionary Thinking in Darwin's Time

By 1831 scientists recognized the reality of the evolution of life forms. They knew that some species alive in the past had gone extinct. They knew that new species came into being.

By the end of the eighteenth century, natural scientists realized that all living things were superbly adapted to their environment and to each other. One such scientist was the Frenchman Jean-Baptiste de Lamarck (1744–1829), who saw life forms as a branching tree. He believed in gradual evolution as a matter of fact. He even suggested that the human race had once lived in trees and was linked to apes. However, he guessed wrong about the mechanism of evolution: He thought structural changes occurred in living things because they adapted to changing environments and then passed on their acquired characteristics to their offspring.

In the early nineteenth century in western Europe thoughtful people were discovering the first remains of prehistoric human beings. In 1829 Paul Tournal (1809–1872), a pharmacist from Narbonne, found fossil human bones with the remains of extinct animals. Marcel de Serres (1780–1862), a lawyer from Montpelier, found some very primitive stone tools. Jacques Boucher de Perthes (1788–1868), a customs officer in northwestern France, reported the accumulated discoveries of flint tools and bones of extinct animals in a three-volume work (1847–1857).[5] This was on the eve of the publication of Darwin's masterpiece.

Early Life of Darwin

Charles Darwin was the son of a well-to-do physician. He was fortunate in that he never had to earn a living. As a boy Darwin had a compulsion to collect beetles—a regular beetlemania. At Cambridge University he studied little but favorably impressed the botany professor, John Henslow. "What a fellow Darwin is for asking questions!" said Henslow. Darwin graduated in 1831.[6]

About this time Captain Robert Fitzroy, a twenty-five-year-old naval officer of (illegitimate) descent from Charles II, was looking for a suitable companion to join him on a proposed five-year voyage.[7] The purpose of the voyage was to map, among other things, the coasts of South America. On his ship, the *Beagle,* Fitzroy had made a previous voyage there and had brought back four natives of Tierra del Fuego to educate and then return to their people.

Fitzroy already had a naturalist, Robert McCormick, for the new voyage, but they did not get along. Henslow recommended Darwin as both a naturalist and a pleasant companion. This was important to

Captain Fitzroy, who suffered from depressions. His uncle, Lord Castlereagh, had become so depressed that he committed suicide a few years before. Fitzroy needed a congenial cabinmate, for by naval custom he could not socialize with his officers. He feared the consequences of a depression during five years of isolation on a ninety-foot vessel. This fear turned out to be justified: He did have a severe depression on the second voyage of the *Beagle,* and his second-in-command had to replace him.

Although still in his early twenties, Charles Darwin was an amiable, unpretentious and well-controlled person. In spite of Fitzroy's hot temper, Darwin managed to get along with him. Fitzroy believed that every word in the Bible was literally true, while Darwin had his doubts.

Darwin took on the *Beagle* the following equipment: microscope, magnifying glass, compass, magnet, and barometer. He also took Charles Lyell's *Principles of Geology.* (When he returned to London he became a friend of Lyell.) In Argentina the backwardness of the Fuegian natives made a deep impression on him. To him they seemed to be of low intelligence and completely lacking in moral principles. He wrote in his journal: "Compare the Fuegians and Ourang-Outang and dare to say difference is not so great."[8] During the five-year voyage he avidly collected specimens of rocks, plants, and animals. His love of science grew.

As he sailed south along the South American coast, Darwin noticed what seemed to be local variations of the same species, adapted to slightly different environments. On the Argentine pampas Darwin found the fossil remains of animals with skin armor like that of modern armadillos. So it appeared that species also changed over time in the same place. It seemed reasonable to assume that through time a species could change gradually.

In the Galapagos he found mockingbirds and finches that differed from one island to another. It seemed impossible that God would create a special species for each island. Once again they seemed like adaptations to slight differences in environment.

When the *Beagle* got back to England in 1836 Darwin and Fitzroy were free to follow separate paths. Captain Fitzroy got married. In 1837 he received a gold medal from the Royal Geographic Society and in 1851 was elected to the Royal Society. His coastal surveys were so accurate that they are still useful today. In 1855 the navy established a meteorological office and put Fitzroy in charge. In 1857 the navy promoted him to admiral. So Fitzroy had scientific credentials.

Darwin brought back from the voyage his collection of specimens and many notebooks full of observations. In 1839 he married his first cousin, Emma Wedgwood, who bore him ten children. Both he and Emma had been brought up as Unitarians, and she continued in that persuasion throughout her life. He loved her and did not wish to offend her. However, Darwin himself ceased to believe in an anthropomorphic God. In his autobiography he said, "Nothing is more remarkable than the spread of skepticism or rationalism during the latter half of my life."[9]

When Darwin read *Essay on the Principle of Population,* by Thomas Malthus, he was impressed. On September 28, 1838, he had a sudden insight: Perhaps the process of selective survival that Malthus described was not tragic but beneficial. Because of the enormous reproductive capacity of living things and the limited supply of food, only the fittest individuals could get enough to eat to survive and reproduce themselves.

Malthus helped Darwin to see the struggle in nature not just as a struggle between different species, but also as a struggle between individuals of the same species. Malthus thought in terms of whole populations; now Darwin did, too.

English animal breeders also influenced Darwin. They improved animal species by artificial selection. Since there were no two horses alike, these breeders thought in terms of the mating of superior individuals. So did Darwin. Individuality was what distinguished living from nonliving things.

Combining the concept of Malthus with the practices and beliefs of animal breeders, Darwin came up with the concept of a variable population composed of unique individuals. In this population natural selection produced gradual improvement without either human or divine intervention. Biological progress was automatic, and in seeming chaos there was order. Nature was self-regulating.[10]

Thus in 1838 Darwin thought out the core of his theory of evolution. However, he showed his work only to a few friendly scientists. Charles Lyell repeatedly urged him to publish his theory lest someone else get the same idea and beat him to it. Darwin ignored this advice. He was painstaking and worked slowly. He supported every assertion with detailed evidence. He probably realized that his theory, when published, would cause an uproar, and he wanted to protect himself from every attack he could conceive of.

In 1858, twenty years after reading Malthus's essay on population, Darwin received a manuscript from a young naturalist, Alfred Wallace (1823–1913). He too had read the work of Malthus and had formulated the same basic theory of natural selection as had Darwin. Wallace, unaware of Darwin's previous formulation, had sent the manuscript to get Darwin's opinion of it.

Darwin's friends had long been warning him that such a development was possible. Now Wallace forced Darwin's hand. Since both men were gentlemen, they agreed to collaborate on a scientific article, summarizing their combined conclusions. This article appeared later in 1858 in the *Journal of the Linnaean Society,* which had a very small circulation. The article provoked little reaction, probably because only a few scientists read it.

Meanwhile Darwin hastened to finish his book-length manuscript *The Origin of Species,* which appeared the next year. It provoked a great reaction. It went through printing after printing and remains in print today. In 1859, after the publication of this book, the British Association for the Advancement of Science invited the Rev. Samuel Wilberforce, bishop of Oxford, to debate Thomas Henry Huxley, a defender of Darwin, concerning the newly published theory of natural selection. This encounter before an elite audience at Oxford University became legendary. At one point the bishop turned to Huxley and asked sarcastically, "Is it on your grandfather's or your grandmother's side that your ape ancestry comes?" Since the bishop had violated the prevailing code of gentlemanly conduct by getting personal, Huxley was elated. He whispered to Sir Benjamin Brodie, surgeon to the queen, "The Lord hath delivered him into mine hands!" When his turn to speak came he said: "I asserted, and I repeat, that a man has no reason to be ashamed of having an ape for a grandfather. If there were an ancestor whom I should feel shame in recalling, it would rather be a man—*[a man of restless and versatile intellect—who, not content with equivocal success in his own sphere of activity, plunges into scientific questions with which he has no real acquaintance, only to obscure them with an aimless rhetoric, and to distract the attention of his hearers from the real point at issue by eloquent digressions and skilled appeals to religious prejudice.]*"[11]

There are many variations of the text, for the uproar was so great no one was sure exactly what Huxley said. However, it was clear that Huxley had dared to insult an English bishop in his own diocese. Lady Brewster fainted. Robert Fitzroy, Darwin's former cabinmate and now an admiral, arose and brandished the Bible above his head, saying that it was the source of all truth.

Joseph Hooker, another friend of Darwin, reported that it was Hooker, not Huxley, who carried the day. He told the audience that the bishop could not possibly have read *The Origin of Species* and knew nothing about botanical science. He told Darwin that after four hours of arguments "our side" had carried the day.

Given the emotion that this debate provoked, it seems likely that Darwin's friends did not in fact carry the day. However, they made it unlikely that Darwin's work would be lightly dismissed or that the issue would be forgotten.

Wallace once commented to Darwin that natural selection is like the centrifugal governor on a steam engine: The system is self-regulating. Here again the two men shared a concept. It was embodied, as we have seen, in the early modern technology of northwestern Europe. It was also operative in English political and economic thinking. It was therefore to be expected that a scientific theory that turned God into an "unnecessary hypothesis" would emerge in a self-regulating decentralized society like this. It was equally to be expected that no such idea would originate in a country ruled by a despot.

This did not change the truism of modern political science that dominant minorities control all organized groups. A dominant minority ran Britain, and Charles Darwin, although not involved in politics, was part of it. Despite Darwin's heresy, his friends were sufficiently powerful to get him buried in Westminster Abbey along with kings and heroes.

By 1859, when Darwin published *The Origin of Species,* there was wide agreement among intellectuals in Britain and western Europe that at a time before the earth took modern form people had coexisted with extinct mammals. People, it seemed, had existed in a time period not covered by the biblical sequence of events. People were present before writing. They did not appear suddenly but developed gradually from hominids—apes that walked habitually on two legs.

In 1857 a man clearing a cave in a deep ravine of the Neander Valley discovered a portion of a skull and limb bones of what later was called Neanderthal man. No rock strata or animal bones were available to help date the find. Six weeks later Dr. Fuhrott, a teacher six or seven kilometers away, saw the skull fragment and limb bones; he noted the prominent, apelike eyebrow ridges on the skull cap. In 1861 an anatomist, Professor Schaaffhausen, published a paper describing the bones.

Even before the appearance of Darwin's book many educated Europeans considered a biological linkage between humans and apes as plausible. They were impressed by the appearance and behavior of primitive peoples that explorers had observed in various parts of the world. In 1871 Darwin published a second tome, *The Descent of Man.* He cited human vestigial organs as evidence of primate origins: the tailbone, muscles to wiggle the ears. "With all his exalted powers," said Darwin, "Man still bears on his bodily frame the indelible stamp of his lowly origin."

If Darwin's view of human descent was accepted, there would no longer be any problem in explaining bestial human behavior. Human beings had been beasts originally, and still behaved that way at times. Darwin made not only the concept of God unnecessary, but also the concept of the Devil.[12]

Recently scientists have found evidence that apes have many of the same emotions as human beings, including compassion. They use social pressure to discipline individuals. Moral "rules" seem to be required to enable primates to live together in groups.[13] The goodness in human nature appears to be as natural as the evil and does not seem to require the image or the action of an anthropomorphic God.

Before Darwin, scientists and theologians made ideological compromises and minimized their differences, and after Darwin a majority continued to do so. As learned people, they had more in common with each other than they had with the common people. If they disagreed, it was usually in private. But in the twentieth century Darwin's dangerous idea began to spread more widely.

For example, before 1900 the middlebrow press in New England paid little attention to Darwinism. From 1859 to 1900 in the weekly *Connecticut Courant* in Hartford no one discussed Darwin's theory. In neighboring New Haven, the site of Yale University, the daily *New Haven Evening Register* first mentioned the theory on May 25, 1885, when summarizing a sermon by Henry Ward Beecher in Brooklyn, New York. A month later it mentioned a speech made by an unnamed Hartford Congregational minister entitled "Christian Evolution, Darwin, Religion's Friend," at a gathering of Congregational ministers at

Fair Haven. The *Register* did not cite Darwin again until May 19, 1894, when it carried a summary of a lecture at Yale by the well-known Protestant minister Lyman Abbott. The Rev. Abbott affirmed that Darwin accepted a Creator at the beginning of evolution and that his ideas strengthened belief in God.

The titles of both these sermons denied reality. In fact, Darwin's idea was very dangerous to the theology that the Rev. Abbott and the Rev. Beecher preached.

Darwin never openly attacked Christian values; if anything, he praised them. He conducted his life in accordance with prevailing expectations of how an English gentleman should behave. He was truthful, upright, kind, and courteous. He could not help it if his work undermined the natural basis for Christian values.

Darwin proposed a new secular explanation for the order and complexity of nature and natural history. Before Darwin clergymen used the existence of the natural order as an argument for the existence of an intelligent Creator. This argument was known as the "argument by design." Darwin, by contrast, believed that design in nature emerged spontaneously and gradually. Nature was orderly, but this did not necessarily imply the existence of any God, much less an intelligent and moral God.

Thoughtful people began to wonder whether an immortal God and Christian moral values would ever prevail in the world if they had no basis in nature. Indeed, nature worked by different principles: elimination of the unfit and selection of the fit and sexually attractive. The principles of natural selection and sexual selection were basic to understanding changes in nature.

Darwin gave greater coherence to scientific thinking about nature. By supplying scientists with simple concepts that they could use to process a large mass of observations, Darwin served as the master scientist of the nineteenth century. His ideas were robust, with wide applications and implications. They were also parsimonious, using a minimum of theory to cover a maximum of facts.

Darwin's intellectual success was not total. There were serious scientific criticisms of his theory of evolution. In his lifetime the most important was the "blended inheritance" problem. Suppose a few individuals happen to have a desirable new characteristic. If the inheritance from mother and father are blended in the gene pool, what is to keep the new characteristic from being diluted out of existence? For this objection an answer was available in Darwin's lifetime but remained hidden from his view. Gregor Mendel (1822–1884) was the son of an Austrian peasant.[14] His parish priest noticed his great intelligence and taught him natural history. He was able to prepare for the university at a gymnasium (high school). In 1843, because of financial need, he entered an Augustinian monastery so as to be able to continue his education. In Altbrunn Monastery there were monks who were botanists, mineralogists, and mathematicians. They grew rare plants in the monastery garden and served as high-school teachers.

In 1851 his order sent him to the University of Vienna to study physics with Christian Doppler. There he also studied botany, plant physiology, experimental methods, combinational mathematics, and probability theory. When he returned to his monastery and began his own experiments, he selected twenty-two edible pea varieties, which he tested and found to be homozygous (that is, they bred true). Using ten thousand hybrid plants and probability theory, he discovered that plant characteristics do not blend; instead, they are particulate, discrete. Some traits are dominant and appear in every generation; some are recessive and may not appear for one or more generations. Thus Mendel's findings suggested that no superior characteristic was going to be lost in a gene pool of less favorable characteristics.

Soon after Darwin's death the evidence of fossil humans increased. Well-preserved skeletons of Neanderthal man were found in 1887 in Belgium, in 1908 in France, and in 1911 in Spain. In the early decades of the twentieth century specimens of a more primitive hominid, *Homo erectus,* were found in Java and near Beijing. In 1994 anthropologists found in East Africa hominid remains going back four and a half million years. Now we know that not one but many links existed between apes and human beings. Genetic evidence shows that the relationship between humans and chimpanzees is close, since they share 98.4 percent of their structural genes (see Fig. 1).

Why Darwin's Idea Was Dangerous

Darwin's idea was dangerous because it served as a "universal acid" eating away at the belief structures of politics, religion, and ethics. These structures included myths that satisfied the wishful thinking of the common people, making it easier for their rulers to manipulate them.[15]

Darwin inspired the foundation of a new discipline, anthropology, in the late nineteenth century. For the first time scientists applied scientific methods to the study of human beings. This was a violation of the unwritten contract between clergy and scientists.

Darwin had an important influence on the religion of the educated elite. He made the anthropomorphic concept of God obsolete—at best it was one of the many symbols for God. The elite no longer accepted the unsupported authority of priests or princes.

These developments did not occur, and probably could not have occurred, before the work of Darwin. Except in the case of Galileo, earlier advances in physics, astronomy, and chemistry had not caused a major disturbance. They had been kept in one intellectual compartment, while religion and morals were kept in another.

After Darwin it was no longer easy to paper over the differences between science and religion, or to lock them in two separate compartments. For when Darwin applied scientific methods to the study of human beings, he broke down the partition between the two compartments. Human beings could be regarded as animals in natural environments. No concept of human beings was so sacred that it could not be questioned, analyzed, and rejected.

Darwin's dangerous idea was an example of the power of knowledge. It served not only to change western European culture, but also to shape an emergent world culture. The power of scientific knowledge became a threat to the myths and traditions of all ethnic groups and social classes. By helping to undermine religious orthodoxy in Europe, Darwinism made it necessary for the aristocracy to find new social controls, especially in cities.

Notes

1. Daniel C. Dennett, *Darwin's Dangerous Idea.*
2. Henry Faul and Carol Faul, *It Began with a Stone,* pp. 106–14.
3. "James Hutton," in Charles C. Gillispie, ed., *Dictionary of Scientific Biography.*
4. "Charles Lyell," in Gillispie, *Dictionary of Scientific Biography.*
5. D.K. Grayson, *The Establishment of Human Antiquity,* pp. 99, 117, 195; John Reader, *Missing Links: The Hunt for Earliest Man,* p. 24.
6. Peter Brent, *Charles Darwin: A Man of Enlarged Curiosity,* p. 94.
7. Ronald W. Clark, *The Survival of Charles Darwin,* pp. 18–19; H.E.L. Mellersh, *Fitzroy of the Beagle,* pp. 40, 135; "Robert Fitzroy," in Gillispie, ed., *Dictionary of Scientific Biography.*

8. R.J. Berry, ed., *Charles Darwin*, p. 18; Brent, *Charles Darwin*, p. 456.

9. Charles Darwin, *The Autobiography of Charles Darwin, 1809–1882*, p. 95.

10. Graham Richards, *Human Evolution*. pp. 115–16; Michael Ruse, *The Darwinian Revolution*, p. 175; Ernst Mayr, *Toward a New Philosophy of Biology*, p. 15; Mayr, *The Growth of Biological Thought*, pp. 484, 495.

11. J.E. Lucas, "Wilberforce and Huxley: A Legendary Encounter."

12. Graham Richards, *Human Evolution*, p. 544; Ernst Mayr, *Toward a New Philosophy*, pp. 89, 196, 346–52.

13. Frans de Waal, *Good Natured: The Origins of Right and Wrong in Humans and Other Animals*.

14. Vitezslav Orel's *Mendel* is the best source on Mendel's life.

15. Daniel C. Dennett, *Darwin's Dangerous Idea, passim*.

13 THE MARRIAGE OF SCIENCE AND TECHNOLOGY

"Once the rockets are up, who cares where they come down?
That's not my department," said Werner von Braun.

—Tom Lehrer

The second period of development in modern technology, sometimes called the second Industrial Revolution, began around 1870 and reached a peak in 1913. In Europe and America this was the beginning of a prosperous period, a time of opportunity. The time of most rapid population growth in London was between 1880 and 1914.

Western governments provided more funding for engineers; it was in their self-interest. Imperialists knew that they needed efficient transportation systems to retain and develop their new territories. They were successful because the railroad and steamship were fast, relatively cheap, and little affected by weather. They could carry many people and bulky goods.

For political reasons the German government led the way in both science and technology. They led the way in all higher education, for the Germans wanted to catch up with and overtake the dominant British. The Germans and Americans attended the wedding of science and technology.

The Influence of Steam Transportation

There were many advantages to steam transportation. After the building of railroads manufacturers no longer had to locate factories on rivers and canals. They could build them near coal mines and other sources of raw materials. Entrepreneurs in towns linked by rail could diversify their activities. Manufacturers could now seek raw materials from far and wide.

With the advent of steam power, river transport cost one third as much as before; sea transport, one seventh as much; and railroad transport, one fiftieth as much as horse-drawn land transport. Overall, between 1800 and 1910 in Europe transport costs fell to one fifteenth of the transport costs of the previous century. This reduction played a major role not only in permitting the explosive growth of cities, but also in increasing the productivity of labor.[1]

In Russia, the St. Petersburg–Moscow rail line opened in 1851, initiating a building boom. Freight traffic in Russia quadrupled between 1865 and 1880; it doubled between 1880 and 1890; and from 1890 to 1900 it almost doubled again. Railroads carried mainly grain, coal, and oil.[2]

Railroads made possible a greater volume of exports. They carried grain from the great "breadbaskets" of the American Midwest, Argentina, Poland, and the Ukraine to more densely populated regions in need of food. They carried coal for steamships to port cities. Railroad construction and maintenance itself stimulated the coal and iron industries.

In large countries such as the United States and the Russian empire, success in spanning the entire territory by rail had important political and military implications as well. The railroad moved troops and brought them supplies. The Trans-Siberian Railroad, built between 1891 and 1905, covered 5,787 miles (9,313 km), from Moscow to Vladivostok, and made possible a modern state spanning much of Eurasia. In the face of Chinese and Japanese pressure this railroad was necessary to carry troops and food into Siberia.[3] The same was true of railroads in the western United States.

Railroads were important as long-distance passenger carriers. They promoted tourism. The first Pullman sleeper car was built in 1859 in the United States and in the 1870s in Europe. For the first time it was comfortable and convenient for tourists to move from one site to another. Railroad travel was the first kind of land travel that was little affected by the weather. In the midst of a storm it was possible to travel on a train in complete comfort, eating and sleeping as usual. Standard tours and guidebooks became popular.

In the late nineteenth century interurban trains enabled suburbs to bloom. It was not long after the first commuters appeared in railroad stations that they faced the din and hustle of rush hour traffic. Affluent families withdrew even farther from the air pollution, noise, and crime of the great city to be among trees, flowers, and birds.

Railroads reached peasants in remote rural areas that had previously been isolated from both national economic transactions and cultural patterns. Peasants could take trips to important cities, where they learned to speak the main vernacular language. They changed from unwashed country yokels into respectable Frenchmen, Germans, Italians, Russians, etc.

In India the British built railroads that knit the country together, helping the elites of many ethnic groups to feel greater solidarity. Railroads made communication more efficient. They replaced the stagecoach as the principal carrier of mail. They also carried books and magazines that drew readers into a single national culture. Every railroad station had a telegraph office.

Inventors tried to adapt the steam engine to water transport. This was because waterways already existed; and unlike roads, the existing canals needed no additional construction. Inventors hoped to build ships that could travel upstream without any wind behind them. In 1787 John Fitch demonstrated a paddle wheel boat driven by steam. In 1807 came the first steamboat that was a financial success: it was built by another American, Robert Fulton, who sent it up the Hudson River at five miles an hour. Soon paddle wheel boats moving at up to fifteen miles an hour became common on American rivers and along coasts. In 1817 in New York there was a steam ferry running from Manhattan to Brooklyn.

Steamships came to Russia early. In 1817 there was one on the Kama River and in 1823 another on the Dnieper. However, barges continued to dominate river and canal travel. Steamships remained scarce until the end of the nineteenth century. Railroads carried mostly east-west traffic. The railroad boom did not ruin Russian inland waterways because these waterways carried mostly north-south freight. Freight movement on waterways was seasonal and only half as fast as on railroads, but it was cheap.[4]

In 1819 an American sailing ship equipped with a steam engine, the *Savannah,* successfully crossed the Atlantic Ocean and proceeded to St. Petersburg. Steam alone was used only 16 percent of the time the ship was moving. The steam capability was useful when a sailing vessel was becalmed and in getting in and out of harbors. The great drawback was fuel. Whereas wind for sailing was free (if unreliable), coal for steampower was not readily available in every port. The British navy built coaling stations.

In 1840 it took thirty days for a sailing ship to cross the Atlantic Ocean, but a steamship could cross the Atlantic in fifteen days. In 1850 this was reduced to ten days.

After 1850, as a result of the rising cost of wood and the falling cost of iron and steel, shipbuilders constructed more and more ships with metal hulls. Wooden hulls were more vulnerable to trauma and explosives and were more endangered by fire and rough seas. Metal hulls were less vulnerable and could withstand the vibrations of big new marine engines.

For structural reasons a wooden ship could not be much more than three hundred feet long. Iron keels could be much longer without breaking. Shipbuilders could make iron hulls thinner, and after 1880 steel hulls were used as well. This provided more cargo space (20 to 50 percent by volume). Shipbuilders could make steamships without masts that were larger and had smokestacks and cabins on deck. Thus the luxury ocean liner came into being.

After 1870 the screw propeller, invented in 1827, replaced the paddle wheel. Unlike the single paddle wheel, the screw propeller did not cause the ship to list to one side, was less vulnerable to enemy fire, and usually stayed underwater when the ship rolled. The new ships had both low-speed thrust and high-speed efficiency. The box boiler, which could withstand higher pressure, replaced the cylindrical boiler. By 1874 ocean steamships could make up to sixteen knots and cross the Atlantic in seven days.

In 1884 a well-educated British aristocrat, Charles A. Parsons, invented a more powerful kind of steam engine, the steam turbine. Parsons was familiar with thermodynamics, a branch of physics. Previous engineers had begun with the reciprocal movement of a piston, which they converted to rotational movement. The steam turbine contained a series of curved blades on a rotating spindle plus pressurized steam. It was lighter in weight than the steam boiler and could achieve eighteen thousand revolutions per minute. In 1897 a British navy ship powered with a steam turbine reached thirty-five knots. Moreover, it achieved this with hardly any vibration or noise. Soon turbines were used both on warships and merchant vessels. Today they still provide power for larger ships.

Steamships and railroads were responsible for delocalizing diet. They brought grain and meat to Europe from Australia, New Zealand, Argentina, and the United States. Steamships also carried tropical products to Northern Hemisphere markets, which helped to pay for railroad building in the Southern Hemisphere. While railroads developed national markets, steamships served to develop international markets.

Automobiles and Electrical Applications

By 1890 the Germans were giving the British strong competition in science and technology. The Germans had seen opportunities to develop markets for new kinds of goods and services, and they used the best scientific knowledge available.

Much earlier, in the late eighteenth century, the Prussians had begun to commit themselves to the principle of meritocracy. They adopted it as an alternative to family status and patronage in the recruitment of government officials. In 1770 they introduced compulsory civil service examinations. In 1807 they established the principle of meritocracy in admitting candidates to take those examinations. In 1871, after the unification of Germany, enrollments in universities expanded in all fields, including science and technology, and the principle of meritocracy was more widely applied.[5]

The Germans had to recruit the best men because they were playing catch-up with the British. They founded a higher technical school in Karlsruhe in 1825, another in Munich in 1868, and a third in Berlin in 1879. The German government poured money into the universities. Engineers and scientists gained prestige, not only in Germany, but also internationally.[6] Young people from America and other parts of Europe went to Germany to earn doctoral degrees in the sciences and engineering.

German businessmen became highly responsive to scientific discoveries. They aimed at producing a quality product so as to increase their market share. Today the names Bayer, Mercedes-Benz, Siemens, and Diesel are household words, and they serve to remind us of the excellence of German industrial projects toward the end of the nineteenth century. Today corporations as a matter of course pay attention to scientific discoveries relevant to what concerns them.

Unfortunately the British neglected technical education. They did not found true technical schools until 1889. By 1914 British industry was starved for engineering talent. Between the decades 1860–1869 and 1900–1909 the increase in British industrial productivity fell from 33 percent per decade to 9 percent.[7]

The best brains in Britain tended to be drawn into the traditional classical curriculum because it was more prestigious and because classical graduates could find positions as officials in the British Empire. High finance and real estate investment attracted a few of them.

In the elite "public" (private) schools of Britain, mathematics was always important, but science was a despised subject. Throughout the nineteenth century the British elite held the view that Oxford and Cambridge should be kept disengaged from industry and any work that dirtied the hands. Until 1900 Oxford offered no scholarships for students in the physical sciences. Until 1919 Greek was compulsory for all science students at Cambridge, as it was until 1920 at Oxford. While physicists at Cavendish Laboratory at Cambridge did brilliant basic research, it had little relevance to the needs of British industry of the time.[8]

The British Quaker scientific and entrepreneurial elites were declining. It is true that during the nineteenth century a large number of Quaker scientists in proportion to their share in the total population continued to do good work. Thirty Quakers to one Anglican were elected to the Royal Society. This began to change after 1871, when Oxford and Cambridge opened their gates to Quakers.[9] Young Quakers and other middle-class individuals began to make contact with young aristocrats and make their way into the most prestigious professions and government offices. Professionals trained in the Greco-Roman classics were not qualified to be scientists and engineers.

In his book *The Lever of Riches: Technological Creativity and Economic Progress,* Joel Mokyr points out that every technologically creative society had an economic lead for only a short period and then lost it. The evidence from Great Britain during the late nineteenth and early twentieth centuries supports this hypothesis.

I suggest this explanation is generalizable to other times and places. If they had the choice, most highly intelligent people preferred to participate in a ruling class and be a big shot. They were not keen to suffer the uncertainties and toil involved in research and invention. The more open the British ruling class was to talent, the more likely the talented would compete for entrance.

As I suggested, perhaps this was part of the explanation for the technological stagnation of China after 1400. Such a hypothesis might also help to explain the sudden failure of physical science and technology in early-nineteenth-century France. At that time it became possible for the gifted and talented to compete for positions in the civil bureaucracy.

Electricity in Industry

From 1870 to 1914 the most important new technologies used electricity. Yet electricity was not a prime mover. It had to be derived from a mechanical generator powered by steam, water, or internal combustion. Faraday had discovered the principle of the generator but not how to build one.

In 1867 Sir William (born Wilhelm) Siemens, a German aristocrat, invented the first commercially practical generator. It depended on the rotation of a continuous coil of conducting wire between the poles of a strong magnet. Turning the coil produced a current in it.

Entrepreneurs in the budding electrical industry first used a steam engine to move the conducting coils in the generator. In 1870 the best that reciprocating steam engines could achieve, a thousand revolutions per minute, was not good enough. The solution lay in the steam turbine.

In the late nineteenth century engineers began to install steam turbines in electric power stations.[10] From generators powered by steam or water came the electric current to run thousands of electric motors such as those in vacuum cleaners, sewing machines, washing machines, and refrigerators. These devices worked on the reverse principle of the generator: electric current supplied to a coil turned a rotor and created mechanical energy. Household appliances could be made small and needed no energy-wasting pulleys, as did steam engines. They could be started and stopped in a moment and were relatively quiet. The electricity that ran them could be brought in from a distant source.

In an electricity-based industrial economy workers needed a better means of lighting. Arc lights were too bright and could only be used in large public spaces. Gas lights and oil lamps were too dim, and they were also dirty, smelly, and potentially toxic. For most interiors a medium-bright, safe device was needed.[11]

In 1879 an Englishman, Joseph Swan (1828–1914), and an American, Thomas Alva Edison (1847–1931), independently invented the electric light bulb. Edison was more successful because he designed a better system for generating and controlling current to go with his bulb.

The electric light bulb was a kind of vacuum tube like the ones physicists used for experimental purposes. The manufacturer pumped out most of the air inside the bulb. In this way the incandescent carbon filaments had little oxygen with which to combine and would not burn out too quickly.

People used illumination mostly at night, however. To use electrical energy capacity fully, entrepreneurs had to find daytime uses for it. One important daytime use was the running of electric streetcars and subway trains in cities. Electric-powered trains were cleaner and quieter than steam-powered ones. In 1879 workers installed an electric tram in Berlin.[12]

Edison was an American hero in his time. In addition to the electric light bulb, he also invented the phonograph, the carbon telephone transmitter, and the motion picture projector. All these inventions involved the use of electricity.

Edison began as a skillful but rather irresponsible telegraph operator with a knack for fixing electrical machines. At the age of twenty-one he read Faraday's journals; later he said that was the turning point in his life. Although untrained in mathematics (he was almost entirely self-taught), Edison organized a team of specialists, including mathematicians, and set up the first industrial research laboratory.

At first he improved on existing machines. The invention that initially brought him fame was the phonograph (1877). The electric light bulb brought him wealth; by 1885 he was a millionaire. He made batteries for Ford cars and became a close friend of Henry Ford.[13]

The development of electrical technology was of great help to Sweden, Norway, and Switzerland, which lacked coal and oil resources. They built hydroelectric plants, which used water to move the turbines that produce electric current.[14]

Another early use of electricity was for the refrigeration of food. In 1869 Henry P. Howard installed the first air-chilling system on board a steamship used to carry frozen beef from Texas to New Orleans. In 1879 a steam-powered refrigerated ship carried mutton from Australia to London and brought Queen Victoria a frozen leg of lamb.[15]

Steam-driven refrigerators were noisy and inefficient, however. When electricity became available as house current, more people bought refrigerators. They could also use house current to provide household lighting and run household appliances.

In the early twentieth century electricity made possible the mechanized business office. By the 1980s engineers used electric current to run computers, telephones, and copiers.

Industrial Chemistry

Modern industrial chemistry began in the middle of the nineteenth century, when chemists sought uses for coal tar, a dark muck left over from the production of coke and coal gas. In 1856 a young English amateur, William Henry Perkin (1838–1907), tried to synthesize quinine from this stuff. While he was cleaning a reaction vessel with alcohol, he saw a purple solution inside. He had discovered a brilliant purple dye, later called mauveine. Perkin managed to raise the capital to bring the dye to market. He retired rich in 1874.

This was only the beginning. The Germans followed Perkin's lead and from coal tar they began to synthesize dyes that had formerly been available only from vegetable sources. These dyes were not only useful in dyeing textiles. They could also be used in staining microorganisms and human tissues. Scientists discovered that particular dyes had an affinity for specific tissues and organisms. This made possible modern bacteriology and, ultimately, the conquest of many infectious diseases.[16]

Until the twentieth century most drugs were natural alkaloids extracted from plants. In the nineteenth century chemists isolated the active agents and physicians determined optimal dosages. As knowledge of biochemistry increased, chemists and research physicians were able to synthesize new drugs. In 1910 Paul Ehrlich announced the synthesis of salvarsan, a safe and effective cure for syphilis.

Entrepreneurs established great pharmaceutical companies such as the Bayer company in Germany. These companies produced safer and more effective drugs to prevent and cure disease. More chemists became involved in their synthesis and production.

The Internal Combustion Engine

While the German and American electrical and chemical industries developed, other engineers turned to a transportation problem. The problem was to find a new source of power for land transport. They wanted to make a machine that was a good substitute for a horse.

Horses were a major source of pollution in cities. In New York in 1900 they produced every day 1,100 metric tons of manure, 270,000 liters of urine, and 20 carcasses.[17] But railroads and steamboats, which were also polluters, could not take passengers door to door.

Both German and American inventors tried steam and electricity to run the needed machine, but neither proved satisfactory. It was an internal combustion engine run on gasoline that finally put the horse out of business.

Nikolaus Otto (1832–1891), the self-taught son of an innkeeper, built the first practical four-stroke internal combustion engine and exhibited it in 1867. Like Watt's steam engine, it was stationary at first; automobiles came later. The fuel burned in the engine itself, not in a separate firebox. Its structure was smaller and more compact than that of a steam engine. That is why it could be light enough to power an early airplane.

Having obtained a patent in 1876, in the next seventeen years Otto produced and sold fifty thousand internal combustion engines, mainly for use in light engineering factories. In 1886 the patent expired and other inventors could build upon Otto's work.

Gottlieb Daimler (1834–1900) and Carl Benz (1844–1929) invented the automobile. First they attended German technical schools. When they began experimenting, gasoline was an unwanted and dangerous product of the petroleum industry. Oil was first used for illumination. Daimler started using gasoline in his machines. He invented the carburetor, which made possible the first high-speed gasoline engine (improving the speed from 130 to 900 rpm).

The inspiration for the automobile body was the bicycle. A four-wheeled car was like two bicycles linked together. In 1886 Daimler and Maybach made a four-wheeled vehicle that went 11 mph.

Daimler's next car (1889) had a belt drive for the wheels, a steering tiller, and a four-speed gearbox. In 1890 he organized the Daimler Motor Company. Ten years later he created the first modern automobile, the Mercedes. After his death, in 1926, his company merged with that of his rival, Carl Benz, to form Mercedes-Benz.[18]

The automobile could not have worked without rubber tires. Natural rubber tends to be sticky, but Charles Goodyear, the son of a storekeeper in New Haven, Connecticut, accidentally discovered that if rubber is mixed with sulfur and dropped on a hot stove, it loses its stickiness. The process of adding sulfur to rubber and heating it was called vulcanization. In 1844 Goodyear got a patent.

The first rubber tires were made of solid rubber and were used on bicycles. In 1887 John B. Dunlop (1840–1921), a Scottish veterinarian, invented a pneumatic tire (filled with air) for his son's bike. The next year he got a patent. The tire had a hard outer casing and a soft inner tube and was inflatable. Dunlop began production in Belfast in 1890.[19]

In 1898 Rudolf Diesel, a graduate of German technical schools, exhibited a new kind of heat engine that worked at very high pressure. Initially it compressed air, not a mixture of air and fuel. When fuel was injected, it ignited spontaneously. Today diesel engines run on heavy oil and have replaced steam engines on most railroads.[20]

By 1914 a stock of 64,000 motor cars was rolling on German roads;[21] in England there were 132,000.[22]

The internal combustion engine reached many farms. In 1892 the first gasoline tractor appeared in the United States. This type of engine became the chief source of power on the farm, supplemented later by electricity.

Henry Ford did not invent the automobile, as many Americans believe, but he did make a mighty contribution to automobile manufacturing and marketing. While working in Detroit as a maintenance supervisor for the Edison Illuminating Company, he came across an article in a magazine, *The American Machinist,* which explained how to build a simple gasoline machine from odds and ends. In 1896, with the help of three buddies, he built a car that could go at 20 mph. Ford went on to build successful racing cars, improving on his designs each time.

After two business failures, in 1902 Ford sold his first Model A to a dentist for $850. The car was an immediate success, and Ford became wealthy at forty-two.

Ford wanted more. He got the idea of building a low-priced car that almost any family could afford. The Model T, which came out in 1908, was both simple and sophisticated in design. He began to produce it in a new assembly plant in Highland Park, New Jersey, built of reinforced concrete and wide expanses of glass windows. This gave him lots of open floor space with a low risk of fire.

Inside the plant Ford began to streamline production methods. Inspired by procedures used in Chicago meat packing plants, in

1913 he installed the assembly line, a moving conveyor belt, just waist high. Workers did no walking or lifting but had to work fast and steadily.

Most of the workers spoke little or no English; they were of European peasant background and not used to steady eight-hour workdays all year round. Ford had a very high turnover rate among his workers until he raised their pay to the unheard-of rate of five dollars a day.

Between 1913 and 1914 the time needed to produce a Ford car fell from twelve hours to one hour and thirty-three minutes. The seemingly insatiable public demand for the Model T, and the more efficient methods of production, made Ford extremely rich.[23]

The internal combustion engine was ideal for early airplanes because it had a high power-to-weight ratio. Aluminum, a light metal ideal for airplane body construction, became affordable, for when cheap electricity became available, it became practical to extract aluminum from ore by electrolysis. This was important because aluminum had a high strength-for-weight ratio.

By this time scientists had accumulated a lot of information about aerodynamics. In 1738 Daniel Bernoulli (1700–1782), a Swiss physicist, mathematician, and physician, discovered the main mechanism of flight. In a book on hydrodynamics he presented the idea that the pressure of moving fluid (gas or liquid) in a tube changed with its velocity: As the speed of flow increased, the pressure decreased.

The flow of air around a forward-moving airfoil creates upward suction. Air moving below the flat underside of the foil moves more slowly and exerts positive pressure (upward) on the foil. Air moving up and over the airfoil moves faster and exerts negative suction (also upward) on the foil. This provides lift.

Obtaining lift was not the only problem the pioneers of aviation had to solve. In 1783 the first men had ridden in balloons high into the clouds. In 1853 George Cayley built the first glider that warm updrafts could lift. Inventors could achieve lift by shaping wings as airfoils.

In the time of the Wright brothers forward thrust could be had from an internal combustion engine. Through calculations and experience the Wright brothers learned that they needed 520 square feet of wing and an 8- or 9-horsepower (hp) engine to carry up to 200 pounds.

The big problems were related to mechanisms for controlling a lightweight aircraft in the air. Airplanes, like bicycles, had to be kept in balance, which meant that the pilot had to control them on the three axes of motion (roll, yaw, and pitch). The Wright brothers began by learning to control gliders that were lighter than air.

To control their aircraft, the Wright brothers would twist the wings so as to offer varying surfaces to the wind (wing warping). Later they added lateral rudders, flaps on wing edges. Then they could bank and turn the plane by turning the flaps down on one wing and up on the other. Today we call such flaps ailerons.[24]

The brothers learned that they could not always trust the calculations given in the literature on aerodynamics. They had to build a wind tunnel and test each airplane part for themselves. In 1900 they took their latest glider for testing to Kitty Hawk, North Carolina, because they knew that there was lots of soft sand along the beach to cushion a fall and the winds were supposed to be steady.

In this way they mastered the problems of stability and control. In 1902 they built their own thirteen-horsepower engine and attached it to a propeller. The propeller was aerodynamically equivalent to an airfoil, or wing: It created suction that propelled the plane forward. The plane had two sets of wings, parallel to each other, and the pilot lay prone on the lower wing. The Wrights spent a thousand dollars building this biplane and on their travel expenses.

In the summer of 1903 they began to test another biplane, *The Flyer,* at Kitty Hawk. In September Orville flew for twelve seconds. On December 17 he remained in the air almost a minute and covered 850 feet. There were only five witnesses. It was the first time in history in which a machine carrying a man raised itself by its own power into the air in full flight, sailed forward without reduction in speed, and landed at a point as high as where it started.

The Wrights did not meet with instant acclaim, nor did they seek it. In 1905 the journal *Scientific American* suggested their achievement at Kitty Hawk was a hoax. Indeed, the Wrights did not have a practical airplane until 1905, when they built one that could fly for at least thirty-nine minutes and take off and land safely. The next year they patented their invention.

In 1907, when Wilbur arrived in France to demonstrate *The Flyer,* the *New York Herald* (Paris edition) headed its story: "Flyers or Liars?" On August 8, 1908, Wilbur flew at Le Mans airfield for two hours and twenty minutes, for a distance of 77.5 miles. The European press and technical community went wild. In 1909 the U.S. Army Signal Corps bought a plane from the Wrights. Wilbur set up the army's first flying school at College Park, Maryland.

The early airplanes were built on frames with lightweight materials and very little metal. The pilot and passengers were out in the open, exposed to the elements. Most planes had only one or two engines. It was in tsarist Russia that a man built the ancestor of the airliners of the future. It had four 100-hp engines, and it could carry sixteen people in an enclosed cabin.

The man who designed it, Igor Sikorsky (1889–1972), was born into the prerevolutionary intelligentsia. Both parents had medical degrees, and his father was a professor of psychiatry in Kiev. Igor attended a higher technical school in St. Petersburg. He was polite, gentle, and cool.

In 1908 he learned of Wilbur Wright's visit to Europe, and within twenty-four hours he decided on a career in aviation. In 1910 he first tried to build a helicopter. In 1911, having built a plane with a 50-hp engine, he went up to the daring height of 1,500 feet and got his first thrill of flying.

In 1913, using money borrowed from his father and sister, he designed the *Grand One,* the first four-engine plane that could fly. The *Grand One* had four German-made Argus engines mounted on the leading edge of its wings. It weighed over four tons and had an enclosed cabin built of wood. Sikorsky was the first to take it up in the air for a test, a practice he continued with all his later models.

After the plane was accidentally damaged beyond repair, Sikorsky built a replacement, the *Ilya Muromets,* named after a medieval Russian knight. It had six windows on each side of the cabin, was heated by radiators filled with exhaust gas, and had electric lights powered by a wind-driven generator. The enclosed area was divided into a pilot's cabin, a passenger cabin, a bedroom, and a toilet. In February 1914 the *Ilya Muromets* carried sixteen people and a dog. Every flight it made over St. Petersburg brought horse-drawn traffic below to a standstill.

In the spring of 1914 Sikorsky used more-powerful engines to build a copy of the *Ilya Muromets.* To prove its value to the Russian army, he decided to try a long-distance flight from St. Petersburg to Kiev, 744 miles to the south. Before dawn on June 30, 1914, with a crew of three, Sikorsky took off from Korpusnoi Airdrome near St. Petersburg. It took eight and a half hours to reach their refueling place at Orsha. Refueling took two hours. Fifteen minutes after taking off from Orsha, a fuel line to one of the four engines broke, and gas leaking out onto the wing caught fire. Two crewmen crawled out on the wing and put out the fire with their overcoats.

Sikorsky decided to make an emergency landing. His men fixed the fuel line and they spent the night in the plane. The next day they took off before dawn and flew into a cloud bank. The air was turbulent, rain was heavy, and visibility was near zero, so they had to use a compass. They dropped suddenly to four hundred meters, caught sight of the ground, and realized they were lost. So they headed west until they caught sight of the Dnieper River. Then they reestablished their flight path.

With much of the gasoline used up, they found it easy now to climb above the clouds to 1,500 meters, where there was no more turbulence. They cruised over the fluffy white ocean of clouds for two hours. When they estimated they were close to Kiev, they descended below the clouds and, by good luck, saw below the famous medieval church of the city. They landed on the field of the Kiev Aeronautical Society, establishing a record for long-distance flight.

The tsar decorated Sikorsky, exempted him from the draft, and awarded him a hundred thousand rubles to develop more and better aircraft. During World War I copies of the *Ilya Muromets* served as reconnaissance planes and bombers for the Russian army.[26]

After the Bolshevik revolution Sikorsky decided to leave Russia. When he departed he left a fortune of half a million dollars behind, but he carried his essential wealth in his head. Early in 1919 he reached the United States, where he at first lived on the edge of starvation, giving lectures on astronomy for a living. In 1923, with help from the loyal Russian émigré community, Sikorsky organized his own aeronautical engineering company. He designed and built an amphibious plane for Pan American Airlines, which went into use in 1931. The helicopter he tested successfully in 1938 became the prototype of subsequent American helicopters. Sikorsky's helicopter went on its first mission of mercy in January 1944, when it took blood plasma from Battery Park, New York, to Sandy Hook, New Jersey, to victims of a ship explosion.[27]

It took big investments to sustain economic development. The instruments of scientific investigation were getting more precise and complicated and therefore more expensive. Teams often succeeded better than solitary individuals in solving scientific and technological problems.

Conclusion

Science and technology are still happily married and will probably remain so. Since 1895 scientific breakthroughs have amazed us, and new technologies, especially in communication, have changed our lives. However, the technologies that originated between 1870 and 1914 have a special importance because they have transformed our everyday lives. The generator, the electric motor, the light bulb, the steady production of new pharmaceuticals and medical appliances, the automobile, the airplane, are the fruit of the insights and ingenuity of that faraway time.

Notes

1. Paul Bairoch, "The Impact of Crop Yields, Agricultural Productivity and Transport Costs on Urban Growth between 1800 and 1910."
2. J.N. Westwood, *A History of Russian Railways,* p. 78.
3. Steven G. Marks, *Road to Power: The Trans-Siberian Railroad and the Colonization of Asian Russia, 1850–1917.*
4. Westwood, *History of Russian Railways,* pp. 17–26.
5. Hans Rosenberg, *Bureaucracy, Aristocracy, and Autocracy: The Prussian Experience, 1660–1815,* pp. 178–211.
6. Charles E. McClelland, *State, Society and University in Germany, 1700–1914.*
7. Michael Sanderson, *The Universities and British Industry, 1850–1970,* p. 9.
8. W.F. Connell, *A History of Education in the Twentieth-Century World,* p. 50; Detlef K. Muller et al., *The Rise of Modern Educational Systems,* pp. 154–59; Sanderson, *Universities and British Industry,* pp. 33–51.
9. M.W. Kirby, *Men of Business and Politics: The Rise and Fall of the Quaker Pease Dynasty of North-East England, 1700–1943;* Elizabeth Isichei, *Victorian Quakers,* pp. 158–73.
10. Trevor I. Williams, *A Short History of Twentieth-Century Technology, c. 1900–c. 1950,* p. 5; Williams, *The History of Invention,* pp. 162–68; Isaac Asimov, *Asimov's Chronology of Science and Discovery,* pp. 286–87.
11. George Basalla, *The Evolution of Technology,* p. 47.
12. Maxwell G. Lay, *Ways of the World: A History of the World's Roads,* p. 134.
13. Matthew Josephson, *Edison.*
14. Thomas K. Derry, *A History of Scandinavia,* p. 254.
15. James Burke, *Connections,* pp. 238–42.
16. Aaron J. Ihde, *The Development of Modern Chemistry,* pp. 454–62.
17. Lay, *Ways of the World,* p. 132.
18. Anthony Feldman and Peter Ford, *Scientists and Inventors,* pp. 180–84, 200–1; Williams, *History of Invention,* pp. 164–65.

19. Williams, *History of Invention,* pp. 196–97.
20. W.H.G. Armytage, *A Social History of Engineering,* p. 191.
21. Ibid., p. 191.
22. Edward Royle, *Modern Britain: A Social History, 1750–1985,* p. 17.
23. Robert Lacey, *Ford: The Man and the Machine.*
24. Steven H. Guyford and James J. Haggerty, *Flight,* pp. 14–59.
25. Fred Howard, *Wilbur and Orville;* Tom D. Crouch, *The Bishop's Boys.*
26. K.N. Finne, *Igor Sikorsky: The Russian Years.*
27. Igor I. Sikorsky, *The Story of Winged S;* Frank J. Delear, *Igor Sikorsky: His Three Careers in Aviation.*

14 BREAKTHROUGHS IN SCIENCE

1895 to 1997

We are an intelligent species and the use of our intelligence quite properly gives us pleasure. In this respect the brain is like a muscle. When it is in use we feel very good. Understanding is joyous.

—Carl Sagan

Of all scientific disciplines in the twentieth century, which have made the greatest progress? Why?

Early modern scientists such as Newton referred to themselves as "dwarfs standing on the shoulders of giants." The shoulders they had in mind were Aristotle and other ancient Greeks whom they respected. The truth is that some twentieth-century scientists have been more like giants standing upon the shoulders of dwarfs. Ernest Rutherford, Edwin Hubble, Alfred Wegener, James Watson, and Francis Crick are not household names—but they are scientific giants.

The habit of historians has been to include the seventeenth-century scientific revolution in physics and astronomy in their European world history texts but to ignore the multiple scientific breakthroughs of the twentieth century. Historians tend to put the history of science in a compartment at the margin of "real" history.

The Social Context of the New Scientific Revolution

Climate. In this breakthrough period the climate was generally warm. This is relevant because climate was favorable to the survival of babies and children. The larger the population, the greater the number of potential geniuses.

It is generally believed that mathematicians and scientists do their best work when they are in their twenties and thirties. This suggests that the larger the number of young people in a population, the more likely it is that there will be innovations in mathematics and science.

Investigative Technologies. Collecting new information is one of the basic functions of communication technologies. After the marriage of science and technology people in both areas interacted to produce new investigative technologies. These included the electron microscope, radioactive dating, X-ray crystallography, and the radio telescope. With the invention of the transistor in 1948, computers entered the lives of scientists. Then there were spacecraft and earth satellites, all of which collected scientific data. New medical technologies included magnetic resonance imaging, CAT (computerized axial tomography) scans; and PET (positron emissions tomography) scans to explore a living human body.

The more scientists knew, the better they could advise engineers, who created new technologies for them. The better the investigative technology, the more scientists knew. The result has been a continual positive feedback with no end in sight.

Political Elites. As in the seventeenth century, twentieth-century scientists required the acceptance and sponsorship of political elites. Governments were protective in wider and wider areas in the globe. Political elites responded to the possibility that scientists might create more efficient military weapons and better electronic surveillance technologies. It took little imagination to conceive how new technologies might create wealth.

Tradition. As I have proposed, the medieval university, printing with movable type, and the construction of new communication systems served to accelerate scientific progress. By the end of the seventeenth century, scientists had developed traditions of their own. They had rules of investigation and interpretation. They agreed that the supernatural had no place in the understanding of nature. Each major scientific discipline had its own history, which served to legitimize its current activity. They now had heroes of their own.

Physics

In 1895 physicists had a well-established body of theory. They believed in the conservation of matter and energy. They were familiar with the electromagnetic spectrum of radiation. However, they were not familiar with the inside of an atom or with radioactivity.

It was in this context that Wilhelm Roentgen (1845–1923), a physics professor at the University of Wurzberg in Germany, began his experiments with a vacuum tube. This tube was a major instrument of scientific investigation in his time. Inside the tube there was a cathode that could discharge electric current. When the air or gas pressure in the tube was very low, almost a perfect vacuum, physicists would turn on the current. The current, in making its journey across the tube to the anode at the other end, caused the remaining gas and even the glass walls of the tube to become radiant. Each gas had its own delicate color.

At low pressure the electric current came into contact with fewer atoms than normal and applied high energy to them. Some gas atoms acquired so much additional energy that they released previously unknown radiation.[1]

On November 8, 1895, Roentgen was experimenting in his laboratory with a vacuum tube. He intended to analyze the gases in the tube by turning on the current and using a spectroscope to determine their chemical structure.

In order to get a better view of the light inside, he covered most of the tube with black cardboard and turned on the current. The gas in the tube glowed. Then he noticed that a nearby cardboard screen coated with barium platinocyanide (a luminescent substance) was glowing. The cardboard screen was opposite the covered cathode in the tube. He turned off the current and the screen darkened. He turned it back on and the screen glowed. Then he realized that "cathode rays" could not be responsible for the glow.

Roentgen put his hand between the end of the tube and the screen. He saw the bones of his own hand on the screen. He reasoned that some unknown kind of penetrating rays were emerging from the end of the tube. He called them X rays because they were unknown.

For seven weeks Roentgen did experiments with the unknown rays. On December 22 he could wait no more. Using a photographic plate he took a picture of his wife's hand showing her bones and wedding ring. Using this as proof of his discovery, he released the news to the public. Since vacuum tubes were standard equipment in physics laboratories, other physicists quickly confirmed these results.[2]

X rays had an immediate practical use. Within a few weeks physicians put them to use in setting broken bones. By using X rays they could also find metal objects such as bullets and safety pins inside the body.

Reading this news, Henri Becquerel (1852–1908), a French physicist who specialized in luminescent rocks, started an experiment with a piece of natural potassium uranyl sulfate. He knew that it glowed after exposure to ultraviolet light, so he put it on his balcony so that the sun would "charge" it. Under it he placed a photographic plate wrapped in thick black paper to shield it from the sun. Would the sunlight make the rock emit X rays? Sure enough, at the end of the day the plate had gray smudges under its wrapping.

Elated by this result, Becquerel planned to repeat the experiment the next day. However, the sky clouded over. So he put his rocks and covered photographic plates in a file drawer. A week later, on March 1, 1896, Becquerel opened the drawer and on impulse developed a photographic plate. Again he saw blotches on the plate, only darker ones. He realized that the rocks had emitted radiation. He did not know that they emitted a whole spectrum of radiation, not just X rays. Becquerel had discovered natural radioactivity.[3]

Others continued Becquerel's experiments. J.J. Thomson (1856–1940), director of Cavendish Laboratory at Cambridge University, discovered electrons. His successor, Ernest Rutherford (1871–1937), together with Frederick Soddy, discovered natural isotopes, intermediate elements that broke down at a fixed rate until they became a stable element. For example, in dating early hominid remains, scientists used nearby rocks containing potassium 40 (an unstable isotope) and the stable element argon (a gas). Potassium 40 broke down at a fixed rate. They measured the amount of potassium 40 still left in relation to argon and then estimated the age of the rock.

Living organisms contain a stable amount of the isotope carbon 14. In dating organic remains such as wood, bone, and parchment, scientists could measure the amount of carbon 14 in relation to nitrogen. In this way they could estimate when the organism had died. Rutherford also discovered protons, which appeared to be an essential part of all atoms, together with electrons. In 1911 Rutherford proposed a "solar system" model of the interior of an atom. He came to the conclusion that electrons determine the chemical properties of an element, while its nucleus (containing protons) determines its radioactive properties. In 1919 Rutherford finally fulfilled the dream of medieval alchemists who sought to transmute "base elements" into gold. By bombarding the nucleus of nitrogen atoms with alpha particles, he transmuted nitrogen into oxygen plus hydrogen.[4]

Meanwhile, in 1912 a German physicist, Max von Laue, invented a new X-ray investigative technology. A crystal of a molecule acts as one giant molecule because of the regular spacing of its constituent atoms. While passing through a crystal of the molecule being studied, X rays form a characteristic image. It reveals the shape of molecules and the distance between the atoms of the molecule. Later X-ray technology made possible the analysis of the molecular structure of DNA —the genetic material. This in turn revolutionized genetics.

Astronomy

At the beginning of the twentieth century astronomers were not sure that galaxies other than our own (the Milky Way galaxy) existed. The universe as they understood it was coextensive with our galaxy. But astronomers were now turning their big glass eyes up to the night sky. They were puzzling over the fuzzy shapes they called nebulae (clouds).

In 1912 an American astronomer, Vesto Slipher (1875–1969), studied what was at the time called the Andromeda (M-13) Nebula. Using the spectroscope he found that this nebula was apparently moving toward Earth.

Edwin Hubble (1889–1953) was the greatest astronomer of the twentieth century. He was bright and athletic and won a Rhodes Scholarship to Oxford. On returning home he decided to become an astronomer and entered the graduate program at the University of Chicago. In 1919 he arrived at the Mount Wilson observatory in California to use the new one-hundred-inch telescope.

In 1924 he found evidence that the so-called Andromeda Nebula was really a galaxy. By studying stars of variable brightness (Cepheid variables) that he found in this "nebula" he learned that it was farther away from Earth than the diameter of our galaxy. Therefore it had to be a separate galaxy. He studied other nebulae and found that they too were galaxies. These entities produced hot emission spectra, indicating the presence of bright stars. Nebulae, which are clouds of gas and dust, do not produce hot emission spectra.

After studying all known nebulae, most of which were receding from Earth, in 1929 Hubble formulated his law: the more distant a galaxy, the faster it is receding from us. Apparently the universe (which I shall call the cosmos hereafter) was expanding.

Hubble's discoveries increased the plausibility of the big bang theory of cosmic history. This history began with a great explosion that occurred between ten and twenty billion years ago. Both Newton and Einstein had assumed that the cosmos was unchanging; Hubble found it to be dynamic. The cosmos had a past and a future.[5]

By 1934 astronomers realized that there were as many galaxies as foreground stars, perhaps hundreds of millions. Each galaxy might include billions of stars. The scale of the cosmos was huge compared to that of our galaxy. But was there any proof of this hypothesis?

In May 1964 two radio astronomers, Robert Wilson and Arno Penzias of the Bell Telephone Laboratory at Holmdel, New Jersey (now part of Lucent Technologies), tested their equipment by turning it toward a "quiet" place in the sky.

Instead of a near-total lack of radio noise, which would be an indicator of near-absolute-zero cold, they found unexpected heat—3 degrees above absolute zero. They couldn't understand what they had found. They retested their equipment, turning to various places in the sky, and got the same result. They rechecked their equipment and went inside their antenna to remove traces of pigeon droppings—to no avail.

Meanwhile, sixty miles away at Princeton, New Jersey, a group of astronomers led by Jim Peebles and Robert Dicke were looking for photons that they expected to find as vestiges of the big bang explosion. They did not know that what they were seeking had already been found six months earlier. Fortunately, the two New Jersey groups made contact with each other and in May 1965 jointly published a paper about their discovery.[6]

Geology

After physicists discovered radioactivity, progress in geology took a great leap forward. It was possible to determine the age of the earth and of the various kinds of rocks on earth.

In 1893 a physicist, Lord Kelvin, calculated the age of the earth with the assumption that it had originally been as hot as the sun today. He believed that this heat was dissipated at a steady rate. In this way he calculated that the earth's crust might be only a hundred million years old. This was too short a time frame to contain the geologists' tale, much less Darwin's outline of evolution. If Lord Kelvin was correct, there would not have been enough time in the past for the geologists' tale to unroll.

In 1907 Bertram Boltwood, a scientist at Yale University, was the first to suggest that it might be possible to date the earth's crust by measuring the relative amounts of lead and an unstable isotope of uranium in rocks, which decays into lead.

At the age of twenty-one Arthur Holmes (1898–1965) began a quest for radioactive dating methods. In 1904 he heard Rutherford speak at Yale, and his interest was fanned to a passion. In 1926 he wrote 70 percent of a report of a committee of the U.S. National Research Council affirming that radioactive dating was the only reliable geologic dating method. By 1931 Holmes was able to convince most scientists.[7]

Today's dating of the age of the earth is based on the dating of rocks. Holmes realized that the earth dissipates not only the heat from the time when the solar system was formed, about 4.6 billion years ago, but also from radioactive rocks. The age of the earth is estimated by analyzing both earth rocks containing uranium and lunar rocks. The rocks containing uranium were 4.5 billion years old and the lunar rocks were 4.6 billion years old.[8] That is long enough for the tale proposed by geologists to have taken place.

In the early twentieth century geologists and paleontologists were familiar with many anomalous facts. For example, what was a fossil amphibian doing in Antarctica? What was a fossil marsupial doing there? Why was there evidence of Paleozoic glaciers in tropical Africa, and no evidence of glaciers in Canada or Siberia? Why were fossil animals in Brazil so like those of Africa?[9]

Another puzzle was the youthfulness of fossil life found on the ocean floor. Fossils of marine life found on land went back two billion years, while those of marine life in the ocean went back only two hundred million years. In this case, current geologic theory was not modified but rather discarded and replaced. A new paradigm was born.

In 1915 Alfred Wegener (1880–1930), a German meteorologist, proposed a radical explanation for these anomalies. He was the son of an evangelical preacher and had a bit of scientific evangelism in him. He was also an adventurer who loved ballooning and exploring in Greenland. It seems predictable that such a man would tackle the most important scientific problem he could possibly study.

Wegener's book was entitled *The Origin of Continents and Oceans.* He called attention to the surprising fit, like two marriageable jigsaw puzzle pieces, of the eastern coast of South America and the western coast of Africa. He also drew attention to the presence of similar animals, living and extinct, on both sides of the Atlantic. He inferred that all the world's continents had once been joined in a common land mass (Pangaea). Then, he suggested, this land mass split and its pieces became mobile. Today they are considered as separate continents.

Many geologists rejected Wegener's idea, in part because he was a meteorologist and had no credentials in geology. Some geologists liked his idea. However, no one had any idea of a mechanism that could make continents separate and move apart. Nor did they understand how portions of the earth's crust could separate without leaving holes.

Wegener became a Greenland specialist and made four exploratory visits there. On the fourth trip, in 1930, he died of exhaustion and cold.[10] Had he lived another forty years, he would have been delighted to see that his idea had provoked a revolution in geology.

How did this revolution happen? After 1945 geologists began to study natural magnetism in rocks. Basalt from volcanic eruptions is fairly rich in iron, and as it cools it becomes weakly magnetized by Earth's magnetic field.

Geologists learned that in past epochs there were reversals in Earth's magnetic poles. That meant that at times a compass needle (if it had existed then) would have pointed south instead of north. These periods of magnetic reversal were worldwide: All rocks of the same age showed the same polarity no matter what their source. Half of the earth's crust was reversely magnetized in alternating bands; that is, the northern magnetic pole might be replaced by the southern magnetic pole and vice versa. It followed that rocks could be matched by the alternating magnetic strata in them.

After World War II scientists made a concerted effort to study ocean floors. A turning point was the International Geophysical Year, 1957–1958, when scientists undertook the systematic mapping of ocean floors. Geologists discovered these floors were made mainly of basalt and were thus volcanic in origin. They discovered underwater volcanoes. Ocean rocks were indeed quite young. In the midst of these young rocks in the Atlantic Ocean was a north-south ridge. On each side of the ridge the sea floor was spreading apart. Now geologists had an answer for the question of how portions of the earth's crust could separate without leaving tears and holes: New material from inside the earth rose to fill the gap.

Among geologists the idea spread that ocean floors and continents were separate and real entities that moved in relation to each other. By 1960 they had found that magnetic bands in the floor on both sides of the ridge were symmetrical. By 1968 geologists concluded that the surface of the earth was made up of six tectonic plates and twelve subplates. The movements of these plates were responsible for the movements of continents and ocean beds. The plates were something like paving stones on the move. They accepted Wegener's hypothesis that in the distant past all continents had been part of one land mass.

Genetics

Geneticists have also revolutionized their discipline. Knowledge of genetics began to grow in 1900, when English-speaking scientists became interested in the work of the late Austrian monk Gregor Mendel. Hugo de Vries argued that evolution proceeded by sudden mutations in genetic material.

In 1907 T.H. Morgan and his associates at Columbia University began their work on the genetics of fruit flies, which produced a new generation every ten to fourteen days. Within three years they established that some traits might be sex-linked. They suggested that heredity was determined by particles called genes. However, until the development of sufficiently powerful electron microscopes in the late 1960s, no one saw a gene.

In 1928 Frederick Griffith, a public-health bacteriologist, observed that certain strains of bacteria acquired new characteristics that remained present in their offspring when grown in an extract from another strain possessing these characteristics, showing that genetic information is transmitted by a chemical compound. Was this something a protein? Proteins were complex molecules that might do the complicated work of genes. No, the genetic material was not a protein, said O.T. Avery (1877–1955), a physician doing research at the Rockefeller Institute Hospital in New York. He argued that the genetic material was relatively simple deoxyribonucleic acid (DNA). It had been first isolated in 1869 by Friedrich Miescher, a Swiss biochemist, who found it in the remnants of cells in pus. It was found only in the nuclei of cells. Before Avery, scientists thought DNA was merely a helper to some complex protein that really did the job.[11]

Two ambitious young men, Francis Crick (1916–) and James Watson (1928–), sought to decipher the molecular structure of DNA.

Watson, a biologist, felt encouraged when he learned that DNA could be crystallized, because he knew that every crystal has a pattern, and any pattern can be detected. Crick, a physicist, was familiar with X-ray crystallography. He was a friend of Maurice Wilkins, who was using X-ray technology to study DNA crystals. Wilkins's colleague, Rosalind Franklin, was taking greatly improved X-ray photographs of those crystals. However, she could not explain the pattern that she saw.

The intellectual assets of Crick were complementary to those of Watson. The two of them also had good interpersonal chemistry; Crick said that they were both arrogant, ruthless, and impatient with sloppy thinking. "If either of us suggested a new idea," he said, "the other, while taking it seriously, would attempt to demolish it in a candid but non-hostile manner. This turned out to be quite crucial." They were able to discard untenable ideas quickly and persist in the search.

In 1953 Watson and Crick used the information in an X-ray photograph taken by Rosalind Franklin that her superior, Maurice Wilkins, had showed to them without her permission. Watson and Crick then used Tinker Toys to create a model of a DNA molecule.

As many theoretical geneticists had predicted, DNA produced a complementary substance, RNA, which fitted DNA as a key to a lock. RNA served as a template (or mold) for the formation of proteins. The sequence of DNA bases determined the sequence of amino acids along the proteins.

How could such a simple substance do all this? The reason that DNA contained all the complexities of genetic information was that the information was contained in its extremely variable *sequence* of bases, rather than in a *variety* of bases.[12]

The resulting explosion in genetics research has already increased appreciation of the role of heredity in human intelligence and personality traits. For example, psychologists studying identical twins reared separately found that their intelligence was much the same as that of identical twins reared together.

Biochemistry

Scientists believe that the controls in an organism are of two kinds. The first, provided by the nervous system, is rapid and automatic: Neurotransmitters are relatively simple substances and go very short distances. The endocrine glands, which produce hormones, provide the second kind of control. They work more slowly, regulating growth and providing gradual adjustments to functional and seasonal changes.

The two kinds of controls are coordinated. Both rely on chemical messengers. The body is self-regulated.

Most of the communication within the body is outside the realm of human consciousness. We cannot find out by introspection alone what is going on in our head. Our brains did not evolve so as to make us conscious of the chemical mechanisms of our own body.

Our unconscious, automatic data processing enables us to focus attention on unusual, dangerous, more informative, and more important events in our experience. It enables us to think about long-term problems. In this way, when old strategies fail we can devise new ones. If we had to regulate by conscious decisions everything going on in our bodies, we would suffer from severe information overload. In many cases we would be unable to respond quickly enough. So the greater part of brain functioning is automatic: A lot is going on in our heads, but we have little awareness of it.

The study of biochemistry began in earnest in 1897. Eduard Buchner (1860–1917) was a professor at the College of Agriculture in Berlin. Like Pasteur and other "vitalists," he believed that living things had to be present to cause fermentation. He thought that fermentation, like other biological processes, could not be explained solely in terms of chemical mechanisms. There had to be some "life principle" at work.

In 1893 Buchner tried to prove his point by pulverizing yeasts and extracting fluid from their very dead remains. In 1896 he mixed this fluid with a concentrated sugar solution, thinking that no fermentation would occur and no alcohol would be produced. However, cell-free fermentation did occur. A cell-free extract of yeast, the enzyme zymase, could convert sugar into alcohol. This result was the opposite of what Buchner had expected. His "failure" was among the most significant negative results in the history of science.

After this scientists felt ready to tackle the study of chemical processes in living cells, for they had come to believe that there was no mysterious, unanalyzable "vital principle" in living things.[13] In 1902 scientists recognized that chemicals secreted by certain glands into the bloodstream served as "messengers" within the body.

To describe such secretions, in 1905 E.H. Starling coined the word *hormone* (from the Greek *hormao,* "to stimulate"). Progress in identifying hormones was slow until the 1950s, when radioactive isotopes became available for research. They harmlessly served as tracers within the body.

If there is a master gland in the human body, it is the hypothalamus, a part of the brain. It translates messages from the rest of the brain into electrical impulses and hormones.[14]

Now scientists are studying the genetics and biochemistry of the brain. This wonderful organ constitutes only 2 percent of body weight but requires more than half of the human genome to code for it. In 1975 Hans Kosterlitz and John Hughes discovered endorphins, the brain's own opiatelike hormones. Runners can explain "runner's high" in terms of such secretions. It is possible to become addicted to the chemical byproducts of one's own activity.

In 1981 Roger Sperry won a Nobel Prize for his discovery that pattern-dependent thinking occurs mainly in the right side of the brain. Much creative thinking probably depends on recognizing patterns and discrepancies in patterns. This may be the part of the brain that gives us hunches and "smells a rat."[15]

In 1984 scientists discovered that brain cells, like glandular cells, can replace themselves. New neurons are made all the time. In May 1989 Solomon Snyder, director of neuroscience at the Johns Hopkins School of Medicine, announced that scientists could grow brain tissue in the laboratory.[16]

Psychiatrists now use psychoactive drugs to help troubled patients. They have been especially successful in lifting people out of depressions with doses of serotonin, a natural product of the body. New useful drugs for mental distress are in preparation.

Conclusion

What has happened to science in the twentieth century?

1. The most radical changes have occurred in nuclear physics, astronomy (especially cosmology), geology, biochemistry, and genetics. These disciplines include much more fundamental knowledge than they did before 1895.

2. Cosmology became a historical science. Cosmologists no longer confined their search to unchanging principles and laws. Geologists, stimulated by Wegener's idea, changed their paradigm. Their science, which had been historical since James Hutton, became even more so.

3. Brain research undermined the belief that the soul was distinct from the mind, that the mind was distinct from the brain, and that the brain was distinct from the rest of the body.

Did the souls of the dead reach heaven up in the sky? Outer space appeared to be more like hell than heaven.

Did God make human beings in his image? We now know that human beings are members of the primate family and behave in much the same ways (good and bad) as their cousins. Our primate cousins have not yet perceived that we are more divine or more beautiful than they are.

The science with the most practical consequences is genetics. We are beginning to harvest new pharmaceuticals based on progress in molecular biology. The most feared present diseases, cancer and AIDS, show signs of yielding to scientists.

Notes

1. A.E. McKenzie, *The Major Achievements of Sciences,* vol. 2, p. 278; Alex Keller, *The Infancy of Atomic Physics,* pp. 36–40; E.N. Jenkins, *Radioactivity,* p. 2.

2. "Wilhelm Roentgen," in Charles C. Gillispie, ed., *Dictionary of Scientific Biography.*

3. Robert P. Crease and Charles C. Mann, *The Second Creation: Makers of the Revolution in Twentieth-Century Physics,* pp. 10–12; "Henri Becquerel," in Gillispie, ed., *Dictionary of Scientific Biography;* L. Badash, "Chance Favors the Prepared Mind: Henri Becquerel and the Discovery of Radioactivity."

4. David Wilson, *Rutherford: A Simple Genius;* Crease and Mann, *Second Creation,* pp. 15–19.

5. Rocky Kolb, *Blind Watchers of the Sky,* pp. 194–96, 213–18. See also Gale E. Christianson, *Edwin Hubble.*

6. Kolb, *Blind Watchers,* pp. 240–42, 253–59.

7. Claude C. Albritton, *The Abyss of Time;* Lawrence Badash, "The Age of the Earth Debate."

8. I. Bernard Cohen, *Revolution in Science,* pp. 446–66.

9. Martin Schwarzbach, *Alfred Wegener.*

10. James D. Watson, *The Double Helix*; Francis Crick, *What Mad Pursuit*; Allen, *Life Science,* pp. 189–96, 209–21.

11. Garland Allen, *Life Science in the Twentieth Century,* pp. 42–69, 196–208; "Oswald Avery," in Gillispie, ed., *Dictionary of Scientific Biography.*

12. Watson, *The Double Helix;* Crick, *What Mad Pursuit,* pp. 70, 74; Allen, *Life Science,* pp. 189–96, 209–21.

13. Allen, *Life Science,* pp. 147–84; "Eduard Buchner," in Gillispie, ed., *Dictionary of Scientific Biography.*

14. Lawrence Crapo, *Hormones: The Messengers of Life,* pp. 4–16; Isaac Asimov, *Asimov's Chronology of Science and Discovery,* pp. 422, 463, 481.

15. Richard Bergland, *The Fabric of the Mind,* p. 10.

16. *The New York Times,* August 15, 1989, Science section.

15 THE THIRD COMMUNICATION REVOLUTION

We have decided to call the entire field of control and
communication theory, whether with the machine or in the
animal, by the name Cybernetics, which we form from the
Greek [for] steersman.

—Norbert Wiener

The first communication revolution occurred in the mid-fourth millennium B.C. in the Nile and Tigris-Euphrates Valleys. It was a well-developed phonetic writing system. The second communication revolution began in the 1840s when the first telegraph systems were built. Then communication at the speed of light appeared.

The third communication revolution began as a response to military needs, such as decoding secret German messages and guiding rockets to their targets. After World War II population and markets grew in the United States and Eurasia. Business managers needed more efficient information collection, processing, storing, retrieval, and transmission methods. They also needed new forms of mass media to sell their goods and services.

Politicians speaking to millions of constituents also had to use mass media. For most people, television became the most important source of political information (and disinformation).

From Radios to Computers

The principal twentieth-century innovations in communication, in chronological order, were radio, cinema, television, computers, earth

satellites, and fiber-optic cables. Paper became less important because electronic devices stored, processed, retrieved, and transmitted
information. Now by means of satellites and computers people can
send telephone calls and electronic mail to any place in the world.
These messages travel at the speed of light and do not pollute the
environment.

The process of innovation in mass communication began in 1888,
when Heinrich Hertz (1857–1894), a German physicist, discovered the
radio frequency band in the electromagnetic wave spectrum. In so
doing, as H.G.J. Aitken pointed out, Hertz discovered a new communication continent.[1] It contained no land for agriculture and no fossil
fuels, but it was rich in resources for communication.

Hertz began with scientific theory. Following a prediction of the
mathematician James Clerk Maxwell, he looked for waves longer than
light waves. He tried to generate them by setting up an electric circuit
that made sparks oscillate through the air across a gap between two
metal balls. To detect any long waves that might be emitted, Hertz
used a loop of wire with a gap at one point. He calculated that as the
current between the two balls in the first circuit sent out radiation, that
radiation ought to give rise to a current in the loop of wire.

His prediction came true: small sparks jumped across the gap in the
detector loop. Hertz found that the waves were about 66 cm (22
inches) long, a million times the wavelength of visible light. They
traveled at the speed of light.

Another physicist, Oliver Lodge, using a closed instead of an open
circuit, discovered how to detect radio waves by tuning. That is, Lodge
made his receiver resonate at the same frequency as his transmitter.
This amplified the radio waves between transmitter and receiver.

A wealthy Italian amateur, Guglielmo Marconi (1874–1937), took
the next step. He wanted to find a way to communicate over long
distances by using radio waves as a signal carrier. By 1899 he could
send a Morse code message across the English Channel by radio waves
in pulses. Marconi did not stop there. He refused to believe that if he
broadcast a radio beam out across the Atlantic Ocean it would inevitably get lost in outer space.

Marconi's experiments had suggested that for some unknown reason radio waves would follow the curvature of the earth. To achieve
greater distance he used longer vertical antennas. They produced
longer wavelengths at lower frequencies with high voltage (intensity).

In 1901 Marconi set up a broadcasting station in Cornwall, England, and a receiving station in Newfoundland, Canada. He ordered the Cornwall station to broadcast the letter *S* in Morse code during certain hours. On a blustery day, December 12, he picked up a faint *S* on his receiver, probably coming from Cornwall, two thousand miles away. At the time scientists had not known this was possible.

In the 1920s Marconi pioneered the use of short waves at high frequency, which skipped between ionosphere and earth and went even greater distances. However, these shortwave messages were still limited to Morse code.[2]

It was Reginald Fessenden (1866–1932), a Canadian-born American physicist, who in 1901 first modulated (changed) radio carrier waves to carry a wide array of sound signals, that is, music and the human voice. On Christmas Eve in 1906 he broadcast Christmas music from Brant Rock on the Massachusetts coast. Men on nearby ships, who had radio receivers aboard for security reasons, were astonished to hear the music.[3]

In the late nineteenth century Thomas Edison had made the observation that electricity flows from a heated metal through space (the Edison effect, discovered in 1883). This observation helped solve the problem of converting alternating current (AC), which is more easily transported over long distances, to direct current (DC). Direct current is less transportable, but it must be used with radio receivers. A device used for such a conversion is called a rectifier. Early radios used a crystal for rectification. Engineers did not know how the crystal changed AC to DC.

In 1904 John A. Fleming created a new rectifier in the form of a partial vacuum tube. In this tube a hot metal filament transferred electrons to a positively charged anode (hence the word *electronic*). This transference involved the Edison effect, which was stronger in such a tube. Vacuum tubes do not depend merely on the flow of electricity, as does an electric motor. They also control the behavior of electrons.

In the year 1906 Lee De Forest invented the triode vacuum tube. In this tube an electronic gate, in the form of a grid, acted like a venetian blind, shutting the current on and off, changing alternating to direct current and amplifying it when desired. This made commercial radio broadcasting possible.[4]

In 1919 shortwave radio transmission began. It was especially important in the Soviet Union and the United States, both of which stretched across several time zones. In 1920 the first regular public radio longwave broadcasts began in the United States and the United Kingdom.

Engineers adapted radio waves to other uses. In 1935 a British team headed by R.A. Watson-Watt developed radar to detect the approach of enemy ships, planes, and later ballistic missiles. During the thirties pioneering astronomers began to receive natural radio waves from outer space, and in 1942 Grote Reber made the first radio maps of the universe.

We now turn to the transmission of visual images. Motion pictures, which first appeared in the 1890s, were based on the principle that the brain retains the images of the eye for an instant longer than the eye actually records them. Hence a series of images tends to fuse into a continuous impression.

In 1889 W.K.L. Dickson developed the first film and projector. Between 1895 and 1900 Europeans, notably the brothers A. and L. Lumière, developed them further. The Lumière brothers displayed their first motion picture in public in 1895.

The next breakthrough came in 1927 with the shooting of the first feature film with sound, *The Jazz Singer*. Color films caught on commercially in the 1950s.

In the twentieth century motion picture producers have made films mostly for entertainment. Others have used motion pictures to document crime, revolutions, and the horrors of war. Whether recording fact or fiction, motion picture films are very realistic. This is why they are dangerous: Con artists and propagandists can exploit them, too.

The television era began in 1926, when J.L. Baird of the United Kingdom first demonstrated a television apparatus. He was also responsible for the first international television broadcast, from London to New York in 1928.

The most outstanding figure in the development of this medium was a refugee from Soviet Russia, Vladimir Kosma Zworykin. He was born in 1889, the son of a riverboat merchant. He attended the St. Petersburg Institute of Technology, where a teacher, Boris Rosing, inspired him to think about the creation of television. After doing graduate work in physics in France, he returned home to serve as a radio officer for the imperial army during the First World War. After the Bolsheviks seized power he fled to the United States.

When Zworykin arrived, all the television systems that anyone had devised were electromechanical, not electronic. He joined the Westinghouse Electric Corporation in 1920. In 1923 and 1924 he filed patent applications for a television transmission tube and a receiver—the first all-electronic television system. Both parts used large vacuum (cathode ray) tubes in which a stream of electrons was magnetically deflected to scan a screen.

In 1928 Zworykin obtained a color television patent. The next year he joined the Radio Corporation of America as a senior researcher. In 1929 he produced a picture tube that users could operate without specialized knowledge and could view under normal lighting conditions.

After 1945 television, which was free of charge as long as electricity was available and the set worked, quickly replaced cinema as the principal form of mass entertainment in the Western world. In 1951 color television broadcasting began in the United States.

Television has become a source of up-to-date information—political, economic, and scientific. It displays stock market prices second by second (on CNBC) and reports news continuously (on CNN). Technically it is a child not of photography, like the movies, but of the radio, for like the radio it is an electronic device and permits instant communication by live transmission.

The Computer Revolution

From the nineteenth century through World War II many individuals built computers. Computers used during the war contained thousands of vacuum tubes as switches. But the man who foresaw what lay ahead was a former child prodigy.

Norbert Wiener (1894–1964), a professor at MIT, developed much of the mathematics that made computing possible. Wiener was an unlikely culture hero. He was short, round, and myopic, with bulging eyes and a beard.[5] He was also notoriously absentminded. When he started on an errand he would forget what business he was about and ask a passerby, "Where am I going?" People loved to tell stories like that because Wiener had an awesome intellect.

Wiener was a child prodigy. He had the fortune and misfortune to be educated at home. His brilliant father tore him down as he built him up. Leo Wiener, a German Jew, was professor of Slavic languages at Harvard. Norbert had to struggle to maintain his self-respect in dealing with his father.

At the age of eighteen months Wiener learned the alphabet. At three he could read and write. He learned from his father until he reached the age of nine, when he entered high school. Two years later he graduated. In 1906 he enrolled in Tufts College, from which he graduated at the age of fourteen with a degree in mathematics. He earned a doctoral degree in philosophy from Harvard University at the age of eighteen.

During World War I he prepared firing tables for the army. Without computers, it was necessary to make ten thousand to a hundred thousand calculations to work out the trajectory of a single type of shell.

In 1919 Wiener joined the Mathematics Department at the Massachusetts Institute of Technology and stayed there all his working life. Ironically, he was a poor communicator, being a bad listener and a disorganized lecturer. Yet his research on communication brought glory to MIT.

During World War II he worked on artillery problems again, calculating how to point a gun to fire at a moving target. He also worked on the development of computers.

Wiener and a group of engineers, physiologists, and mathematicians first met together at Princeton in the late winter of 1943–1944. There they developed the concept of feedback. In 1948 Wiener published his influential book *Cybernetics*. He coined that word from the Greek word for "steersmanship" and used it to refer to the science of communication and control in living and nonliving systems.

His mathematical principles helped free him from the confines of mechanics. He saw that a machine that processed information was essentially made of information. It was a system of information transfer and could be constructed of any materials.

In the nineteenth century engineers had thought that the way to control a machine was to constrain its motion. They used devices such as cams, clutches, screws, and belts that were part of the mechanical infrastructure of gears and levers. Twentieth-century engineers developed instead electronic control devices that were physically and conceptually distinct from the machine.

Historically, computers have been of two types, analog and digital. Analog computers such as thermostats and speedometers measure a continuum of values. These values represent physical variables by means of electrical and mechanical substitutes. For example, the speedometer measures generator voltage, which represents the speed of the car. Analog computers work in real time. Their defect is that they are affected by the environment and qualities of the materials of which they are built.

Digital computers, on the other hand, measure only discrete values, usually binary signals (off-on, 0–1). These values represent letters, numbers, and other signs. Each signal equals a bit; eight bits equal a byte. Signals do not represent physical variables in real time, but rather inputs from the users at whatever time they choose. Digital computers are not affected by the environment and the qualities of the materials of which they are built.

During World War II British mathematicians and engineers devised a number of machines for decoding German messages. The Colossus, developed by a team headed by Alan Turing, was wholly electronic and used Boolean logic successfully. It was not a general-purpose computer.

During World War II American mathematicians and engineers at the University of Pennsylvania built ENIAC, a computer for making ballistic calculations (ENIAC stands for Electronic Numerical Integrator and Computer). It was faster than its predecessors and program-controlled. However, it weighed thirty tons, occupied fifteen hundred square feet of floor space, and contained eighteen thousand vacuum tubes, which often failed. It generated so much heat that it could be run only one hour at a time. During that hour the lights of Philadelphia would dim.

After the war American military men wanted to use computers to guide ballistic missiles. ENIAC was hopelessly heavy, and so miniaturization was needed. This was the motivation behind the development of the transistor as a substitute for the vacuum tube.[6]

The year 1948 was not only the date of publication of *Cybernetics* but also the year when the transistor (the word comes from *transfer* plus *resistor*), a device for amplifying and controlling electric currents, was invented. Three physicists at Lucent Technologies, William B. Shockley, Walter Brattain, and John Bardeen, were responsible. The three men found that some crystals, such as germanium, rectified and amplified electron flows better than others. To make a transistor they used germanium first, and later selenium and silicon with certain impurities. The transistor could serve as a switch, rectify current (make it go in one direction), and amplify it.

The transistor was tiny compared to the vacuum tube. It was said to have a "solid state" compared to the emptiness in the low-pressure vacuum tube.

The transistor generated little heat and used little power. It did not burn out like the vacuum tube. It was cheap, small, durable, and immune to vibration and shock. So important was it that its inventors received the Nobel Prize in physics in 1956.

By 1950 American and British computers had became electronic, digital, automatic, general-purpose, and program-controlled. They used binary arithmetic, which could be traced back to the ancient Greeks but was developed by G.W. Leibniz (1646–1716).

They also used certain logical gates—"and," "or," and "not"— invented by George Boole (1815–1864), a poor, self-taught Irish mathematics teacher.

In 1951 a Stanford University engineering professor, Frederick Terman, laid the foundations for the computer industry in northern California. He persuaded the university to assign some of its land to an industrial park. Then two of his former graduate students, William Hewlett and David Packard, built a plant in this park. It became the most successful industrial park in the world: the core of Silicon Valley. Hewlett and Packard became billionaires.

In 1955 William Shockley moved to Palo Alto and started manufacturing transistors. Two years later people began to use them to run computers. Monster-sized computers soon shrank.

In 1956 IBM developed the first computer language, FORTRAN, and programmers began to produce software. Before this engineers had to put the program of a computer in its hardware.

In nearby Mountain View in 1957 a group of scientists and engineers founded Fairchild Semiconductor Corporation. It made silicon chips containing transistors. Then some Fairchild leaders left and formed the Intel Corporation, which produced a chip that the user could program.

Robert Noyce of Fairchild Semiconductor invented the integrated circuit in 1959. He found that a conductive circuit board could be photoprinted on a silicon chip. It became possible to increase the speed and efficiency of these circuits, which contained many tiny transistors, by miniaturizing them and cramming them into a single chip.

In 1971 Marcian Hoff of Intel Corporation invented the microprocessor: a whole central processing unit on a single silicon chip. This is the brain of a computer. The industry-standard chip of 1990 held a half million transistors in the same space occupied by a single transistor in the early 1950s. Engineers installed chips to control watches, bathroom scales, gasoline pumps, microwave ovens, washing machines, elevators, automobiles, and airplanes.

Thus control over machines shifted from mechanical devices that were part of the infrastructure of the machine, to the vacuum tube, and then to silicon chips full of integrated circuits. This made possible the production of personal computers composed of a central processing unit (now contained in a silicon chip), a memory chip, and input and output devices. In 1967 engineers added a keyboard to computers for the input of data. In 1970 they devised the floppy disk for storing data.[7] The first personal computer to achieve great commercial success was the Apple II, built by Steve Jobs and Steve Wozniak and marketed in 1977. When their company went public in December 1980, its market value was $1.2 billion.

IBM, meanwhile, had not been left behind. In 1945 it was the leading business machine company in the world. It built electronic computers for the armed forces first, since these huge machines were too expensive for commercial consumption. Then in 1952 IBM began to produce machines for the open market. At first they were large machines that only big businesses could afford. Then in 1981 IBM came out with its personal computer. Two years later it marketed the first personal computer with a hard disk drive, programmable with commands from various kinds of software.

The personal computer can perform all information operations: collection (through its input facility), processing, storage (on tape or disks), retrieval, and transmission (through its modem and telephone lines or fiber optic cables). Instead of moving paper, modern transmitters of information move electrons. This requires very little energy and does not pollute the environment. So fax machines are eclipsing photocopiers; electronic mail is eclipsing letter writing. Telecommunication systems are changing from analog to digital. In the near future it will no longer be necessary to use a modem to convert digital signals from digital computers into analog signals for transmission.

Computer systems analysts now assemble various pieces of equipment as a workstation. They also connect workstations into a company network. Meanwhile universities, scientific institutions, business organizations, and individuals are getting connected with each other via the Internet.

The speed of information exchange is increasing, which predicts more rapid scientific and technological breakthroughs. Scientists are using computers to simulate everything from astronomical collisions to molecular reactions. Computers are not just handy devices to improve business efficiency: they stimulate the growth of many sciences as well.

Since 1965 silicon chips have doubled in power every two years. For the past two decades computing and communication technologies have been growing both more powerful and more cost-effective.[8]

Consequences

We know now that we live in the midst of a communication revolution. Its consequences continue to unfold.

Linking personal computers to office machines by telephone lines enables professionals and some corporate employees to telecommute. People who work at home can save on driving expenses, the cost of business clothes, cleaning bills, and restaurant checks. Parents can be near their children, especially when they are sick. Many managers are pleased with the arrangement: Mountain Bell says that its telecommuters are 35 to 40 percent more productive than their in-office counterparts.

Computers have made it possible to study quantitatively things that have many causes, such as the weather in a given place, historical events, economic trends, public opinion, criminal behavior, and academic performance. Once the data is entered into the computer, the computer can complete multiple regression analysis in a matter of seconds; formerly this analysis took days or weeks of laborious calculations.

Computers have opened up data bases, such as Medline (recent articles and books on health), and research library catalogs. One can correspond by e-mail with individual researchers on the cutting edge of their field.

However, computers have contributed to the increasing inequality of wealth and power in developed societies. In both working-class and middle-class families it is often necessary for both parents to work, for one parent to hold two jobs, or even for both parents to hold two jobs. Only in this way can they maintain their standard of living and pay for their children's college education. Illiterate and unskilled workers are less and less employable except in businesses paying less than the minimum wage (sweatshops) and in harvesting crops.

Between 1945 and 1973 commentators saw only the underclass as "not needed." Beginning in 1973, as manufacturing industries dwindled in developed countries, manufacturers saw more and more blue-collar and no-collar workers as "not needed." Those who remained in their jobs suffered a gradual decline in their standard of living.

In the 1980s in industries employing many white-collar workers, executives began to buy large numbers of personal computers without reducing their white-collar work force. The result was that the machines produced more documents but worker productivity did not increase. By 1990 many executives resolved to make better use of computers by making permanent reductions in their work force, or "downsizing." Then white-collar workers too felt the pain of being "not needed." Some lost their jobs; if they found another job, it was often part time and/or at lower pay. Even middle managers suffered.

Simultaneously a "braining" of the economy occurred. People of average intelligence and social skills had more difficulty getting promoted. Only highly intelligent and socially skilled individuals went on the fast track.

Intelligent employees were important because product quality was more important. As the populations of developed and developing countries grew and as markets at home and abroad grew larger, slight improvements in corporate products yielded greater profits, and slight deficiencies caused greater losses. Even expert advertising and aggressive salesmanship might not compensate for a slightly inferior product.

Another related development was that women with college degrees were able to compete for jobs with higher pay and greater power. At last careers were opened to female talents. However, most women who joined the competition paid a penalty: They often had to postpone having children. They had fewer children or none at all. Meanwhile, less motivated and less educated women did not use birth control consistently and got pregnant as teenagers. The welfare system reinforced this tendency. Not surprisingly, the relationship between fertility and education took a dive: the less education, the greater the fertility (about three children per woman); the more education, the lesser the fertility (about one child). This was the opposite of the situation that had prevailed before 1850, when the higher the social rank, the greater the fertility, and the lower the social rank, the lesser the fertility. Instead of being top-heavy, developed societies became bottom-heavy.

The above trend was a dysgenic development, that is, detrimental to the hereditary qualities of our species. It was also expensive, for the people who were least needed in the computerized economy were reproducing at a faster rate than those who were most needed.[9] Consequently the social burden of the poor and the criminal increased. As the baby boom generation begins to retire, the increasing proportion of elderly persons in the population will add to the social burden.

The need for 80 percent of the work force is declining much faster than their net reproduction rate. What good will it do to send more people to college if suitable jobs for them do not exist?

Conclusion

Judging from the past, the impact of a new communication technology depends on the degree to which it is user-friendly, its affordability, and the proportion of literates (or computer literates) in a population (which equals the market for information). For maximum business activity, the people in the market must be literate in a standardized vernacular language.

If the new technology is user-friendly, affordable, and finds a large market, it will greatly facilitate other innovations. These innovations will be technological, economic, political, scientific, and literary.

Notes

1. Hugh G.J. Aitken, *The Origins of Radio,* p. 32.
2. Stanley Leinwold, *From Spark to Satellite: A History of Radio Communication,* pp. 1–58.
3. Helen M. Fessenden, *Fessenden, Builder of Tomorrows,* p. 153.
4. Larry Hirschhorn, *Beyond Mechanization,* p. 34.
5. Norbert Wiener, *Ex-Prodigy: My Childhood and Youth;* Wiener, *I Am a Mathematician.*
6. David Ritchie, *The Computer Pioneers,* pp. 62–107; Stan Augarten, *Bit by Bit: An Illustrated History of Computers,* p. 90; Ronald W. Clark, *Works of Man,* pp. 284–87.
7. Joel Shurkin, *Engines of the Mind: A History of the Computer,* pp. 300–10.
8. Michael A. Dertauzos, "Communications, Computers, and Networks," pp. 62–69.
9. Richard Herrnstein and Charles Murray, *The Bell Curve,* p. 349.

CONCLUSION

In the introduction I suggested four major causes of breakthroughs in world history. They were climatic change, change in communication and transportation technology, competition between political elites, and scientific discoveries. Why did I choose these four and exclude so many other factors?

Breakthroughs in world history were my subject matter, not all of world history. I did not try to describe everyday life, state and local history, or the struggles between political factions within a state or between political elites of different states. Such material serves to describe the fabric of human life; it does not explain fundamental changes in that fabric.

There are always many causal factors at work in any situation. To consider all of them would be to describe how a society worked, not to explain how it changed. My aim was to choose and use only a minimum of causal factors, not to make a market list.

These factors were the most important that I could identify. What I did resembles what statisticians do at the end of an analysis. In the last multiple regression run they include only the predictor variables that account for at least 5 percent of the variance in the criterion variable. In my experience, these predictor variables, two to five in number, account for 60 to 80 percent of the variance.

The following are my justifications for excluding other causal factors.

1. *Other important technologies: military, productive (agricultural and industrial), and medical.* Improvements in communication and transportation technology increase the speed at which facts and ideas spread. This increases the options and resources of inventors in all fields.

There were few medical improvements before 1914. Prior to 1870 artisans devised improvements in military and productive technologies. Innovation was slow and discontinuous. The great leap forward came after technology and science were wed, about 1870.

2. *The role of founders of religion and philosophers.* These people took the "road less traveled by." When they did what was right they were often not rewarded but punished. This is a book about the road more traveled by, however. If I could, I would rather walk with Jesus of Nazareth on the less traveled road than with Augustus Caesar on the more traveled road. But I can't follow both roads in one book.

3. *The role of common people and leaders of revolutions.* Political specialists (now professionals) usually win. They make the big decisions, officially or unofficially. Revolutionary leaders usually lose.

4. *Dietary changes.* They are important but only derivative causes of breakthroughs in world history. Climatic changes, the availability of communication and transportation technology, exploration and discovery, trade, and population growth are probably the most important causes of dietary change.

5. *Accidents.* Some scientific discoveries, such as those of Pasteur, Roentgen, and Becquerel, are in part accidental. But the only people who can recognize an anomaly when they see it are those who know what is typical. Only those who ask a question can recognize the answer when it appears accidentally. As Louis Pasteur said, "Chance favors only the prepared mind."

All good political and military leaders prepare for contingencies. They calculate risks before taking action. They have fallback arrangements. Political and military accidents happen, for better or for worse, but most of them do not cause breakthroughs in world history.

I have not written this book as a guide to policy planning. The explanations in it are retrodictive, not predictive. Yet I think it plausible that climatic changes, changes in communication and transportation technologies, variation in the competition between political elites, and scientific discoveries will continue to be weighty causes of breakthrough in our future.

BIBLIOGRAPHY

Adshead, S.A.M. 1992. *Salt and Civilization.* New York: St. Martins.

Aitken, Hugh G.J. 1976. *Sparks and Syntony: The Origins of Radio.* New York: Wiley.

Albritton, Claude C. 1980. *The Abyss of Time.* San Francisco: Freeman and Cooper.

Alexandre, Pierre. 1987. *Le Climat en Europe au moyen age, 1000–1425.* Paris: Ecole des hautes etudes en sciences sociales.

Allen, Garland. 1975. *Life Science in the Twentieth Century.* New York: Wiley.

Anderson, E.N. 1988. *The Food of China.* New Haven: Yale University Press.

Angle, H. Larry. 1994. *First Among Friends.* Oxford: Oxford University Press.

Aries, Philippe, and Georges Duby, eds. 1988. *A History of Private Life,* vol. 2, *Revelations of the Medieval World.* Cambridge, MA: Harvard University Press.

Armytage, W.H.G. 1961. *A Social History of Engineering.* Cambridge, MA: MIT Press.

Ashtor, Eliyahu. 1983. *Levant Trade in the Later Middle Ages.* Princeton: Princeton University Press.

Asimov, Isaac. 1989. *Asimov's Chronology of Science and Discovery.* New York: Harper and Row.

———. 1982. *Asimov's Biographical Encyclopedia of Science and Technology.* 2d ed. New York: Doubleday.

Augarten, Stan. 1984. *Bit by Bit: An Illustrated History of Computers.* New York: Ticknor and Fields.

Avrin, Leila. 1991. *Scribes, Script and Books.* Chicago: American Library Association.

Badash, Lawrence. 1965. "Chance Favors the Prepared Mind; Henri Becquerel and the Discovery of Radioactivity." *Archives internationales d'histoire des sciences* 18, pp. 55–66.

———. 1989. "The Age of the Earth Debate." *Scientific American* 261 (August), pp. 90–96.

Baillie, Michael G.L. 1994. "Dendrochronology Raises Question about Nature of AD536 Dust-Veil Event." *The Holocene* 4 (2), pp. 212–17.

———. 1988. "Irish Tree Rings, Santorini, and Volcano Dust Veils." *Nature* 332 (6162): 344–46.

Bairoch, Paul. 1988. *Cities and Economic Development: From the Dawn of History to the Present.* Chicago: University of Chicago Press.

————. 1990. "The Impact of Crop Yields, Agricultural Productivity and Transport Costs on Urban Growth Between 1800 and 1910." In *Urbanization and History,* Ad van der Woude et al., eds. Oxford: Clarendon Press, p. 134–51.

Barber, Elizabeth W. 1994. *Women's Work: The First 20,000 Years.* New York: Norton.

Barbour, Hugh. 1964. *The Quakers in Puritan England.* New Haven: Yale University Press.

Basalla, George. 1988. *The Evolution of Technology.* Cambridge: Cambridge University Press.

Beardall, J.M., and Miller, J.D. 1994. "Diseases in Humans with Mycotoxins as Possible Cause." In *Mycotoxins in Grain,* ed. J.D. Miller and H.L. Trenholm. St. Paul: Eagan Press.

Begley, Vimala, and Richard D. De Puma, eds. 1991. *Rome and India: The Ancient Sea Trade.* Madison: University of Wisconsin Press.

Behrens, C.B.A. 1985. *Society, Government and the Enlightenment: The Experiences of Eighteenth-Century France and Prussia.* New York: Thames and Hudson.

Bell, David. 1995. " 'Lingua Populi, Lingua Dei': Language, Religion, and the Origins of the French Revolution," *American Historical Review* 100 (5), pp. 1403–37.

Bergland, Richard. 1985. *The Fabric of the Mind.* Harmondsworth: Penguin.

Bernal, J.D. 1965. *Science in History.* New York: Hawthorn.

Berry, R.J., ed. 1982. *Charles Darwin: A Commemoration (1882–1892).* London: Academic Press.

Betzig, Laura. 1986. *Despotism and Differential Reproduction: A Darwinian View of History.* New York: Aldine, esp. pp. 69–97.

Blanning, T.C.W. 1987. *The French Revolution: Aristocrats Versus Bourgeois?* Atlantic Highlands, NJ: Humanities Press International.

Blumenberg, Hans. 1987. *The Genesis of the Copernican World.* Cambridge: Cambridge University Press.

Boardman, John, et al., eds. 1986. *The Oxford History of the Classical World.* Oxford: Oxford University Press.

Boone, James L. 1986. "Noble Family Structure and Expansionist Warfare in the Late Middle Ages." In *Rethinking Human Adaptation,* R. Dyson-Hudson and M.A. Little, eds., pp. 79–96. Denver: Westview,

————. 1988. "Parental Investment, Social Subordination, and Population Processes Among the Fifteenth- and Sixteenth-century Portuguese Nobility." In *Human Reproductive Behavior,* L. Betzig et al., eds., pp. 201–20. Cambridge: Cambridge University Press.

Bouwsma, William. 1995. "Liberty in the Renaissance and Reformation." In R.W. Davis, ed., *The Origins of Modern Freedom in the West,* pp. 203–34. Stanford: Stanford University Press.

Braithwaite, William C. 1961. *The Beginnings of Quakerism,* 2d ed. Cambridge: Cambridge University Press.

Brandstrom, A., and L.G. Tedebrand, eds. 1988. *Society, Health and Population During the Demographic Transition.* Stockholm: Almquist and Wiksell International.

Braudel, Fernand. 1981. *Civilization and Capitalism, 15th to 18th Century,* vol. 1, *The Structures of Everyday Life.* New York: Harper.

Bray, Francesca. 1984. *Science and Civilization in China,* vol. 6, part 2, *Agriculture.* Cambridge: Cambridge University Press.

Brent, Peter. 1981. *Charles Darwin: A Man of Enlarged Curiosity.* New York: Norton.

Brice, William C., ed. 1978. *The Environmental History of the Near and Middle East Since the Last Ice Age.* London: Academic Press.

Bridenbaugh, Carl. 1968. *Vexed and Troubled Englishmen, 1590–1642.* New York: Oxford University Press.

Brief, K.R., et al. 1990. "A 1400-Year Tree-ring Record of Summer Temperatures in Fennoscandia," *Nature* 346, pp. 434–39.

Brunekreef, Bert et al. 1989. "Home Dampness and Respiratory Morbidity in Children, " *American Review of Respiratory Diseases* 140, pp. 1363–67.

Bulliet, R.W. 1975. *The Camel and the Wheel.* Cambridge: Harvard University Press.

Burke, James. 1978. *Connections.* Boston: Little, Brown.

Burke, Peter. 1972. *The Italian Renaissance: Culture and Society in Italy.* Princeton: Princeton University Press.

Butzer, Karl W. 1958. *Quaternary Stratigraphy and Climate in the Near East.* Bonn: Dummleis Press.

Cardwell, D.S.L. 1972. *Turning Points in Western Technology.* New York: Science History Publishers.

Casson, Lionel. 1984. *Ancient Trade and Society.* Detroit: Wayne State University Press.

Chadwick, Owen. 1975. *The Secularization of the European Mind in the Nineteenth Century.* Cambridge: Cambridge University Press.

Chaffee, John W. 1986. *The Thorny Gates of Learning in Sung China: A Social History of Examinations.* Cambridge: Cambridge University Press.

Chandler, Alfred D. 1965. *The Railroads.* New York: Harcourt, Brace, World.

Chang, Chiachen, and Lin, Zhiguang. 1992. *The Climate of China.* New York: Wiley.

Chao, Kang. 1986. *Men and Land in Chinese History: An Economic Analysis.* Stanford: Stanford University Press.

Chartier, Roger, ed. 1989. *A History of Private Life: Passions of the Renaissance.* Cambridge, MA: Harvard University Press.

Christensen, Clyde M., and Richard A. Meronuck. 1986. *Quality Maintenance in Stored Grains and Cereals.* Minneapolis: University of Minnesota.

Christianson, Gale E. 1984. *In the Presence of the Creator.* New York: Free Press.

———. 1995. *Edwin Hubble: Mariner of the Nebulae.* New York: Farrar, Straus, Giroux.

Cipolla, Carlo. 1980. *Before the Industrial Revolution: European Society and Economy, 1000–1700,* 2d ed.. New York: Norton.

Clark, Ronald W. 1985. *Works of Man.* New York: Viking.

———. 1984. *The Survival of Charles Darwin.* New York: Random House.

Clutton-Brock, Juliet. 1992. *Horse Power: A History of the Horse and Donkey in Human Societies.* Cambridge: Harvard University Press.

Cohen, I. Bernard. 1985. *Revolution in Science.* Cambridge, MA: Belknap Press.

Cohen, Mark N. 1989. *Health and the Rise of Civilization.* New Haven: Yale University Press.

Collins, E.J.T. 1975. "Dietary Change and Cereal Consumption in Britain in the Nineteenth Century, " *Agricultural History Review* 23 (part 2), pp. 97–115.

Connell, W.F. 1980. *A History of Education in the Twentieth-Century World.* New York: Teachers College Press.

Coote, Robert B. 1990. *Early Israel.* Minneapolis: Fortress.

Crafts, N.F.R., and C.K. Harley. 1992. "Output Growth and the British Industrial Revolution: A Restatement of the Crafts-Harley View," *Economic History Review* 14 (4), pp. 703–30.

Crapo, Lawrence. 1985. *Hormones: The Messengers of Life.* New York: W.H. Freeman.

Crawford, E. Margaret, ed. 1989. *Famine: The Irish Experience, 900–1900.* Edinburgh: J. Donald.

Crease, Robert P., and Charles C. Mann. 1986. *The Second Creation: Makers of the Revolution in Twentieth-Century Physics.* New York: Macmillan.

Crick, Francis. 1988. *What Mad Pursuit.* New York: Basic Books.

Crone, Patricia. 1986. "The Tribe and the State." In *States in History,* John A. Hall, ed., pp. 47–77. Oxford: Blackwell,

Crossan, John D. 1991. *The Historical Jesus: The Life of a Mediterranean Jewish Peasant.* San Francisco: Harper.

Crouch, Tom D. 1989. *The Bishop's Boys.* New York: Norton.

Crowley, Thomas. 1991. *Paleoclimatology.* New York: Oxford University Press.

Crumley, Carole L. 1994. "The Ecology of Conquest, Contrasting Agropastoral and Agricultural Societies' Adaptation to Climatic Change." In *Historical Ecology,* Carole L. Crumley, ed., pp. 183–202. Santa Fe: School of American Research Press.

Curtis, Richard K. 1982. *Evolution or Extinction.* Oxford: Oxford University Press.

Dales, R.E., et al. 1991. "Respiratory Health Effects of Home Dampness and Molds Among Children, " *American Journal of Epidemiology* 134, pp. 199–203.

———. 1991. "Adverse Health Effects in Adults Exposed to Home Dampness and Molds." *American Review of Respiratory Diseases* 143, pp. 505–9.

———. 1994. "Immunotoxic Effects of Mycotoxins." In J.D. Miller and H.L. Trenholm, eds., *Mycotoxins in Grains,* pp. 339–58. St. Paul: Eagan Press.

Damasio, Antonio R. 1994. *Descartes' Error.* New York: G.B. Putnam.

Darwin, Charles. 1985. *The Autobiography of Charles Darwin, 1809–1882.* New York: Norton.

Davis, John Bunnell. 1817. *A Cursory Inquiry into some of the Principal Causes of Mortality among Children.* London, n.p.

Deane, Phyllis. 1979. *The First Industrial Revolution,* 2d ed.. Cambridge: Cambridge University Press.

De'er, Zhang. 1994. "Evidence of the Medieval Warm Period in China," *Climatic Change* 26 (2–3), pp. 289–97.

Delear, Frank J. 1969. *Igor Sikorsky: His Three Careers in Aviation.* New York: Dodd Mead.

Dennett, Daniel C. 1995. *Darwin's Dangerous Idea.* New York: Simon and Schuster.

Derry, Thomas K. 1979. *A History of Scandinavia.* Minneapolis: University of Minnesota Press.

Dertauzos, Michael A. 1991. "Communications, Computers, and Networks," *Scientific American* (September), pp. 62–69.

de Waal, Frans. 1996. *Good Natured: The Origins of Right and Wrong in Humans and Other Animals*. Cambridge, MA: Harvard University Press.

Dickinson, H.W. 1936. *James Watt: Craftsman and Engineer*. Cambridge: Cambridge University Press.

————. 1973. *Matthew Boulton*. Cambridge: Cambridge University Press.

Dictionary of Scientific Biography. 1981. Ed. Charles C. Gillispie. New York: Scribners. "Oswald Avery," vol. 1, pp. 342–43; "Henri Becquerel," vol. 1, pp. 558–60, "Eduard Buchner," vol. 1; "Robert Fitzroy"; "Galileo Galilei," vol. 5, pp. 237–50; "James Hutton," vol. 6, pp. 577–89; "Charles Lyell"; "Wilhelm Roentgen," vol. 11, pp. 529–31.

Dijkstra, Lyanne, et al. 1990. "Respiratory Health Effects of the Indoor Environment in a Population of Dutch Children." *American Review of Respiratory Diseases* 142, pp. 1172–78.

Dols, Michael. 1977. *The Black Death in the Middle East*. Princeton: Princeton University Press.

Doyle, William. 1988. *Origins of the French Revolution,* 2d ed. Oxford: Oxford University Press.

Duby, George. 1977. *The Chivalrous Society*. London: Arnold.

Dyson-Hudson, R., and M.A. Little, eds. 1986. *Rethinking Human Adaptation*. Denver: Westview Press.

Eastman, Lloyd F. 1988. *Family, Fields and Ancestors: Constancy and Change in China's Social and Economic History, 1550–1949*. New York: Oxford University Press.

Eisenstein, Elizabeth L. 1979. *The Printing Press as an Agent of Change: Communications and Cultural Transformations in Early Modern Europe,* 2 vols. Cambridge: Cambridge University Press.

Elwin, Mark. 1973. *The Pattern of the Chinese Past*. Stanford: Stanford University Press.

Fairbank, John K. 1992. *China: A New History*. Cambridge: Harvard University Press.

Fang, Jin-Qi, and Guo Liu. 1992. "Relationship Between Climatic Change and the Nomadic Southward Migration in Eastern Asia During Historical Times," *Climatic Change* 22 (2), pp. 151–168.

Fang, Jin-Qi, and Pao-Kuan Wang. 1980. "On the Relationship between Winter Thunder and Climatic Change in China in the Past 2200 Years," *Climatic Change* 3, pp. 37–46.

Faul, Henry, and Carol Faul. 1983. *It Began with a Stone*. New York: Wiley.

Feldman, Anthony, and Peter Ford. 1979. *Scientists and Inventors*. New York: Facts on File.

Ferris, Timothy. 1988. *Coming of Age in the Milky Way*. New York: Morrow.

Fessenden, Helen M. 1974. *Fessenden, Builder of Tomorrows*. New York: Arno Press.

Feuerwerker, Albert. 1990. "Chinese Economic History in Comparative Perspective." In *Heritage of China,* Paul S. Ropp, ed. Berkeley: University of California Press.

Fink-Gremmels, J. 1990. "Mycotoxins: The Situation in Europe with Special

Emphasis on West Germany," *Veterinarian and Human Toxicology* 3, pp. 40–41.

Finne, K.N. 1987. *Igor Sikorsky: The Russian Years.* Washington, D.C.: Smithsonian Institution Press.

Floud, Roderick, and Donald McCloskey, 1981. *The Economic History of Britain since 1700,* vol. 1. Cambridge: Cambridge University Press.

Fox, George. 1911. *The Journal of George Fox,* 2 vols. Cambridge: Cambridge University Press.

Fowler, Brenda. "Find Suggests that Weaving Preceded Settled Life." *New York Times,* May 9, 1995, pp. C1, C10.

Frankfort, H., and H.A. Frankfort. 1946. *The Intellectual Adventure of Ancient Man.* Chicago: University of Chicago Press.

Fridlizius, Gunnar 1988. "Sex Differential Mortality and Socio-economic Change: Sweden, 1750–1910." In *Society, Health and Population during the Demographic Transition,* A. Brandstrom and L.G. Tedebrand, eds. Stockholm: Almquist and Wiksell International.

Gabriel, Richard A. 1990. *The Culture of War: Invention and Early Development.* New York: Greenwood Press.

Garnsey, Peter, and Richard Salter. 1987. *The Roman Empire: Economy, Society, and Culture.* Cambridge: Cambridge University Press.

Garrison, Ervan. 1991. *A History of Engineering and Technology.* Boca Raton: CRC Press.

Gascoigne, John. 1990. "A Reappraisal of the Role of the Universities in the Scientific Revolution." In *Reappraisals of the Scientific Revolution,* David C. Lindberg and Robert Westman, eds., pp. 207–260. Cambridge: Cambridge University Press.

Gauthier-Pilters, Hilde. 1981. *The Camel: Its Evolution, Ecology, Behavior, and Relationship to Man.* Chicago: University of Chicago Press.

Gellner, Ernest. 1983. *Nations and Nationalism.* Ithaca: Cornell University Press.

Geyer, Felix, and J. van der Zouwen. 1986. *Sociocybernetic Paradoxes: Observation, Control and Evolution of Self-Steering Systems.* London: Sage Publications.

Geymonat, Ludovico. 1965. *Galileo Galilei.* New York: McGraw Hill.

Gille, Bertrand. 1986. *The History of Techniques,* vol. 1. New York: Gordon and Breach.

Gimbutas, Marija. 1991. *The Civilization of the Goddess.* San Francisco: Harper.

Goldstone, Jack. 1991. *Revolution and Rebellion in the Early Modern World.* Berkeley: University of California Press.

Goubert, J.P. 1989. *The Conquest of Water: The Advent of Health in the Industrial Age.* Princeton: Princeton University Press.

Grant, Edward. 1984. "Science and the Medieval University." In J.M. Kittelson, ed., *Rebirth, Reform, and Resilience: Universities in Transition, 1300–1700.* Columbus: Ohio State University Press.

Grayson, D.K. 1983. *The Establishment of Human Antiquity.* New York: Academic Press.

Griffiths, Jeremy, and Derek Pearsall. 1989. *Book Production and Publishing in Britain, 1375–1475.* Cambridge: Cambridge University Press.

Grigg, David. 1982. *The Dynamics of Agricultural Change.* New York: St. Martin's.

Guenee, Bernard. 1985. *States and Rulers in Later Medieval Europe*. London: Blackwell.

Gumilev, L.N. 1967."Heterochronism in the Moisture Supply of Eurasia in the Middle Ages." *Soviet Geography.*

Gunn, Joel D. 1994. "Global Climate and Regional Biocultural Diversity." In *Historical Ecology,* ed. Carole L. Crumley, pp. 67–99. Santa Fe: School of American Research Press.

Guyford, Steven H., and James J. Haggerty. 1965. *Flight.* New York: Time Books.

Hale, John R. 1971. *Renaissance Europe: Individual and Society, 1480–1520.* New York: Harper and Row.

Hall, Rupert. 1983. *The Revolution in Science, 1500–1750,* 2d ed. London: Longmans.

Hammer, C.U., et al. 1980. "Greenland Ice Sheet Evidence of Post-glacial Volcanism and Its Climatic Impact," *Nature* 288, pp. 230–35.

Harline, Craig E. 1987. *Pamphlets, Printing and Political Culture in the Early Dutch Republic.* Dordrecht: Nijhoff.

Harris, Marvin. 1985. *Good to Eat: Riddles of Food and Culture.* New York: Simon and Schuster.

Harris, William V. 1989. *Ancient Literacy.* Cambridge, MA: Harvard University Press.

Hassan, F.A., and B.R. Strecki. 1987. "Nile Floods and Climatic Change." In *Climate: History, Periodicity, and Predictability*, ed. M.R. Rampino et al., pp. 37–46. New York: Van Nostrand.

Hawkins, G.S. 1965. *Stonehenge Decoded.* New York: Delta Dell.

Headrick, Daniel R. 1981. *The Tools of Empire: Technology and European Imperialism in the Nineteenth Century.* New York: Oxford University Press.

————. 1991. *Telecommunication and International Politics, 1851–1945.* New York: Oxford University Press.

Heers, Jacques. 1977. *Family Clans in the Middle Ages.* New York: North Holland Press.

Helden, Albert van. 1977. *The Invention of the Telescope.* Philadelphia: American Philosophical Society.

Henry, Donald O. 1989. *From Foraging to Agriculture: The Levant at the End of the Ice Age.* Philadelphia: University of Pennsylvania Press.

Herlihy, David. 1973. "Three Patterns of Social Mobility in Medieval History," *Journal of Interdisciplinary History* 3 (4), pp. 623–47.

Herlihy, David, and Christiane Klapisch-Zuber. 1985. *Tuscans and Their Families.* New Haven: Yale University Press.

Herrnstein, Richard, and Charles Murray. 1994. *The Bell Curve.* New York: Free Press.

Heyerdahl, Thor. 1979. *Early Man and the Ocean.* Garden City: Doubleday.

Hill, Christopher. 1972. *The World Turned Upside Down.* New York: Viking.

Hillel, Daniel J. 1991. *Out of the Earth: Civilization and the Life of the Soil.* New York: Free Press.

Hingham, Charles, ed. 1989. *The Archaeology of Mainland Southeast Asia.* Cambridge: Cambridge University Press.

Hirschhorn, Larry. 1984. *Beyond Mechanization.* Cambridge, MA: MIT Press.

Hobsbawm, Eric, and Terence Ranger, eds. 1983. *The Invention of Tradition*. Cambridge: Cambridge University Press.

Hoffman, Philip T., and Kathryn Norberg. 1994. *Fiscal Crisis, Liberty, and Representative Government*. Stanford: Stanford University Press.

Hollister, C. Warren. 1991. *Roots of the Western Tradition: A Short History of the Ancient World*, 5th ed. New York: McGraw Hill.

Holmberg, Scott D. 1990. "The Rise of Tuberculosis in America before 1820," *American Review of Respiratory Diseases* 142 (5), pp. 1228–32.

Hourani, Albert. 1991. *The History of the Arab Peoples*. Cambridge, MA: Harvard University Press.

Howard, Fred. *Wilbur and Orville*. 1987. New York: Knopf.

Huff, Toby E. 1993. *The Rise of Early Modern Science: Islam, China, and the West*. Cambridge: Cambridge University Press.

Hunt, Lynn. 1984. *Politics, Culture and Class in the French Revolution*. Berkeley: University of California Press.

Ihde, Aaron J. 1964. *The Development of Modern Chemistry*. New York: Harper and Row.

Isichei, Elizabeth. 1970. *Victorian Quakers*. Oxford: Oxford University Press.

Israel, Jonathan. 1995. *The Dutch Republic: Its Rise, Greatness, and Fall, 1479–1806*. Oxford: Oxford University Press.

Jacob, Margaret. 1988. *The Cultural Meaning of the Scientific Revolution*. Philadelphia: Temple University Press.

Jenkins, E.N. 1979. *Radioactivity*. London: Wykeham Publications.

Josephson, Matthew. 1959. *Edison*. New York: McGraw Hill.

Keller, Alex. 1983. *The Infancy of Atomic Physics*. Oxford: Clarendon Press.

King, Henry C. 1955. *The History of the Telescope*. Cambridge, MA: Sky Publishers.

Kirby. M.W. 1984. *Men of Business and Politics: The Rise and Fall of the Quaker Pease Dynasty of North-East England, 1700–1943*. London: Allen and Unwin.

Kittelson, J.M., ed. 1984. *Rebirth, Reform, and Resilience: Universities in Transition, 1300–1700*. Columbus: Ohio State University Press.

Koenigsberger, H.G. 1987. *Medieval Europe, 400–1500*. London: Longman.

Kolb, Rocky. 1996. *Blind Watchers of the Sky*. New York: Addison-Wesley.

Kuiper-Goodman, T. 1990. "Risk Assessment to Humans of Mycotoxins in Animal-derived Products," *Veterinary and Human Toxicology* 12, pp. 6–13.

Lacey, Robert. 1986. *Ford: The Man and the Machine*. Boston: Little Brown.

Ladurie, Emmanuel Le Roy. 1971. *Time of Feast, Time of Famine: A History of Climate Since the Year 1000*. New York: Doubleday.

Lamb, Hubert H. 1970. "Volcanic Dust in the Atmosphere, with a Chronology and Assessment of Its Meteorological Significance," *Philosophical Transactions, Royal Society of London*, Ser. 1, 266, pp. 425–533.

———. 1977. *Climate, Present, Past, and Future*, vol. 2. London: Methuen.

———. 1982. *Climate, History and the Modern World*. London: Methuen.

Langford, Jerome J. 1971. *Galileo, Science and the Church*, rev. ed. Ann Arbor, MI: University of Michigan Press.

Lay, Maxwell G. 1993. *Ways of the World: A History of the World's Roads*. New Brunswick, NJ: Rutgers University Press.

Leakey, Maeve, et al., 1995. "New Four Million Year Hominid Species from Kanapoi and Alia Bay, Kenya," *Nature* 376 (6541), pp. 555–71.

Leakey, Richard. 1994. *The Origin of Humankind.* New York: Basic Books.

Leighton, Albert C. 1972. *Transport and Communication in Early Medieval Europe,* A.D. 500–1100. New York: Barnes and Noble.

Leinwold, Stanley. 1979. *From Spark to Satellite: A History of Radio Communication.* New York: Scribners.

Lemonick, Michael D. 1994. "How Man Began," *Time,* March 14, pp. 80–87.

Lewis, Bernard. 1995. *The Middle East: A Brief History of the Last 2000 Years.* New York: Scribner.

Lewit, Tamara. 1991. *Agricultural Production in the Roman Economy,* A.D. 200–400. Oxford: B.A.R.

Lowe, Rudolf. 1985. "Adam Smith's System of Equilibrium Growth." In *Essays on Adam Smith,* A. S. Skinner and T. Wilson, eds. Oxford: Oxford University Press.

Lucas, J.E. 1979. "Wilberforce and Huxley: A Legendary Encounter," *Historical Journal* 22, pp. 313–30.

Lyons, M. 1989. "Weather, Famine, Pestilence and Plague in Ireland, 900–1500." In *Famine: The Irish Experience, 900–1900,* E. Margaret Crawford, ed. Edinburgh: J. Donald.

Mabee, Carleton. 1969. *The American Leonardo: A Life of Samuel F.B. Morse.* New York: Knopf.

McClelland, Charles E. 1980. *State, Society and University in Germany, 1700–1914.* Cambridge: Cambridge University Press.

McEvedy, Colin, and Richard Jones. 1978. *Atlas of World Population History.* Harmondsworth: Penguin.

McKenzie, A.E. 1960. *The Major Achievements of Sciences,* vol. 2. Cambridge: Cambridge University Press.

MacMullen, Ramsay. 1988. *Corruption and the Decline of Rome.* New Haven: Yale University Press.

McNeill, William. 1987. "The Eccentricity of Wheels, or European Transportation in Historical Perspective," *American Historical Review* 92 (5). pp. 1111–26.

McNeish, Richard S. 1992. *Origins of Agriculture and Settled Life.* Norman: University of Oklahoma Press.

Marks, Steven G. 1991. *Road to Power: The Trans-Siberian Railroad and the Colonization of Asian Russia, 1850–1917.* Ithaca: Cornell University Press.

Mass, Clifford F., and David A. Portman. 1989. "Major Volcanic Eruptions and Climate: A Critical Evaluation," *Journal of Climate* 2 (6), pp. 566–93.

Matossian, Mary K. 1985. "Death in London: 1750–1909," *Journal of Interdisciplinary History* 16 (2), pp. 183–97.

———. 1986a. "Climate, Crops, and Natural Increase in Rural Russia, 1860–1913." *Slavic Review* 45 (3), pp. 457–69.

———. 1986b. "Did Mycotoxins Play a Role in Bubonic Plague Epidemics?" *Perspectives in Biology and Medicine* 29 (2): 244–56.

———. 1989. *Poisons of the Past.* New Haven: Yale University Press.

———. 1991. "Fertility Decline in Europe, 1875–1913: Was Zinc Deficiency the Cause?" *Perspectives in Biology and Medicine* 34 (4), pp. 604–16.

————. 1996. "Effects of Natural Fungal Toxins on Fertility and Mortality in Connecticut, 1660–1900," *Journal of Nutritional and Environmental Medicine* 6, pp. 285–300.

Maxwell, Mary. 1990. *Morality Among Nations: An Evolutionary View.* Albany: SUNY Press.

Mayr, Ernst. 1982. *The Growth of Biological Thought.* Cambridge: Harvard University Press.

————. 1988. *Toward a New Philosophy of Biology.* Cambridge: Harvard University Press.

Mayr, Otto. 1986. *Authority, Liberty and Automatic Machinery in Early Modern Europe.* Baltimore: Johns Hopkins University Press.

Mellersh, H.E.L. 1968. *Fitzroy of the Beagle.* London: Hart Davis.

Meyer, F. 1977. "Evolution de l'alimentation des français, 1781–1972," *Gastro-Enterologie Clinique et Biologique* 12, pp. 1043–51.

Miller, J.D., and H.L. Trenholm, eds. *Mycotoxins in Grains.* St. Paul: Eagan Press.

Miskimin, Harry. 1977. *The Economy of Late Renaissance Europe, 1460–1600.* Cambridge: Cambridge University Press.

Mitchell, B.R. 1980. *European Historical Statistics, 1750–1975,* 2d ed. New York: Facts on File.

Moise, Edward 1977. "Downward Social Mobility in Pre-revolutionary China," *Modern China* 3, pp. 3–32.

Mokhtar, G., ed. 1990. *General History of Africa,* vol. 2. Berkeley: Unesco.

Mokyr, Joel. 1985. *The Economics of the Industrial Revolution.* Totowa, NJ: Rowman and Allan.

————. 1990. *The Lever of Riches.* New York: Oxford University Press.

Muirhead, James P. 1858. *The Life of James Watt.* London: J. Murray.

Muller, Detlef K., et al., 1987. *The Rise of Modern Educational Systems.* Cambridge: Cambridge University Press.

Multhauf, Robert P. 1978. *Neptune's Gift: A History of Common Salt.* Baltimore: Johns Hopkins University Press.

Murray, A. 1978. *Reason and Society in the Middle Ages.* Oxford: Oxford University Press.

Myers, A.R. 1975. *Parliaments and Estates in Europe to 1789.* London: Thames and Hudson.

Neumann, J. 1993. "Climatic Changes in Europe and the Near East in the Second Millennium B.C.," *Climatic Change* 23, pp. 231–45.

Nicholas, David. 1992. *The Evolution of the Medieval World: Society, Government and Thought in Europe, 312–1500.* London: Longman.

Nissen, Hans J. 1988. *The Early History of the Ancient Near East, 9000–2000 B.C.* Chicago: University of Chicago Press.

North, Douglass. 1995. *The Paradox of Freedom.* Stanford: Stanford University Press.

Notestein, Wallace. 1954. *The English People in the Era of Colonization, 1603–1630.* New York: Harper.

Nutzel, W. 1976. "The Climatic Changes of Mesopotamia and Bordering Areas, 14,000 to 2,000 B.C.," *Sumer* 32, pp. 11–24.

Oddy, D.J. 1976. *The Making of the Modern British Diet.* London: Croom Helm.

Okie, Susan. 1995. "Monkey See, Monkey Do," *Washington Post,* April 12.

Orel, Vitezslav. 1984. *Mendel.* Oxford: Oxford University Press.

Ozment, Steven. 1980. *The Age of Reform, 1250–1550.* New Haven: Yale University Press.

Patterson, Orlando. 1991. *Freedom in the Making of Western Culture.* New York: HarperCollins.

Perren, R. 1978. *The Meat Trade in Britain, 1840–1914.* London: Routledge, Kegan and Paul.

Pestka, James J., and Genevieve S. Bond. 1990. "Alteration of Immune Function Following Dietary Mycotoxin Exposure," *Canadian Journal of Physiology and Pharmacology* 68 (7), pp. 1009–16.

———. 1994."Immunotoxic Effects of Mycotoxins." In J.D. Miller and H.L. Trenholm, eds., *Mycotoxins in Grains,* pp. 339–358. St. Paul: Eagan Press.

Pier, A.C., and McLoughlin, M.E. 1985. "Mycotoxic Suppression of Immunity." In *Trichothecenes and Other Mycotoxins,* ed. John Lacey, pp. 507–19. New York: Wiley.

Piggott, Stuart, 1983. *The Earliest Wheeled Transport.* Ithaca: Cornell University Press.

———. 1992. *Wagon, Chariot, and Carriage* London: Thames and Hudson.

Platt, S.D., et al. 1989 "Damp Housing, Mould Growth, and Symptomatic Health State." *British Medical Journal* 298, pp. 1673–1678.

Powell, Barry B. 1991. *Homer and the Origin of the Greek Alphabet.* Cambridge: Cambridge University Press.

Price, Roger. 1983. *The Modernization of Rural France.* New York: St. Martins.

Pryor, John H. 1988. *Geography, Technology and War: Studies in the Maritime History of the Mediterranean, 649–1571.* Cambridge: Cambridge University Press.

Putnam, George H. 1962. *Books and Their Makers During the Middle Ages.* New York: Putnam.

Rampino, M.R., et al., eds. 1987. *Climate: History, Periodicity, and Predictability.* New York: Van Nostrand.

Raymond, Robert. 1986. *Out of the Fiery Furnace: The Impact of Metals on the History of Mankind.* University Park, PA: Pennsylvania State University Press.

Reader, John. 1981. *Missing Links: The Hunt for Earliest Man.* Boston: Little Brown.

Rensberger, Boyce. 1993. "Severe drought doomed earliest empire," *Washington Post,* August 20.

Richards, Graham. 1987. *Human Evolution.* London: Routledge, Kegan, Paul.

Ridder-Symoens, Helde de. 1992. *A History of the University in Europe,* vol. 1. Cambridge: Cambridge University Press.

Rightson, Keith. 1982. *English Society, 1580–1680.* New Brunswick, NJ: Rutgers University Press.

Ritchie, David. 1986. *The Computer Pioneers.* New York: Simon and Schuster.

Ropp. Paul S., ed. 1990. *Heritage of China.* Berkeley: University of California Press.

Rosenberg, Hans. 1958. *Bureaucracy, Aristocracy, and Autocracy: The Prussian Experience, 1660–1815.* Cambridge, MA: Harvard University Press.

Royle, Edward. 1987. *Modern Britain: A Social History, 1750–1985.* London: E. Arnold.

Ruse, Michael. 1979. *The Darwinian Revolution.* Chicago: University of Chicago Press.

Sack, Robert D. 1986. *Human Territoriality: Its Theory and History.* Cambridge: Cambridge University Press.

Sakaguchi, Yutaka. 1978. "Climatic Changes in Central Japan Since 38,400 y BP." *Bulletin of the Department of Geography,* University of Tokyo (March), no. 10, pp. 2–30.

Salaman, Redcliffe N. 1949. *The History and Social Influence of the Potato.* Cambridge: Cambridge University Press.

Sanderson, Michael. 1972. *The Universities and British Industry, 1850–1970.* London: Routledge and Kegan Paul.

Santillana, Giorgio de. 1955. *The Crime of Galileo.* Chicago, University of Chicago Press.

Sar Desai, D.R. 1989. *Southeast Asia, Past and Present,* 2d ed. Boulder, CO: Westview Press.

Scham, Simon. 1989. *Citizens: A Chronicle of the French Revolution.* New York: Knopf.

Schierbeek, Abraham. 1959. *Measuring the Invisible World: The Life and Works of Anton van Leeuwenhoek.* London: Abelard.

Schmandt-Besserat, Denise. 1992. *Before Writing: From Counting to Cuneiform,* vol. 1. Austin, TX: University of Texas Press.

Schwarzbach, Martin. 1986. *Alfred Wegener.* Madison, WI: Science and Technology Press.

Senner, Wayne M., ed. 1989. *The Origins of Writing.* Lincoln: University of Nebraska Press.

Shapin, Steven. 1994. *A Social History of Truth: Civility and Science in Seventeenth-Century England.* Chicago: University of Chicago Press.

Shurkin, Joel. 1984. *Engines of the Mind: A History of the Computer.* New York: Norton.

Sikorsky, Igor I. 1967. *The Story of Winged S.* New York: Dodd Mead.

Simkin, Tom, and Lee Siebert. 1994. *Volcanoes of the World,* 2d ed. Tucson, AZ: Geocience Press.

Simmons, Frederick J. 1990. *Food in China: A Cultural and Historical Inquiry.* Boca Raton, FL: CRC Press.

Simon, Edith. 1966. *The Reformation.* New York: Time Books.

Singer, Charles. 1985. *A History of Technology,* vol. 4. Oxford: Oxford University Press.

Sjostak, Rick. 1991. *The Role of Transportation in the Industrial Revolution.* Montreal: McQueens University Press.

Skinner, A.S., and T. Wilson, eds. 1985. *Essays on Adam Smith.* Oxford: Oxford University Press.

Smiles, Samuel.1868. *The Life of George Stephenson and His Son Robert Stephenson.* New York: Harper.

Smith, Bruce D. 1992. *Rivers of Change: Essay on Early Agriculture in Eastern North America.* Washington, D.C.: Smithsonian Institution Press.

Smith, F.B. 1988. *The Retreat of Tuberculosis, 1850–1950.* London: Croom Helm.

Smoragiewicz, W., et al. 1993. "Trichothecene Mycotoxins in the Dust of Ventilating Systems of Buildings," *International Archives of Occupational and Environmental Health* 65 (2), pp. 113–17.

Spitz, Lewis W. 1985. *The Protestant Reformation, 1517–1559*. New York:
Harper and Row.

Steinberg, S.H. 1974. *Five Hundred Years of Printing*, 3d ed. Harmondsworth:
Penguin.

Stevens, William K. 1993. "Dust in Sea Mud May Link Human Evolution to
Climate," *New York Times*, December 14.

Stone, Lawrence. 1965. *The Crisis of the Aristocracy, 1558–1641*. Oxford: Oxford University Press.

———. 1969. "Literacy and Education in England, 1640–1900," *Past and Present* 42, pp. 61–139.

Strayer, Joseph. 1970. *On the Medieval Origins of the Modern State*. Princeton:
Princeton University Press.

Struik, Dirk J. 1981. *The Land of Stevin and Huygens: A Sketch of Science and
Technology in the Dutch Republic During the Golden Century*. Dordrecht:
Reidel Publishing.

Sutherland, Donald M.G. 1985. *France, 1789–1815: Revolution and Counterrevolution*. Oxford: Oxford University Press.

Tanner, William F. 1992. "An 8000-Year Record of Sea-Level Changes from
Grain-Size Parameters Data from Beach Ridges in Denmark," *The Holocene* 2
(3), pp. 220–31.

Te Brake, William H. *Medieval Frontier: Culture and Ecology in Rijnland*. College Station: Texas A&M University Press.

Temple, Robert. 1986. *The Genius of China*. New York: Simon and Schuster.

Tilly, Charles. 1975. *The Formation of Nation States in Central Europe*.
Princeton: Princeton University Press.

Todd, Emmanuel. 1985. *The Explanation of Ideology*. Oxford: Blackwell.

———. 1987. *The Causes of Progress*. Oxford: Blackwell.

Totman, Conrad. 1993. *Early Modern Japan*. Berkeley: University of California Press.

Twigg, Graham. 1984. *The Black Death*. New York: Schocken.

Tzu, Sun. 1963. *The Art of War*. Oxford: Oxford University Press.

Vance, James E. 1986. *Capturing the Horizon: The Historical Geography of
Transportation Since the Sixteenth Century*. New York: Harper.

Van der Woude, Ad et al. 1990. *Urbanization in History: A Process of Dynamic
Interactions*. Oxford: Clarendon.

Vries, Jan de. 1981. *Barges and Capitalism: Passenger Transportation in the
Dutch Economy, 1632–1839*. Utrecht: HES Publishers.

———. 1984. *European Urbanization, 1500–1800*. Cambridge, MA: Harvard
University Press.

Watson, Andrew. 1983. *Agricultural Innovation in the Early Islamic World*. Cambridge: Cambridge University Press.

Watson, James D. 1968. *The Double Helix*. New York: Atheneum.

Weber, Eugen. 1995. *Peasants into Frenchmen: The Modernization of Rural
France, 1870–1914*. Stanford: Stanford University Press.

Weiss, Barry. 1982. "The Decline of Late Bronze Age Civilization as a Possible
Response to Climatic Change," *Climatic Change* 4, pp. 173–98.

Westfall, Richard S. 1980. *Never at Rest: A Biography of Isaac Newton.* Cambridge: Cambridge University Press.

Westwood, J.N.A. 1964. *History of Russian Railways.* London: Allen and Unwin.

White, Tim D., et al. 1994. "Australopithecus Ramidus, A New Species of Early Hominid from Aramis, Ethiopia," *Nature* 371, pp. 306–12.

Wiener, Norbert. 1953. *Ex-Prodigy; My Childhood and Youth.* Cambridge, MA: MIT Press.

———. 1956. *I Am a Mathematician.* Cambridge, MA: MIT Press.

Wilde, Emerson. 1965. *Voice of the Lord.* Philadelphia: University of Pennsylvania Press.

Wilford, John N. 1994a. "Enduring Mystery Solved as Tin Is Found in Turkey," *New York Times,* January 4, p. C1.

———. 1994b."Remaking the Wheel: Evolution of the Chariot." *The New York Times,* February 22.

———. 1996. "In the Annals of Winemaking, 5000 B.C. Was Quite a Year." *New York Times,* June 6.

Williams, Trevor I. 1982. *A Short History of Twentieth-Century Technology, 1900–1950.* Oxford: Clarendon Press.

———. 1987. *The History of Invention.* New York: Facts on File.

Wilson, David. 1983. *Rutherford: A Simple Genius.* Cambridge, MA: Harvard University Press.

Wilson, L.G. 1990. "The Historical Decline of Tuberculosis in Europe and America," *Journal of the History of Medicine and Allied Sciences* 45 (3), pp. 366–96.

Wrigley, E.A. and R.S. Schofield. 1981. *The Population History of England, 1541–1871.* Cambridge, MA: Harvard University Press.

Wu, X.D. 1995. "Dendrochronological Studies in China." In *Climate Since A.D. 1500,* ed. R.S. Bradley and P.D. Jones, pp. 432–45. London: Routledge.

Zhang, J., and Thomas J. Crowley. 1989. "Historical Climatic Records in China and the Reconstruction of Past Climates," *Journal of Climate* 2 (8), pp. 833–49.

Zielinski, G.A., et al. 1994. "Record of Volcanism since 7000 B.C. from the G1SP2 Greenland Ice Core and Implications for the Volcano-climate System," *Science* 264, pp. 948–52.

INDEX

Page numbers in italics refer to illustrations.

Mary Kilbourne Matossian grew up in Los Angeles, California, during the depression and World War II. Two years after the first nuclear bomb was dropped on Japan she entered Stanford University. After graduation she studied at the American University in Beirut, Lebanon, where she earned an M.A. degree. Returning to Stanford, she obtained a Ph.D. with distinction and then received a postdoctoral fellowship from Harvard University, where she was associated with the Russian Research Center and the Center for Middle Eastern Studies. She taught for thirty-one years at the University of Maryland at College Park. This is her fourth scholarly book.